Cooking with Pomiane

EDOUARD DE POMIANE was born in Paris, the son of Polish émigrés. One of the twentieth century's greatest cookery writers, he lectured at the Institut Pasteur and wrote a number of classic books including *Cooking in Ten Minutes* and *The Jews of Poland: Recollections and Recipes*. He died in 1964.

D1148738

BY THE SAME AUTHOR

Cooking in Ten Minutes
The Jews of Poland: Recollections and Recipes

Cooking with Pomiane

Edouard de Pomiane

Edited and translated from the French by
Peggie Benton

Serif
London

First published in 1993 by
Serif
47 Strahan Road
London E3 5DA

Originally published by Bruno Cassirer
and distributed copyright © Faber and Faber in 1976.

All rights reserved. No part of this publication
may be reproduced, transmitted or stored in a
retrieval system, without permission in writing
from the publisher.

British Library Cataloguing-in-Publication Data.
A catalogue record for this book
is available from the British Library.

ISBN 1 897959 03 6

Printed and bound in Great Britain by
Cox & Wyman Ltd, Reading

Foreword

by ELIZABETH DAVID

I love Docteur de Pomiane's work. I owe him a great debt. It was he who taught me that while anyone can sometimes fail in preparing even the most familiar of dishes, anyone can also understand the mistake he has made, and how to avoid making it the next time. Read, for example, his investigation into the making of mayonnaise. You will see, in a couple of brief paragraphs, why egg yolks and olive oil fuse. When the sauce goes wrong and the fusion doesn't happen, you will understand why. There are no involved technical details. We are not wearied with chemical formulas nor bombarded with scientific terms. In a few graphic words Docteur de Pomiane has told us just what we need to know. When he leaves us on our own to complete the sauce, to choose our seasonings and exercise our judgement as to its consistency, it is with a new understanding of a basic technique. He has made us understand our actions. We know what we have done right – it is just as important – as well as where we may have gone wrong.

Many writers before Docteur de Pomiane had attempted to explain the everyday happenings of cookery in scientific terms. They had succeeded only in turning both science and cookery into the deadliest of bores. Pomiane, like all good teachers, makes light of his learning, and so makes learning easy for his readers. He takes the mystique out of cookery processes and still contrives to leave us with the magic.

Another aspect of Pomiane's teaching, more relevant today than it has ever been, was his insistence on the composition of a sane and balanced meal. Caring not a jot for convention and the 'classic' French menu of his day, Pomiane told his radio listeners and his readers that their meals were over-heavy and illogically composed. He did this not by telling them to count the calories and assess the vitamin content of their food but by pin-pointing the

5

absurdity inherent in the accepted order of all middle-class French meals:

> As to fish, everyone agrees that it must be served between the soup and the meat. The sacred position of the fish before the meat course implies that one must eat fish *and* meat. Now such a meal, as any dietician will tell you, is far too rich in nitrogenous substances, since fish has just as much assimilated albumen as meat, and contains a great deal more phosphorous ...

In the 1930s those were liberating words. Not enough people paid attention to them. Even now, forty years later, when it is generally accepted that a prosperous minority eats unwisely and to excess while the rest of the world goes hungry, the remorseless progress from soup to fish, from fish to meat and on, senselessly on, to salad, cheese, a piece of pastry, a chocolate mousse or an ice cream, still constitutes the standard meal throughout the entire French-influenced world of hotels and catering establishments. It is a waste of resources, a waste of effort, a pointless adherence to a tradition long outdated.

The faults of the orthodox menu were by no means the only facet of so-called classic French cooking upon which Docteur de Pomiane turned his critical intelligence. Recipes accepted as great and sacrosanct are not necessarily, as he observes, compatible with sense. Before you buy scarce and disproportionately expensive ingredients to cook according to some famous formula, listen to Docteur de Pomiane on one such dish: *homard à l'américaine* 'is a celebrated dish, but it offends a basic principle of taste'. No wonder that this provocative rebel questioning the holy rites of the 'white-vestured officiating priests' of established French cookery – and he not even a Frenchman born – was unpopular among the more reactionary of his colleagues, no wonder that he was feared by the phoney – and loved by his pupils, his readers, his radio audience.

Docteur de Pomiane is a subtle writer. He doesn't labour his points. Passing swiftly from the absurdities of *haute cuisine* to the shortcomings of folk cookery, he provides a gentle warning to these writers whose reverent genuflections before every least crumb of peasant cookery lore promise such fruitful copy for the satirists of the future. In Pomiane's day there was scarcely a French gastronomic writer who was not gravely debating the precise historic origins and exact composition of every regional dish in France. Today we ourselves are going through just such a phase. The attempt to put English country cooking back on the map has assumed the proportions of a national epidemic. Pomiane's approach to rustic recipes may help us to retain a sense of humour on the subject. From a village baker woman of venerable age he has obtained an ancestral recipe for a cherry tart made on a base of enriched bread dough. He gives us the method and warns us not to expect too much.

> When you open the oven door you will have a shock. It is not a pretty sight. The edges of the tart are slightly burnt and the top layer of cherries blackened in places ... Don't be discouraged ... try it. What a surprise! The tart is neither crisp nor soggy ... the cherries have kept all their flavour, and the juice is not sticky – just pure cherry juice. They had some very good ideas in 1865.

The first time I read that description, many years ago now, I found it irresistible. I still do. Every year I look forward to the cherry season so that I can make a cherry tart on bread dough. And I can tell you that M. de Pomiane's impish dig notwithstanding, it seems to me a very pretty sight.

I think I have said enough to show why I find Docteur de Pomiane such a beguiling writer, why to me his brief explanations, his methodically organised recipes unburdened with excess detail but invariably embodying the vital touch of the artist, are worth volumes of weighty expertise. I know of no cookery writer who has a greater mastery of the capitivating phrase, the detail indelibly imprinted on our memories. You or I might explain, for example, that to make a certain sauce we need a large bunch of parsley. A pedantic teacher will specify so many ounces or grammes, so many cupfuls and fractions of cupfuls. It will be a bore, we think, to wash and chop and weigh and measure all that parsley. What Dr de Pomiane tells us is that we need a bunch of parsley the size of a bunch of violets. No wonder indeed that we love him. With that one little phrase he has coaxed us into trying his recipe (it is for a date sauce to go with boiled beef), he has contrived to give the whole process a delightful taste and in our minds he has implanted forever the delicious image of that bunch of parsley transmuted into a bouquet of violets.

Elizabeth David
March 1976

Contents

Introduction   9
Soups   29
Eggs   35
Some Cheese Dishes   40
Savoury Tarts, Pancakes and
Other Delicacies   46
Sea Fish   62
Frogs, Snails and Freshwater Fish   80
Meat   94
Poultry and Game   127
Vegetables   146
Salads   181
Sauces   186
Sweet Dishes   192
Jam   224
A Few Drinks   225
Food to Remember   228

Index   241

The recipes in this book are intended for 4 people.

The Duties of a Host

It is much easier to accept an invitation to dinner than to receive guests at your own table.

To accept an invitation to dinner may or may not be pleasant but, in any case, it is only a question of passing pleasantly, or unpleasantly, an hour or two.

On the other hand, to invite relations, friends or business contacts to a meal is a most complicated business. You must, according to Brillat-Savarin's formula, be responsible for their entire happiness whilst they are under your roof.

But the guest's happiness is a matter of infinite complexity. It depends on the host himself, on his humour, his health, his business interests, his pastimes, the character of his wife, his education, his appetite, his attitude towards his neighbour at table, his artistic sense, his inclination to mischief, his good nature, and so on and so forth.

So it is really not worth worrying too much, or the problem of inviting guests to dinner would become insoluble.

First of all, there are three kinds of guests: 1. Those one is fond of. 2. Those with whom one is obliged to mix. 3. Those whom one detests.

For these three very different occasions one would prepare, respectively, an excellent dinner, a banal meal, or nothing at all, since in the latter case one would buy something ready cooked.

To prepare a dinner for a friend is to put into the cooking pot all one's affection and good will, all one's gaiety and zest, so that after three hours' cooking a waft of happiness escapes from beneath the lid.

A dinner prepared for a business contact is meant to impress him and to 'pay back' hospitality. Horrible expression!

For my part, I have never 'paid back' a dinner. The people who invite me are richer than I am. They would find my table too modest, and they don't come, because they are not invited.

Those whom I do invite like my savoury casserole and *they* don't pay *me* back because they prefer to return and enjoy it another time.

To make a dinner for people one can't bear is to try and keep up with the Jones's, as you say in English. Whatever you do, you are bound to be criticized, so it is better to buy ready cooked food and let the supplier be criticized instead.

Having established these facts, let us begin.

For a successful dinner there should never be more than eight at table. One should prepare *only one good dish*. This should be preceded and followed by some little thing, then cheese and a sweet course if you are in France or pudding and cheese if you are in England. Finally dessert, good coffee, and a glass of cognac or natural spirits.

For the dinner to be really good the host must feel a glow of inward joy during the whole of the week which precedes it. He must await with impatience the day of the party. He must ask himself every day what he can do to improve it, even if it is only a question of a simple *pot-au-feu*.

Whatever such a host offers to his guests, I am sure that it will be good, because he will have enjoyed the anticipation of it for a week beforehand and he will feel this same joy for a week afterwards in his pleasure at having charmed his guests.

The dinner which you are obliged to give is almost always banal, but one should take trouble with it all the same, for perhaps amongst the guests there is someone who is worth while and perhaps the host will find in him a future friend.

In spite of this, however, such a dinner is never outstanding because one can never really please people whom one doesn't know.

The menu should be varied and the dishes neither insipid nor too highly spiced; neither too colourful, too classic nor too exotic. The guests must be able to talk about them as one talks about the latest film for which one has to book seats weeks in advance.

Poor host. I really pity you!

And now for the third category, the 'smart' dinner. I can assure you that on such a day my telephone works overtime. My wife is still in bed. She rages at the telephone exchange who have cut her off between ordering Lobster Thermidor and Chicken Demidoff. "Engaged again. Just my luck. I shall never have time to arrange this wretched dinner. . . ."

And yet, in the evening, when the guests arrive, the hostess will say to them smiling, "How nice of you to come! Let me have your coat, darling . . ."

The Duties of a Guest

In my youth I always said, and later on I repeated, that one should never refuse an invitation to lunch or dinner, for one never knows what one may have to eat the next day.

This being established, I, like all the believers in this maxim, have very frequently found myself at other people's tables.

As soon as one is seated at table between fellow guests, one is torn by conflicting feelings—a desire to enjoy the meal to the full whilst respecting the claims of good manners, and a reluctance to ruin one's digestion.

My considerable experience authorizes me to offer a little advice to young *gastronomes*, on the way in which they should conduct themselves at table.

First of all, don't expect too much. In this way you will not be disappointed at the end of the meal—a thing which is very harmful to the digestion. The day before the party, assess your host at his true value. Calculate, and I am afraid this is a little cynical, just what you are likely to get.

If your host cooks himself, if he is a *cordon bleu* . . . see that your preceding meal is a very light one, or skip it altogether.

On the other hand, if you have accepted, from a sense of duty, the invitation of a culinary ignoramus, have a drink before you leave home and a small snack. In this way you will arrive suitably fortified and you will avoid the pangs of hunger, so delightful before a good dish but so dangerous a prelude to a doubtful dinner.

Don't make a bloomer on arrival. If the house is luxurious, let your coat fall carelessly into the hands of a waiting servant, pull off your gloves and make your *entrée*.

If the household is a modest one your hostess will greet you in the hall, which is much more cosy. In this case, have the courage to air your opinions and if a delicious smell of roast meat is seeping under the kitchen door, dilate your nostrils, sniff it appreciatively and express your delight to your hostess. This behaviour, and you know this as well as I do, would be very much out of place if the occasion were more formal because then it would be very bad form to talk about food at all, and especially about what you could smell in the hall.

Now you sit down to table. What do you do with your table

napkin? I always slip the corner between my neck and my collar. It is a matter of taste, but a matter on which no one agrees with me. Personally, I feel that the moment one tucks in one's napkin is one of the joys of the meal . . . Now one waits.

One waits for the soup . . . or one doesn't wait, if it is already in one's soup plate. In this case, it will be cold—and detestable.

If the soup is piping hot and fragrant, compliment your hostess, but don't ask for more. You would overload your stomach. Hold back for what is to follow. As to what follows, you may or may not like it. You must know how to restrain yourself and accept things gracefully.

Whoever may be your neighbour at table, remember that you came for the purpose of eating. Keep your attention fixed on this weighty occupation, but, at the same time, take care. Very often the day after such a dinner is spoilt by a bad night. So watch how you go at table.

Above all, drink very little. For a *gourmet* wine is not a drink but a condiment, provided that your host has chosen it correctly.

And what about conversation? The art is not to neglect either of your neighbours. And this is not easy. Generally, one talks to them in turn, but as soon as the less agreeable of the two begins to talk to her other neighbour, one leaves her to him and becomes unilateral.

First of all, talk about what is on your plates. The subject is there under your nose and will suggest all sorts of reminiscences and anecdotes. According to the temperament of your neighbour you will steer the conversation in one direction or another—but beware of the fumes of the wine. They are very dangerous . . .

A Word or Two about the Menu

During the past fifty years there has been a trend towards simplicity in all the arts and the art of cooking is no exception. For years doctors have been of the opinion that over-indulgence was the cause of many ailments and now the price of food has obliged all but the rich to cut down their meals to a more modest level. It is no longer possible for an ordinary family to offer their friends the lavish dinners of years ago. The educated public is far more sensitive than before, and recognizes as art the inventive spirit which finds new and interesting ways of presenting various materials.

The young housewife is now as proud of the dish which she has produced as of the embroidery she may have designed or the sweater she has knitted. This dish which she has created must be appreciated by her guests, so she tries to provide a suitable background for it. She must not distract attention by numerous dishes each better than the last. The chosen dish must not, of course, constitute the whole meal. It must be framed by something very light and simple, carefully chosen as a foil to the principal course, which is the highlight of the meal.

It is not easy to choose this main dish. It must please each of the guests. Have they all the same tastes? The hostess must know this. In this matter of choosing the dish she must call into play all her perspicacity and her instincts as a psychologist.

She must know how to blend her guests and group them according to common characteristics which so often lead to similar tastes in food. Having first done this, she must make her choice. The dish can be, according to the circumstances, rustic and copious or subtle and exquisite.

Don't be afraid of departing from the classic menu. If your guests love fish and sunshine, prepare a *bouillabaisse* which need not be followed by any meat dish. Your guests will not complain, and they will take away with them an unforgettable memory of your party.

Don't blush to offer a *cassoulet*. Have the courage to serve the most homely dish provided it is perfect of its kind.

It is usual to begin lunch with *hors d'oeuvres* and dinner with soup. Stick to these customs provided you don't overdo the *hors d'oeuvres* as they do in restaurants. Such an excess of rich salads and sausage and so on requires the accompaniment of quantities of bread and makes the beginning of the meal too heavy.

As for soup, portions are getting smaller and smaller. Serve a good *consommé* which is always welcome and, according to the physiologists, stimulates the digestive juices.

These preliminaries to the meal can be followed at lunchtime, if you wish, by a dish of scrambled eggs, and by a little boiled fish in the evening. Don't tax your ingenuity over these dishes. The simpler and more natural they are, the better.

Concentrate all your efforts on the main dish and let it be abundant. Your guests will enjoy a second helping since you will have used all your art in its preparation.

Follow this with a few leaves of salad and, in the order in which you prefer them, cheese and your sweet dish. Remember that men, in general, are greedier than women, and will enjoy a pudding. To be strictly fair, the women may have been out to tea and eaten all sorts of cakes and would really be quite happy with some fruit. . . .

Serve with the meal your usual wine supplemented by a bottle of something special to accompany the main dish which you will have illuminated, *Madame,* with your own special grace and your charming smile.

Culinary Traditions

What would our lives be like without tradition? What terrible fatigue would overwhelm humanity if it only had to concern itself with the future? Tradition represents a momentary pause in the course of toil—repose and the backward glance towards the past—the comparison of today with yesterday. Tradition is the memory of happy moments which have vanished, and their ephemeral return to life.

Without tradition the past would be dead. Tradition brings back to life those whom we have loved, those to whom we owe the present and, by consequence, the future.

What, after all, is a museum? It is just an exhibition of monuments of the past. In every age civilized men collected mementoes of the past so that living and future generations could draw from them inspiration founded on a solid basis.

Daily life is a struggle. Tradition is peace of mind. And that is why we continually create new traditions by instinct if not through feeling.

All artistic manifestations are somehow based on tradition. Tradition perpetuates the moralistic religions. Tradition elevates everything it touches. Tradition even directs the art of eating. Each country has its own culinary traditions, even if they only consist in the arrangement of meals. An English breakfast is quite different from the French morning *café au lait.* Why? By tradition. One might say that the difference is due to climate. But no, since the traditional Englishman, even when he is living in Bangkok or Bahrein, sticks doggedly to his eggs and bacon, toast, and so on.

It is tradition which makes us eat pancakes on Shrove Tuesday. It was tradition which, for centuries, obliged Russians of all levels of society to exchange hard-boiled eggs at Easter saying as they did so "*Khristós Voskrése*"—Christ is Risen.

Sometimes culinary traditions are dictated and transmitted by religions. Sometimes, older even than our present religions, they are relics of paganism. The *Galette des Rois* is a relic of the Roman Saturnalia and there are many other survivals of pagan traditions.

The various religions laid down gastronomic restrictions and obligations the origins of some of which we shall never know. In some cases certain animals or forms of vegetable life were held to be sacred and it was naturally forbidden to eat them.

In other cases the prohibition of certain foods, perhaps on special days, were based on rules of hygiene dictated by the great moral legislators who were the founders of the religions.

What does it matter? It is a fact that in France even the most lukewarm Christians go without meat on certain days of the year, and especially on Good Friday. On Good Friday even unbelievers eat *morue*, and during Holy Week formidable quantities of this excellent dried and salted cod are consumed.

Is this culinary tradition based upon hygiene? Certainly, since it is a very good thing to go without meat from time to time. This is both a prevention and a cure for arterio-sclerosis, high blood pressure and other pathological states aggravated by over eating. The Jews and the Mahommedans are forbidden to eat pork. This is wise prohibition in countries where trichinosis and other maladies transmitted from pigs to humans are prevalent.

Let us respect these traditions, therefore, both because they represent religious obligations and because they are customs whose benefits have been demonstrated by their suvival through the centuries.

By following traditions we commemorate those who have transmitted them. We bring back to life those who are no longer with us and we perform a good deed, since the Dead are not altogether dead as long as there are those amongst the living who evoke their memory.

The Psycho-Physiology of Gourmandise

If gluttony is a deadly sin, a certain healthy greed or a love of good food which we in France call *gourmandise* is a most important instinct since it prompts us to choose food which we enjoy.

Certainly, this choice could be considered to satisfy desires which are quite unrelated to the needs of the body. This, however, is not the opinion of the physiologists who have studied, in the case of animals, the relation between the psyche and the digestion.

The experiments of Pavloff are quite convincing on this point. The celebrated Russian physiologist operated on dogs to create an opening from the stomach to the exterior. When the dogs were completely restored, and after months during which they had lived and eaten like other dogs, it was possible to collect the secretions from their stomachs and study them at will, both as regards quantity and quality.

These secretions consist of gastric juices. Now it is well known that the gastric juices contain both hydrochloric acid and pepsin, that is to say the substances necessary for the digestion of meat and anything containing albumen.

If there is a scarcity of gastric juice in the stomach, digestion will be poor. This is easy to understand.

Furthermore, the gastric juices secreted by the stomach flow into the intestines. When they come into contact with the mucous lining of the intestine they provoke the formation of a substance called secretine. This is absorbed by the intestine, passes into the blood and stimulates the liver and the pancreas. Bile, reaching the intestine from the liver, emulsifies the fats. The pancreatic juices digest albumen, starch and fat, that is to say all foodstuffs.

Thus the digestion of a meal is governed by the quantity of gastric juice produced in the stomach.

Now let us return to Pavloff's dog. Let us watch it and observe its preferences for different kinds of food. This dog, ignorant of the list of deadly sins, is frankly greedy. He loves meat soup and doesn't try to hide it. When he sees it he quivers with excitement and his delight is perfectly evident as he hurls himself on the bowl and devours his meal.

The next day, try showing him a bowl of boiled rice or simply some starch paste. Our poor dog, unless he is starving, will simply sniff it and leave it severely alone.

This dog has definite preferences. He is greedy for meat and a total abstentionist as regards boiled rice.

How does his stomach react to these very different meals?

At the sight of the meat the gastric juices flow freely into his stomach. Faced with the boiled rice, his stomach does not react at all, or at the most yields a few drops of gastric juice.

Thus just the sight of a good meal is enough to prepare

one's organism for digestion. A bad meal, once taken, will be poorly digested.

In this experiment the greed of our dog paid off. Another dog might, perhaps have preferred a meal without meat. But why does one dog prefer meat, and another prefer bread? Because, for the sake of his organism he needs nitrogenized substances; the other dog requires carbo-hydrates.

Whether it is a question of a man or a dog, no two individuals have exactly the same needs. The idea that an ideal diet can be chosen just on the basis of the calories it contains is an illusion. There are no two human motors which are exactly alike.

The same diet will make one person put on weight whilst another will be quite unaffected by it. A question of temperament, one says. It is just this question of temperament which is at the root of the matter.

Each organism is drawn to the substances of which it has need, and this attraction is the basis of *gourmandise*.

A diabetic is greedy for water. Let him drink. This need for water corresponds to an urgent requirement of his organism. The diabetic has an excess of glucose in his blood and of acid derivatives which are poisoning him. He drinks water in order to dilute the poisons.

Watch some children at a meal. Some of them make a bee line for fat. Others won't touch it. Should one, on the pretext of discipline, restrain the first and force the second to eat the fat which they detest? No; it would be, from the physiological point of view, a waste of effort.

Each of these groups of children has need of different kinds of body-building materials. These needs are shown by the preference for one substance or another which is so often stigmatized as greed.

Children run and jump and play. They need the foods which serve as fuel for their muscles. Amongst these, the most valuable is sugar. Now children love sugar in its various forms, from the most elaborate pudding to the simple lump of sugar which they crunch. Should one refuse them these sweet things on the grounds that they are bad for their teeth? Yes, says the hide-bound theorist. No, says the physiologist, who knows that sugar is a dynamogenic food of the greatest value.

In general, children love butter and fruit. They will even eat unripe fruit too, because they crave for the vitamins which it contains.

Now let us leave the dog and the child. The latter is too often the victim of experiments in any case. We return to the adult, to the *gourmand* with his round tummy and his jolly, red face.

The *gourmand* arrives at your house for dinner. He sniffs appreciatively at the smell of cooking in the hall. You apologize but he stops you, for he is charmed. This delicious smell has stimulated all his internal secretions. You can be sure that he will do honour to your dinner. He will digest his food and assimilate it perfectly. Tomorrow you will hear that he has woken up with a mouth as fresh as if he had eaten nothing but a boiled egg and a plate of chicory cooked in water.

For a *gourmand* there is no need to produce complicated dishes with fancy names. Prepare for him raw materials of good quality. Transform them as little as possible and accompany them with suitable sauces and you will have produced a meal which is just right.

The *gourmand* is always happy and cheerful. He is always in a state of pleasant well-being. Not surprising, since what he has eaten has been assimilated and absorbed into his individual being. The *gourmand* is in harmony with the outside world. He is, in fact, a normal person.

The 'non-*gourmand*' is afraid of eating this and that as he will not be able to digest them. When he has finished eating he will be out of sorts. He is out of step with the world and, in fact, abnormal. That is why he is unhappy, embittered, pessimistic, disagreeable, and even dangerous for those around him.

How should one satisfy one's natural greed? To the extent to which it is not harmful to health. That is to say with art and moderation.

Art, to merit the title, must always be balanced if it is static, or rhythmic if it is in motion. Art, in my opinion, should never be tormented, agitated, a-rhythmic.

The *gourmand* should follow these precepts. His meals should be simple, very simple. One should not complicate things for the sake of originality. Don't imagine that it is as easy to create a new dish as to write a new symphony.

With the seven notes of the musical scale one can compose millions of different musical symphonies. With the far more numerous notes of the culinary scale one ought to be able to compose millions of culinary symphonies. Even if we include the every-day dishes, however, these are far less numerous than their musical counterparts. Why? Because music only touches the spirit, whilst cooking touches not merely the spirit but the whole of our physiological economy as well.

One can write music in a whole range of different keys. One can get used to chords which, yesterday, seemed complete discords.

But it is impossible, for the sake of originality, to salt a soup more than a certain amount. After a time our organism would suffer serious disturbances. Our physiology would refuse to adapt itself. Gastronomy is the only art which touches our organism in two realms so closely linked—in its psycho-physiological functioning.

The natural instinct which impels us to enjoy this salutary art is—and again I am forced to use the French word for want of a true English equivalent—*gourmandise*.

Rapid Cookery

The progress of feminism has led to a culinary crisis. Modern women tend to simplify cooking as much as possible, if not even to dispense with it altogether. How can it be otherwise when so many women nowadays are in factories, or offices, shops or their own consulting-rooms?

Because of this and of the upheavals caused by the War, eating habits have changed considerably. A working woman, and I maintain that nowadays every woman works, either in the home or out of it, is often obliged to steal the time for cooking from the hours which she feels should belong to her share of leisure. With all the activities and obligations of the modern woman—and man—there is often only an hour in which to prepare and eat a meal and allow for the precious moments of calm and repose which should follow. These are the moments in which the process of digestion begins and they are valuable, even necessary, for a cultivated person who believes that eating is not just a means of providing fuel for the human motor, but a satisfaction of his artistic senses.

The time allowed for eating a meal can hardly be reduced beyond twenty minutes. In the case of our busy man or woman, this leaves only forty minutes for preparation and the quiet time which follows the meal. Modern facilities have made everything easier, and it is possible, in a few minutes not only to open a tin or warm up some frozen food but to prepare a whole range of dishes from the simple to the luxurious.

This is a subject on which I feel so deeply that I have

devoted a whole small book to it. For this reason I shall develop it no further here. If you are interested I recommend to you *Cooking in Ten Minutes*. Perhaps you have it already.

The Mystery of Cooking

Cooking should no longer be a mystery. The mystery can be solved by the application to foodstuffs of six principles of chemistry and physics which relate to boiling, frying, roasting and grilling, braising, thickening liquids and producing emulsions of fat.

These six principles cover most situations, and if you understand them the theory of cooking will present no difficulties.

Let us first of all study the mysteries of cooking food in water and see what happens during the process of boiling.

Boiling

The classic *pot-au-feu* is a mixture of beef and vegetables cooked for a long time in salt water.

Now meat is an albuminous substance. Everyone knows of the albumen in eggs and realizes that they harden during cooking. When one plunges meat into boiling water its surface also hardens. Since the surface has hardened (or coagulated as the chemists say) it does not allow anything to pass from the inside of the meat into the boiling water.

But, you will protest, to make a stew one goes about things in just the opposite way. One plunges the meat into cold water and lets the temperature rise slowly. Why? Because one wants to enrich the broth with the goodness of the meat. For this reason one tries to delay the coagulation of the surface to allow it to remain more permeable. Thus, during the early stages of cooking the juice inside the meat exudes into the hot water and that is the secret of a good *bouillon*.

When the temperature of the water reaches boiling point, part of the substances which have seeped from the meat coagulate in their turn and form a scum. One skims this off because it is unsightly. Then one adds the vegetables which, in their turn, yield their flavour to the broth.

But the albumen which hardens at the outset of cooking softens under the effect of prolonged heat. It undergoes a process of digestion similar to that which occurs in the

stomach, and is partially transformed into agreeable substances called peptones.

So, during three hours cooking meat begins by toughening
and coagulating and then becomes tender due to the presence
of peptone.

Boiled beef is too often a disappointment, being simply over-
cooked and stringy. If you take a cube of rump steak and
plunge it straight into fast-boiling salted water, the surface
will coagulate immediately and all the juice will be sealed
inside the meat. In this case don't expect to find the meat
cooked through. The inside will be deliciously red and juicy
and you will have a marvellous *Boeuf à la Ficelle* which I shall
describe to you in a later chapter.

To resume, if you wish to conserve all the fragrance and
flavour in meat, fruit or vegetable, plunge them straight into
boiling water for a short time.

If, on the other hand, you wish to obtain a rich, savoury
broth, let the temperature rise slowly and cook your dish for
several hours.

Frying

When you fry in deep fat you must try to see that the substance in question is cooked, and at the same time to achieve
a lovely crisp, crackling result.

This crisp texture can never be achieved through boiling in
water, partly because the water softens the food, and also
because the maximum temperature reached is only 212°F,
which is not sufficient to drive the moisture out of the foodstuffs.

Fat, on the contrary, can be heated to temperatures between 225°F. and 395°F. according to the type of material
employed. In the course of heating in this fat the albumen in
the food coagulates and the starch is transformed into caramel.
These various transformations are the cause of the crispness.

Having understood this, let us see what happens when you
fry potatoes, for example. Suppose you put onto the fire a deep
fryer containing suet. The fat melts. Measure it with a thermometer. You see that the temperature rises to 250°F.,
270°F., 300°F.

Should you let it rise indefinitely? No, because at a certain
moment you will experience a very unpleasant sensation in
your throat and eyes. You will cough, and begin to cry.

These annoyances are caused by the fumes which you can see above the surface of the bath of fat.

This smoke is a sign of the decomposition of the fat into substances which are irritating to the mucuous membrane. And this fat will be as bad for your stomach as for your throat.

It is therefore natural not to heat fat to a temperature above that when it begins to decompose. The first moment that smoke appears measure the temperature. It is 380°F. It is at this maximum temperature that you must work. This is the principal rule for frying. Wait until the fat *begins* to smoke.

This is the moment to put your potatoes in, and this will cool the fat. It ceases to smoke.

Can one fry whole potatoes, you ask? No, because at this high temperature the surface will brown quickly whilst the inside remains raw. Hence the second rule for frying: *Only fry food in small pieces.*

Cut the potatoes in slices about an eighth of an inch thick.

What will happen at this high temperature if the slices of potato are wet? The water which surrounds them will turn suddenly to steam and be forced out of the pan, taking with it the greasy smoke. It is a catastrophe. Which brings me to the third law of frying: *Only fry food which has been carefully dried.*

Dry the slices with a cloth before putting them into the fat.

Unfortunately there are some kinds of foods which remain moist even after having been dried—fish, for example, and one must use another method to dry them. Dip them into a dry powder; flour is excellent. Fourth rule for frying: *Dip into flour food which is difficult to wipe dry.*

Let us return to the slices of potato. They have been in smoking fat for five minutes. They are ready, but they are still soft. Why? The thermometer explains this.

Plunge it into the fat and see that the temperature is only 285° F. Why? Because all the heat of the fire is employed in the physical and chemical transformation of the potatoes. What must you do? It is quite simple. Lift the potatoes out of the fat and continue to heat. The temperature rapidly mounts to 380° F. The fat begins to smoke once more. Put the potatoes back again. Almost at once they turn golden brown and become crisp. And here is the fifth rule for frying: *Cook the food in smoking fat until it is soft enough to be squashed between your fingers. Lift it out of the fat and then put it back again for a few minutes.*

Take out the potatoes and drain them. Sprinkle them with fine salt. They are perfect.

So these are the mysteries which occur in the deep-frying-pan.

Grilling and Roasting

First of all, let us define these two terms. Grilling a piece of meat consists in exposing it to the radiation of a burning fire or red-hot plate situated properly below, but nowadays often above, the meat.

Roasting, is to cook a joint by placing it in front of the fire, traditionally on a spit, or inside a closed space which is heated from outside or around. In both these cases, cooking is achieved by the use of *dry heat*.

Let us look into each of these methods in turn.

Grilling

A cutlet of mutton grilled over a charcoal fire can be a marvel, or altogether detestable.

In the first case, the surface is golden brown and crackling whilst the inside is red and juicy.

In the second, the surface is soft and greyish while the inside is pallid and bloodless.

What is the secret of success? It can be deduced from the comparison which we have just made.

In order that the juice shall remain in the cutlet one must prevent it from getting out. To succeed in this one must procure the formation, on the surface of the meat, of an impervious layer. This is formed when the albumen coagulates under the influence of heat.

What is the cause of the beautiful golden brown of a well-cooked cutlet? The caramel which is produced by the action of the heat on the sugar which is always contained in the meat.

But to make caramel the sugar must be heated without any water. The surface of the cutlet must, therefore, be quite dry. It will never remain dry if you salt it before cooking, since the salt causes water to ooze from the meat.

From all this one can establish the rules for grilling:

1. First of all open the windows of the kitchen so as not to fill the room with smoke.
2. Make a hot fire.
3. Heat the grill beforehand.

4. Rub the meat lightly with oil or fat to prevent it from sticking to the grill.
5. Brown the meat first on one side and then on the other.
6. Sprinkle it with fine salt and serve immediately.

As for the cooking time: 10 minutes for each pound of beef-steak; 5 minutes for a nice cutlet.

Roasting

Unfortunately, one cannot grill a piece of meat which weighs more than $1\frac{1}{4}$ lbs for it is too thick. The surface would burn whilst the inside was still raw.

One must, therefore, roast it.

Cooking a good roast is based on the same principles as those for grilling. That is to say, fire *very hot*, meat *lightly greased*, *very rapid* coagulation and caramelization of the surface.

But when the surface has reached just the right stage of browning the inside is still raw. What must one do? Must one stop the cooking? No, one need only baste the surface continually with butter or with dripping from the roast. This fat constitutes, on the surface of the meat, a screen which filters the heat, and your roast will cook under the best conditions.

Let us resume. To cook a *good* roast you must:

1. *Sear* the meat at a high temperature.
2. *Baste* continually as it cooks and turn the joint so that it is exposed to the heat all over.
3. If you are making a pot roast, *never put the lid on* as otherwise the meat will be cooked in steam and become flabby.

If you like your meat rare, roast it for 13 to 15 minutes for each pound. For the first pound you will need at least 30 minutes' cooking, however.

Only when the joint is cooked, salt it and dilute the caramel which has formed in the pan with a little boiling water. This is called the *déglaçage*, and this operation will produce a delicious gravy.

And those are the mysteries of the grill and the oven.

Braising and the Mystery of Boeuf Mode

In the preceding pages we have discussed the mysteries which take place in a saucepan or deep fryer during the relatively simple operations of boiling, frying and so on.

We have only tried to modify, by the use of heat, the physical texture and chemical composition of food. We have brought about the coagulation and peptinsation of albumen and the caramelization of sugar.

These are primitive proceedings in which human creative genius plays little part.

Now we are going to investigate a much more subtle form of cooking in the course of which we shall explore the genesis of new flavours and unfamiliar sensations of taste.

We are going to discuss braising. Now you know that this long, slow form of gentle cooking represents the acme of culinary art. This method of cooking, which requires time, is disappearing from our lives, for we have got into the habit of living in a perpetual flurry. Instant cookery is replacing more and more the good old custom of simmering for long hours. But enough of philosophizing. Back to our saucepans and let us make together an imaginary *boeuf mode*.

For this dish one should use a *cocotte*, which is a heavy iron pan with two ears. It has a heavy lid which forms a hollow on top. You will probably have to use an iron casserole instead.

We shall need 3 lbs of beef (roll of silverside, for example) cut in the shape of a cube and larded by the butcher.

When the casserole is on the fire we will melt some pork fat, preferably from the back, cut into very small pieces, with a large knob of butter. As soon as the fat begins to smoke it will have reached its maximum usable temperature so we shall put the meat into the casserole.

In contact with the hot fat the meat changes colour. First it turns pale as the albumen coagulates, then it becomes brown as the sugar turns to caramel. We will turn the meat so that it browns on all its six sides, then sprinkle it with salt and add a glassful of hot water, afterwards putting the lid on the pan.

Suppose that we leave the casserole for 4 hours over a low fire, what happens? It fills with steam, the temperature of which rises rapidly to 212° F. As the lid is very heavy it is scarcely lifted by the pressure of the steam, which accumulates inside.

The meat, when subjected for 4 hours to this same heat, becomes tender and full of peptone like the meat in a stew. This fragrant peptone exudes through the softened surface of the meat and through the slits made in the process of larding.

It dissolves in the liquid in the pan and a gravy is formed. Will this gravy be tasty? No, it will simply have the flavour of peptone. So we must modify our technique, or at least render it more artistic.

So let us abandon this experimental *boeuf mode* and make another. Let us start again at the point where the beef is sizzling in the *cocotte*, browned on all its sides, sprinkled with salt and baptised with the glass of hot water.

Now we are going into action as artists. We are going to add all the frangances which we can find in the vegetable kingdom: onion, garlic, shallots, thyme, bayleaves, parsley, chervil, tarragon, carrots, pepper, nutmeg, ginger, cloves, rosemary, fennel, coriander and marjoram.

We can improve on things still more and replace the water by burgundy and even add, at the last moment, a glass of *armagnac*.

In the course of cooking, the steam becomes perfumed with all these essences and impregnates the meat with them. As for the gravy, it will be more than fragrant. It lacks one thing, however—a velvety smoothness. We shall remedy this by adding gelatine. To this end, from the outset of cooking, at the same time as the herbs, spices and vegetables we shall add half a calf's foot and some bacon rinds.

During the hours in which the *boeuf mode* is cooking these will yield their gelatine and when the juice is cold it will set in a jelly.

During all these long hours of preparation all you will have to do is to lift the lid every half-hour and add a little hot water if the gravy has reduced too much by evaporation.

But each time you will be rewarded for your pains as you sniff the delicious smell which you have been able to create and blend and concentrate.

Just shut your eyes and let your mouth water as you antici-pate the moment when your wonderful *boeuf mode* will melt in your mouth.

We have now discussed four of the six basic principles of cooking. The other two, that of thickening a sauce and of making an emulsion, I shall describe to you in the short chapter on sauces.

Critical Temperatures in Cooking

The action of heat upon foodstuffs during cooking is sometimes useful and sometimes destructive.

Heat coagulates the albumen in meat, fish and eggs and makes them digestible.

In the presence of water, heat turns dry starch into a paste and prepares it for digestion.

Heat, in the absence of water, transforms sugar into caramel which gives an agreeable colour to food and arouses our appetite.

But heat applied without discretion burns food, curdles sauces, destroys vitamins and is very harmful.

It follows, therefore, that the intelligent use of heat is of the first importance in cooking.

When one heats a foodstuff one causes its temperature to rise. By means of a thermometer one can sometimes judge the temperature necessary to achieve certain results in cookery. For instance, it is easy to plunge a thermometer into boiling water and see that it marks 212° F. This is therefore a critical temperature for water. So is 32° F., the point at which water freezes. Everyone is familiar with these temperatures, but very few people have studied the critical temperatures as regards other substances.

Here are a few critical temperatures which I have discovered in the course of my investigations:

Chemists tell us that albumen coagulates at 150° F. Now, supposing I add two yolks of egg to a quart of *bouillon*. I heat and stir the liquid. The egg yolk contains albumen. I watch the thermometer which is plunged in the *bouillon*. The mercury rises and passes 147° F. It passes 175° F. and the egg yolk has not coagulated. At 185° F. the soup curdles.

I have now established that albumen diluted in water coagulates, for the cook, at 185° F. and not at 150° F. One can, therefore, heat a soup thickened with egg to a temperature of about 175–180° F. without curdling it.

If, instead of diluting the egg with broth I dilute it with milk, the temperature at which it coagulates is different again. I can heat to a much higher temperature without curdling it. In fact, in these conditions, yolk of egg only coagulates at just under 205° F.

This mixture of yolk of egg and milk, more or less sweetened,

27

constitutes a custard. This cream, heated to 185° F. thickens in the correct way, but only curdles at 205° F. So it is not difficult to avoid spoiling a custard. You only need to heat very slowly once the custard begins to thicken, and you must keep stirring in order that the liquid shall heat evenly throughout.

If, to this mixture of milk, sugar and yolk of egg I add a little, but only a very little flour (one small teaspoonful to each good pint and a half of milk) the custard will thicken at 175° F. Now this temperature is considerably lower than 205° F., the critical temperature for a real custard, or *crême anglaise*, as we call it in France.

Conclusion: always add a little flour to your custard and you will never have it curdle, since it will thicken at a temperature well below the one which is critical for coagulation.

Here are some other critical temperatures which it is as well to know:

Oil for frying begins to smoke at 195° F. and this is when you must use it. Suppose I fry a *wiener schnitzel*. It is done. I lift it out of the fat. Quickly I insert the thermometer. It marks about 165° F. We are far from the temperature at which vitamins are destroyed, that is to say between 212 and 250° F.

In the same fat I prepare an apple fritter. I remove the fritter and dip the thermometer into the fat. It marks about 150° F.

I will also give you the internal temperature of a large joint of roast beef which has been for an hour in an oven heated to 475° F. I take the joint out of the oven, and insert the thermometer into the centre. Only 137° F.!

The centre of a loaf of bread as it comes out of the oven is in the neighbourhood of 130° F.

All these temperatures seem very low, and this is the reason. To cook something to exactly the right degree is a delicate operation which requires *great care*, scientific interest, and art —that is to say, love.

SOUPS

Pumpkin Soup.

Sometimes I feel that I am very old. When I consider all the changes which have occurred over the long years since I was a child I feel like a stranger even in the Paris where I was born.

The din of the traffic has put the street songs to flight. One is no longer woken by the cry of the groundsel sellers. The raucous song of the oyster man no longer reminds one that it is Sunday which must be celebrated round the family table with a feast of oysters.

The shops have changed too. Only the windows of the butter, egg and cheese shops have kept their character, and on the pavement just beside the door one can still admire the giant pumpkin with gaping sides squatting on its wooden stool and seeming to say to passers-by, "Why not make some pumpkin soup? And you will need some milk for it too. Come inside and buy some."

Certainly in my young days there was no wooden stool. The pumpkin was balanced on top of two other uncut pumpkins which were the *rendezvous* of all the dogs in the neighbourhood who stopped there . . . for a moment or two. The stool is a triumph of modern hygiene.

If you are making pumpkin soup, buy a slice weighing about 1 lb. You will need 1½ pints of milk and 2 ozs of rice as well.

Peel the pumpkin and cut the flesh into small pieces. Put them into a saucepan with a tumblerful of water. Boil for about 15 minutes, then mash the pumpkin to a purée. Add the milk and bring it to the boil. Now pour in the rice and season with salt and pepper. Simmer for 25 minutes.

At this moment the rice should be just cooked. Adjust the seasoning to your taste adding, if you like it, a pinch of caster sugar. *I* prefer a sprinkling of freshly-milled black pepper.

Chilled Soup.

This is my version of a Russian *kholodets* which I have adapted to suit my own taste and pocket.

> 1½ *lbs very ripe tomatoes, a medium-sized cucumber,* ½ *oz very fine semolina,* 1 *tablespoon thick cream, a bunch of chervil and tarragon.*

Cut the tomatoes in pieces and put them into a saucepan. Add 1½ pints of water and boil for 15 minutes. Rub the tomatoes through a coarse sieve.

Add another pint of water, stirring well. Bring to the boil and season lightly with salt and pepper. While the soup is boiling pour in the semolina, stirring all the time. Let it boil, uncovered, for 10 minutes. The soup thickens. Add the cream, stir, and lift it off the fire. Cool the soup for half an hour and while it is cooling, peel the cucumber, cut it in two lengthwise and remove the seeds. Slice the cucumber thinly and chop the herbs. Stir them into the soup and set it to chill.

This soup is delicious in hot weather.

Barley Soup with Goose Giblets

> *Goose giblets,* ¾ *lb carrots,* ½ *lb turnips,* 3 *leeks,* 6 *ozs pearl barley.*

Put the neck, gizzard, liver, feet and wing tips of a goose into a large saucepan with 5 pints of cold salted water. Add the carrots and turnips, peeled and sliced, and the leeks split, carefully washed and tied into a bundle.

Bring the soup to the boil and skim it carefully, then pour in the barley. Lower the heat and cover the pan. Let it simmer for at least 8 hours, adding a little boiling water when necessary.

The smell of the soup as it cooks is subtle and pervasive.

Just before serving, lift out the leeks and the bones and any skin of the goose. Adjust the seasoning. The soup is velvety and smooth but with the unexpected interest of the grains of barley which are still just firm. A soup like this is a meal in itself.

Fish Soup.

For this soup use any fish with a firm flesh—conger eel, for example.

1½ lbs fish, ½ lb Dublin Bay prawns, 3 cloves garlic, 2 onions, ½ lb potatoes, parsley, thyme and fennel, ¼ pint olive oil, slices of fried bread.

Cut the fish into six pieces and each of the Dublin Bay prawns into two. Chop the garlic finely and the onions into small pieces. Peel the potatoes and slice them.

Heat 4 tablespoons of olive oil in a heavy saucepan and fry the garlic and onion a beautiful golden brown.

Add 2½ pints of water and, when it is boiling, the potatoes. Season with salt and pepper. Cover the pan and boil for 20 minutes.

Pour the broth through a sieve and work the potato and onion through with a wooden spoon so that they form a purée which you stir into the broth. Add the fish and the prawns and when they have boiled for 20 minutes, the herbs chopped fine. Boil for 5 minutes more. Meanwhile, fry the slices of bread in olive oil.

Pour the soup into a tureen and carry it to table. Help each person generously, seeing that they have their share of fish. Top each helping with crisp slices of fried bread.

Ideally, this soup should be eaten at the midday meal as it is a little heavy for the evening.

Ruby Soup.

3 pints meat stock, 10 chipolata sausages, ½ lb beetroot, 3 teaspoons vinegar.

If you have some meat stock or 2 Swiss *bouillon* cubes you can make this excellent soup.

Bring the liquid to the boil. Drop in the sausages and cook them for about 10 minutes. When they are done, lift them out and add the beetroot, chopped finely. Boil for 3 minutes and add the vinegar.

The soup turns a brilliant ruby red. Strain it into a tureen over the chipolatas. Give each of your guests a ladleful of soup and a couple of sausages.

Neapolitan Fish Soup with Rice.

Thirty years ago I arrived at Naples for the first time, by sea, and was enchanted by the view of the Bay, and by the peasant women in their brilliant clothes thronging the narrow alleys.

Recently, arriving by train, I had to struggle through

clanging commercial streets before I could enjoy the blue of the sea and the distant *grisaille* of Vesuvius with its plume of smoke.

Thirty years ago I used to feast on spaghetti in dim little restaurants; now I am afraid to go into these places with their dubious cleanliness. I fear I am getting older and a little spoilt. My ideas have grown more luxurious, but in the places where I now eat the spaghetti no longer tastes as good.

In restaurants near the sea and by the Castel del Uovo I have, however, eaten some excellent dishes. Here, when you arrive, a feast is spread before you—shell-fish in nests of crushed ice, fish soup, enormous mussels of a size quite unknown in the North, fried octupus, fish of all sorts alive from the sea, and goodness knows what else.

As darkness falls, in that evocative atmosphere of hot oil and saffron, you enjoy the dish you have chosen, whilst singers, to the twanging of guitars, pour out *Funiculì Funiculá* and *Santa Lucia* and all those tunes which have not changed for the last thirty years.

In such a restaurant I enjoyed two special soups, one of fish and rice and the other of mussels. Now I shall tell you how to make them.

For the fish and rice soup take:

> 1 *lb fish*, 2 *ozs rice*, ½ *lb tomatoes*, 3 *cloves garlic*, 2 *table-spoons olive oil*.

For this soup you can use any fish with firm flesh. Fillet the fish and cut it in pieces the size of a hazel nut. Crush the garlic beneath the blade of a large knife. (This is more easily done if the garlic is first chopped roughly and mixed with a little salt.) Halve the tomatoes, scoop out the seeds and cut them in pieces.

Put the fish, rice, garlic, tomatoes and the backbone of the fish into a saucepan and pour in 2 good pints of water. Bring it to the boil and add the oil and plenty of salt and pepper. Simmer with the lid on for 15 minutes. Try the rice. It is still a little hard. Cook for 3 minutes more and taste again. The rice is just right; the soup too.

Remove the fish bones and pour the soup into a tureen. Scoop each helping from the bottom so that everyone has their own share of fish and rice as well as broth.

With this soup I serve a glass of rough red wine.

Mussel Soup.

> 1 *quart mussels,* 6 *tablespoon olive oil,* 4 *ozs stale bread, a dash of powered saffron,* 6 *shallots chopped finely.*

For this soup you must buy a quart of mussels from a fishmonger whom you trust. Wash them carefully in successive waters, discarding any which are not tightly closed. Scrape all the weed and any excrescences from the shells.

Heat three-quarters of the olive oil, which should be of good quality, in a frying-pan and fry the bread, which you have cut into cubes about the size of poker dice. When they are golden brown, set them on one side.

Pour the water into a heavy iron casserole with the shallots, powered saffron and some pepper, and boil for 5 minutes. Add the rest of the oil.

Drop the mussels into this boiling liquid. Cover them and boil for 10 minutes. Taste the broth and salt it to your liking.

Arrange the mussels in a bowl with the *croûtons* and pour the broth over them.

Whole mussels are served with each portion of soup, so it is a good idea to put a deep dish in the middle of the table to take the shells as they are emptied.

Iced Tomato and Cucumber Soup.

French cookery is not very much concerned with cold soups and the best recipes for these come from Eastern Europe rather than from the Mediterranean. There are wonderful cold soups from Russia and Poland with meat, fish and shell-fish swimming in cream, but these are rather too heavy for our taste. Here is a simpler version of a cold soup:

> 1 *cucumber,* 1 *lb tomatoes,* 1 *oz butter, a trace of Cayenne pepper,* 2½ *ozs thick cream,* 1 *tablespoon tinned tomato purée.*

Cut the cucumber into fine slices, salt it lightly, and leave it under a saucer with a weight on top for an hour or two.

In a covered saucepan, cook the tomatoes with a walnut of butter over a very low fire for 20 minutes. Pour 2 pints of boiling water over them and add a little more salt to please your taste. Boil for 5 minutes.

Pour the soup through a coarse sieve or 'Mouli' and add a trace of Cayenne pepper—about as much as a grain of rice. Stir in the cream and tomato purée. Let the soup boil for 1 minute more, then cool and add the sliced cucumber with its juice. Chill thoroughly. Your guests will remember this soup.

Soupe Aux Tripes.

This is a sort of *pot-au-feu* in which the beef is replaced by tripe.

> 1 *lb tripe, 3 cloves garlic, 6 ozs carrots, 3 leeks, ½ lb tomatoes, 4 tablespoons olive oil, a bouquet of parsley, chervil and basil.*

Scrape the carrots and leave them whole. Wash and trim the leeks and tie them into a bundle.

Mince the garlic and cut the tripe into very thin strips. Chop the herbs finely and slice the tomatoes in two.

Pour the olive oil into a heavy saucepan and fry the garlic golden brown. Add 4 pints of water and bring it to the boil.

Add the carrots, leeks and tomatoes and plenty of salt and pepper and bring them to boiling point once more. Add the tripe and, when it is boiling, cover the pan and simmer for 3 hours. Taste the soup and adjust the seasoning to suit your palate. Remove the vegetables.

Boil for 5 minutes more and then serve to each of your guests a couple of ladles full of tender tripe and golden broth. All but the most snobbish will enjoy this soup.

EGGS

At Easter the shops are filled with boxes of smooth white eggs, whilst the shelves are decked with chocolate eggs which are almost black. For March and April are the months when the hens lay best, and Easter is the time for giving chocolate eggs trimmed with ribbon and filled with sweets. Indeed, throughout the Christian world eggs are exchanged as the symbol of the Resurrection.

Eggs are an almost perfect food. It is easy to appreciate their alimentary value when one realizes that the yolk alone contains sufficient reserves to build the robust little body of the chick.

This fact has been realized for centuries, and even the powdered egg of wartime was no novelty, since in 1386 the troops of Charles VI, who were to invade England, were victualled with salt meat, biscuits, butter and powered yolks of eggs preserved in barrels!

I shall not try to teach you how to produce a boiled egg, an *oeuf mollet*, nor a hard-boiled egg. I do, however, venture to warn you against boiling eggs too long. If an egg is kept more than 12 minutes in boiling water the yolk is subject to a chemical change and produces sulphuretted hydrogen. Even if it is very fresh, the hard-boiled egg then smells bad.

Eggs *sur le plat* need the greatest care, since the white must be completely cooked and the yolk should be hot, whilst remaining fluid. Success depends on the heat of the stove and the rapidity of cooking.

Omelettes and scrambled eggs are gastronomic marvels. An omelette when cooked should still be a little runny inside; scrambled eggs must be creamy.

An omelette, just like scrambled eggs, can form an infinite variety of dishes, depending on what is added. But remember that scrambled eggs with mushrooms must be scrambled eggs with mushrooms and not mushrooms with scrambled eggs— that is to say, whatever one adds to the eggs must not be more than one fifth of the total volume.

Try making omelettes or scrambled eggs with any of the following: mushrooms, prawns, truffles, asparagus tips, *croûtons* of fried bread, artichoke hearts, strips of fried bacon, sauté potatoes, chicken livers, ham, cheese, kidneys, mussels, cockles, herbs, shrimps, cream sauce, onions, garlic, tomatoes, peas, French beans, tunny, salt cod. . . I can't go on. I feel as if I were reading a page of Rabelais.

To Poach an Egg.

A poached egg is cooked in water, after being broken out of its shell. In order that the egg shall keep its shape, the white must not be too runny, and the older the egg, the more fluid its white becomes. The white of a not-so-fresh egg spreads out into the water and your poached egg is ruined.

In order that the white shall coagulate rapidly and completely cover the yolk the egg should be dropped into fast-boiling water to which a little vinegar has been added. Should the water be salted? No, since salt dissolves that part of the white which is called globulin. This, however, is not soluble in unsalted water.

Suppose that I am preparing four poached eggs. I place on the fire a saucepan containing a pint and a half of water to which has been added a tablespoon of vinegar.

The water boils. I break an egg into a cup. Holding the cup by its handle I tip the egg straight into the water. Immediately, it starts to whiten.

I drop a second egg into the boiling water and leave it for a moment while I pour some warm water into a soup plate.

Using a straining-spoon I lift out the two eggs and slip them into the warm water. In this way they keep warm without continuing to cook.

Now I shall cook the other two eggs. First I skim the coagulated albumen from the surface of the water, then bring it to the boil again. I break each egg in turn into the cup and drop it into the saucepan.

This time I am not so lucky. One of the eggs has lost its shape and the yolk is showing. It can't be helped. I let them cook for a minute and then lift them out and slip them into the warm water. The white of the untidy egg can be trimmed. It is not perfect, but it will have to do.

These eggs can be served in various ways.

Œufs Pochés Sur Canapé.

First of all I prepare 4 rounds of bread fried in butter and arrange them on a hot dish. I lift the 4 poached eggs from the boiling water, drain them carefully and place them on the *canapés*, then pour melted butter over them and sprinkle them with paprika or a little red pepper. It is very pretty—and it is very good.

Poached Eggs With Tomato.

I arrange 4 poached eggs on a dish and cover them with a thick tomato purée which I have made by warming and slightly thinning a small tin of tomato purée. I have even added a little olive oil and half a clove of garlic chopped and creamed with a little salt under the blade of a broad knife.

Poached Eggs With Mushrooms.

Before poaching the eggs prepare a purée of mushrooms using:

> 8 *ozs mushrooms*, 2 *ozs butter*, ⅛ *pint double cream*, ½ *tea-spoon flour*, 1 *small truffle*, (*from a tin*).

Clean the mushrooms but do not peel them. Wash them carefully and cut them in slices, then chop them finely on a board, holding the tip of a large kitchen knife in the fingers of the left hand and rocking the blade.

Melt the butter in a saucepan and add the mushrooms. Soon, over the fire, the juice begins to run out. When three-quarters of the juice has evaporated, add salt and pepper and the truffles cut into slices. Then mix the flour and cream in a bowl and stir it into the mushroom mixture. Stir until the sauce thickens slightly.

Put the poached eggs into a dish and pour the creamy sauce over them. Serve them immediately.

This is quite delicious. The whites of the eggs are firm and the yolks soft. The dish is a joy, especially with half a glass of Chablis so cold that the crystal is covered with a mist as evanescent as the morning dew.

Scrambled Eggs With Sorrel.

Make a purée of sorrel in the way I describe on page 178 and keep it hot. For this you will need 1½ lbs sorrel. You will also use:

> 4 *ozs butter*, 4 *slices white bread*, 8 *eggs*.

Fry the slices of white bread in butter. You will have to use at least 2½ ozs for this operation, but it is worth it. When the slices are golden-brown put them in the oven to keep warm.

Break the eggs into a basin. Beat them with a wire whisk and add salt. Melt 1½ ozs butter in a saucepan, pour in the eggs and stir them with the whisk over a low fire. As the eggs thicken, beat rapidly, scraping the sides of the saucepan as you do so. The eggs begin to thicken. They are almost ready. A moment more and you can take the saucepan off the fire, stirring all the time. The eggs are just right. Turn them straight onto a warm, but not hot dish.

Now you must hurry.

Put the slices of fried bread into a warm dish and pile a heaping tablespoonful of sorrel on each. Take another large spoon and cover the sorrel with scrambled egg. Arrange the rest of the egg round the fried bread.

Hurry into the dining room. Your guests should be sitting at table, with a hot plate and a glass of very cold white wine before each of them.

Omelette Basquaise.

> *2 large sweet red peppers, 1½ ozs lard, 5 eggs, a clove of garlic.*

Cut the peppers in half, remove the seeds and chop the flesh finely. Heat half the lard in a frying-pan and melt the peppers in it for 10 minutes. Sprinkle them with salt and turn them onto a plate. Wipe out the frying-pan with soft paper.

Beat the eggs in a bowl. Add a crushed clove of garlic, salt and the peppers.

Heat the rest of the lard in the frying-pan until it is smoking. Pour in the egg mixture and shake the pan to prevent it from sticking. Lift the edges of the omelette so that the liquid egg pours onto the hot surface beneath. When the centre of the omelette is still creamy, fold over the far side. Slip it onto a dish, turning the pan so that the other side folds over.

The omelette is prefectly rolled, golden-brown and smells wonderful.

Carry it to the table and pour into the wine glasses a rough red wine, just as they do in the Basque country.

Omelette With Chipolata Sausages.

This dish should be made with a special Basque sausage called *louquenqua*, but chipolatas make quite a good substitute.

6 *eggs*, 2 *cloves garlic*, ½ *lb chipolata sausages*, 2 *sweet red peppers or* ½ *teaspoon paprika*, 1 *teaspoon lard*

Melt the lard in a large frying-pan and add the chipolatas which you have pricked with a pin to stop them from bursting. Fry the sausages for 5 or 6 minutes. They will exude a great deal of fat.

While they are frying, beat the eggs, season them with salt and add the peppers, finely chopped, or the paprika.

Mince the garlic, throw it into the frying-pan and let it cook for a minute. Cut each little sausage in two and return them all to the pan.

Add the eggs and stir. Shake the pan. The omelette is almost ready. Fold it while the middle is still creamy and slip it onto a warm dish. Its fragrance is most alluring. Your mouth is watering. Quick, a glass of Médoc.

Bouillabaisse of Eggs.

There are some dishes which one hardly dares to mention for fear of looking a fool. *Bouillabaisse* is one of these. In Paris they say that a real *bouillabaisse* can only be eaten in Marseilles, but when I was on the Vieux Port I was astonished to find that each restaurant had its own recipe and no two were the same.

The most extraordinary one I have ever eaten was prepared for me by a sailor from Toulon called Marius. This was a *bouillabaisse* of eggs. Perhaps you would care to try it. You will need:

3 *ozs olive oil*, 2 *teaspoons tinned tomato purée*, 4 *cloves garlic, chopped finely*, 2 *chopped onions*, 4 *eggs*, 12 *slices of stale bread, a pinch of saffron*

Put everything but the eggs and the bread into a saucepan on a medium fire. Add 6 ladlesful of cold water and bring to a fast boil. Add a pinch of freshly-milled pepper and salt.

Cover the pan and boil for another 15 minutes, then lower the heat. Poach the eggs in this liquid for 2 minutes and then lift them carefully onto a warm dish.

Put the slices of stale bread into a tureen and pour the broth over them. Serve each guest with broth and bread and a poached egg and drink to the health of Marius . . . and of me.

SOME CHEESE DISHES

I have never in my life been more ashamed than the day I asked at a shop in Geneva for some "real Emmenthal Gruyère".

The shopkeeper looked at me and said, "Are your French?" "Certainly, Madame", I replied, my national pride stung.

"I can see that", said the good woman, smiling, "but what would *you* say if someone asked you for some real Camembert from Roquefort?"

It was then that I learnt that Gruyère and Emmenthal are two different cheeses coming from two different regions. The shopkeeper then showed me three cheeses of different sizes— Jura, Gruyère and Emmenthal. Outside Switzerland one is usually offered an imitation Emmenthal which comes from the Jura. But never mind. For us, Gruyère will still be the huge cheese with the greyish rind which stares at us with great lop-sided eyes filled with greasy tears.

This cheese can be used not only to finish a meal but for the preparation of a number of interesting dishes. I shall talk about *fondue* later on. Now I shall tell you about some other culinary delights.

Beignets au Fromage.

These are rectangles of Gruyère dipped in batter and deep fried. You will need:

14 *ozs Gruyère,* 6 *ozs flour,* 1 *egg,* ½ *teaspoon baking powder, a good* ¼ *pint dry white wine, oil for frying.*

To make the batter put the flour into a bowl and break an egg into it. Add the baking powder and beat with a fork. Stir in the white wine until the mixture is fairly liquid, but still thick enough to coat a metal spoon.

Heat the oil in a deep frying-pan until it is just smoking.

Meanwhile cut the Gruyère into rectangles about a ¼-inch thick and the size of two fingers. One by one dip them in batter and drop them into the oil. The fritters swell and turn golden-brown. In 5 minutes they are perfectly done.

Lift them out with a straining spoon and put them onto some soft kitchen paper to remove the surplus fat. Finally, sprinkle them with salt and freshly-ground pepper. Try them quickly. They are piping hot and the outside is crisp, whilst the centre is a smooth cream. The sensation is indescribable.

Escalopes de Fromage.

Gruyère, 2 eggs, breadcrumbs, 2 ozs butter.

Cut some Gruyère into rectangles about a ¼-inch thick and the size of half the palm of your hand. Before you are two plates. One contains the eggs, well beaten. The other, breadcrumbs which you have made by grating both the crust and the crumb of some stale white bread.

Put the butter into a saucepan and while this is melting on the stove, dip the pieces of cheese first into the egg and then into the breadcrumbs, pressing them firmly into the crumbs so that the surfaces of the *escalopes* are quite dry. Fry them slowly, first on one side and then on the other and pile them onto a hot plate. Grind some fresh pepper over them and serve them with a glass of white wine. I should choose a *Château Chalon* from the Jura.

Croûtes au Fromage.

If you wish to enjoy this dish to the full, put a bottle of white wine on ice an hour or two before you start cooking. To make the *croûtes* you will need:

10 *ozs fresh breadcrumbs, 4 ozs butter, 8 ozs Gruyère, white bread.*

Cut 4 slices of bread rather less than ½-inch thick and about the size of the palm of your hand.

Melt half the butter in a frying-pan and fry the slices of bread. Turn them over. They have drunk up all the butter. Add some more and let the bread brown on the other side. You will have 4 beautiful slices, golden brown on each surface. Let them get cold.

Now there is just a little butter left. Divide it into bits and dot them over the slices. On each piece of fried bread lay a slice of cheese about ½-inch thick. Then put them onto a dish, already warmed, under the grill. The cheese slowly begins to colour.

Now you must be very careful. If the cheese melts all is lost. While it is golden-brown and still firm whisk the dish from beneath the grill and put each slice onto a hot plate.

Carry them to the table and pour the ice-cold wine into the glasses. The crystal mists over at once. Salt the *croûtes* lightly and give a couple of turns of the pepper mill over each. Your guests are wondering how to eat them. Quite simple. Knife and fork so that they don't burn their fingers, and iced white wine so that they will not burn their tongues.

Tranches au Fromage.

This is a peasant dish, rustic and vigorous. It is not everybody's taste. But one can improve upon it. Let us get to work.

> *Black bread—a huge slice weighing 5–7 ozs (or 4 smaller slices cut thick), French mustard, 8 ozs Gruyère.*

The slice of bread should be as big as a dessert plate and nearly 1-inch thick. Spread it with a thick layer of French mustard, then cover the whole surface of the bread with strips of cheese about ½-inch thick.

Put the slice of bread on a fireproof dish and under the grill. The cheese softens and turns golden-brown. Just before it begins to run, remove the dish and carry it to the table. Sprinkle it with salt and pepper. Cut the slice in four and put it onto four hot plates. Pour out the white wine and taste your cheese slice. In the mountains this would seem delicious, but here it is all wrong.

But you can put it right. Over each slice pour some melted butter. A mountaineer from the Valais would be shocked, but my friends are enthusiastic, and that is good enough for me.

Gougère Comtois.

During the twelfth century the inhabitants of a certain village in the Franche-Comté agreed to take their milk to a co-operative centre to be made into cheese, which was then divided between the members according to the amount of milk they had contributed. This cheese is the ancestor of the present-day Gruyère, and this dish can be made with either Comtois cheese or Gruyère.

Gougère Comtois is *choux* pastry mixed with grated cheese. It is baked in the oven, either in the form of a crown, or shaped like eggs. I am going to make this *gougère* as I saw it made at Besançon.

A good ¼-pint cold water, 2 ozs butter, 6 ozs flour, 5 ozs Gruyère or Comtois cheese, 3 yolks of egg.

Put the water and butter into a saucepan and stir them over the fire. The butter melts and the liquid begins to boil. Draw the pan aside and add, bit by bit, the flour, stirring all the time with a wooden spoon. The result is a thick mass which sticks to the spoon and the saucepan.

Put the saucepan back over a low heat and continue to stir. The mixture dries, comes away from the spoon, and becomes shiny. All this has taken about 4 minutes.

Lift the saucepan from the fire and add an egg, mixing it in with the wooden spoon. It is not an easy thing to do. The egg slips away. Never mind. Persevere and you will succeed. Repeat this manoeuvre with a second and third egg. Now you have a thick, pale yellow paste. Add 4 ozs grated cheese and mix it in thoroughly, still using the wooden spoon.

Using a metal teaspoon arrange the *gougère* paste in little heaps on a greased baking sheet, brushing them with a mixture of equal parts of yolk of egg and water. Top each one with a sliver of cheese and put the baking sheet into a good oven (about 425° F. Gas 6–7). After 10 minutes open the oven door. What a wonderful sight!

The *gougères* have tripled in size and are turning golden brown. If you took them from the oven now, they would collapse pitiably. They must be cooked right through if you want to avoid disaster. Wait 5 minutes more and the *gougères* turn a superb mahogany colour. Take them out of the oven and lift them from the baking sheet. They are served on a hot dish with a glass of wine from the Jura—Arbois for choice.

Fondue.

Brillat-Savarin was a great man, but the *fondue* of which he speaks in the *Physiologie du Goût* is not a genuine one. As his contains eggs, it hardens during cooking, whereas the real *fondue* must remain creamy, from the pan until the moment it is swallowed. Brillat-Savarin's *fondue* is simply an excellent dish of scrambled eggs with cheese.

The real *fondue* is eaten in Switzerland. I saw it made in

Geneva in my early youth by a specialist well known to all the inhabitants of those days. They called her *La Mère Tant Pis*. She died many years ago, may God rest her soul. And may our gratitude be wafted up to her together with the delicious smell of the *fondue* which I am about to make for you, using:

> 14 *ozs Gruyère of really good quality*, ½ *pint very dry white wine, a liqueur glass Kirsch,* ½ *teaspoon potato flour, a grating of nutmeg, freshly-ground white pepper.*

To prepare the *fondue* I use a small earthenware dish with a handle, measuring about 6 inches across. In Geneva this is called a *câclon*.

I shall prepare the *fondue* in the kitchen, beating it with a small wire whisk. In the dining-room I have already laid the table for four. In the middle of it there is a hot-plate. In front of each guest is a soup plate containing about 20 pieces of stale bread, each fairly thick, but small enough to be eaten in one mouthful. Beside each plate, a fork and a glass.

Now, back to the *fondue*. First I rub the inside of my *câclon* with a clove of garlic to perfume it. Then I cut the cheese into tiny pieces. (I never grate it. That would be a sacrilege, I gather.)

I put the *câclon* on a medium heat, pour in the white wine, turn the pepper mill five times over it and add all the cheese. The wine boils and I begin to beat the mixture. I whisk it for 8 to 10 minutes. Gradually the cheese melts and the wine begins to turn milky, but the result is not encouraging. The cheese forms a mass in the middle of the *câclon* and the wine remains obstinately separate. This is the moment to use the potato flour.

I lift the *câclon* from the fire, just long enough to mix the potato flour with a little cold white wine to a milky consistency. I put the *câclon* back on the fire and pour in the creamed flour little by little, beating all the time. Gradually the mixture thickens and the wine mixes with the cheese. Then I add all the Kirsch and continue to beat. The *fondue* is reaching its final texture. I let it boil for a minute, beating all the time. I taste it. The flavour of alcohol is too strong. I beat it again and go on beating for 4 minutes more. I taste it again —delicious.

The *fondue* is superb. It is smooth and smells wonderful. I carry it into the dining-room and set it on the hot-plate. I adjust the flame so that the *fondue* is just bubbling.

My three guests and I sit down, each with our plate and a glass of very cold white wine.

Each of us carries out the same ritual. I spear a piece of bread with my fork and dip it into the *câclon*, turning it so that it is covered with melted cheese. Does the cheese run? No, a good *fondue* should never run.

I open my mouth and savour the first mouthful. It is hot. It is delicious. I drink some white wine.

All four of us continue in the same rhythm. Suddenly, a catastrophe. My neighbour has let his bread fall into the *câclon*. His fork emerges empty. He must pay a penalty—the second bottle of wine! "Never mind", as *La Mère Tant Pis* said. From that moment I can assure you that we are all very careful.

The *câclon* is empty, all but a crust of *fondue*. I remove this crust with the point of a knife. It is for the guest of honour.

Round the edges of the *câclon* there is some dry, crisp cheese. This is called the *dentelle*, and it is my particular share. I have earned this lacy crust since I have taught you how to make *fondue* like *La Mère Tant Pis*.

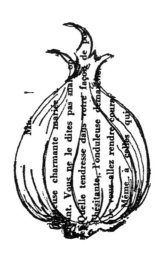

SAVOURY TARTS, PANCAKES & OTHER DELICACIES

Onion Tart.

This is an Alsatian dish which might, in Paris, be considered *bizarre*. A Roman citizen would have called it barbarous, and even I find myself yielding, from time to time, to the temptation of distrusting strange dishes. Whatever you may think, do try this tart and the one which follows.

To make a small tart about 8 inches across you will need to make a *pâte brisée* (the French version of short crust pastry).

Put 7 ozs of flour and 3½ ozs of butter into a basin with a couple of pinches of salt. Add a little water and mix rapidly with your finger tips. If the mixture is too dry, add a little more water, mixing until the pastry no longer sticks to your finger tips. (You will need about 4 tablespoons of water in all.)

Roll out the dough on a floured board until it is quite thin and then line with it a greased flan ring or mould, firming the pastry down with the finger tips and trimming off the edge. The tart will be filled with the following mixture:

> 1 *lb onions, a good ¼-pint thick cream,* 1 *teaspoon flour,* 2 *yolks of egg,* 1 *oz butter.*

Peel the onions and chop them. Heat the butter in a large frying-pan until it smokes. Tip in the onions and stir them with a wooden spoon over a hot fire until they are browned.

Mix the cream with the flour and pour them over the onions. When the mixture begins to bubble pour it into a bowl and cool for 5 minutes. Stir in the egg yolks and spread the mixture into the mould. Bake the tart in a very hot oven (450° F. Gas 8).

This is delicious with a cup of hot *bouillon* or a bottle of Alsatian wine.

Leek Tart or Flammiche.

> 12 *ozs flour,* 8½ *ozs butter,* ½ *lb leeks,* 2 *yolks of egg, a little milk, short crust pastry dough as before.*

46

Make some *pâte brisée* as before, using 6 ozs of the butter and 14 ozs flour. Divide the dough in two unequal parts and use the larger to line a flan ring, leaving the edges of the pastry untrimmed.

Take half a bunch of leeks, trim off the green and slice the white in four lengthwise, washing the leaves in several waters.

Cut the leeks in very small pieces and throw them into boiling water. Leave them for 5 minutes and drain.

Heat the rest of the butter in a saucepan. Add the leeks and stir until their juice has evaporated. Season them with salt and pepper and let them cool, then fill the mould with the buttery leeks.

Cover the tart with the rest of the pastry, rolled out, and pinch the edges together. Prick the top with a fork and make a hole about ½-inch across in the centre. Brush the pastry with a mixture of yolk of egg and water in equal quantities, and bake it in a very hot oven (about 450° F. Gas 8) for 40 minutes.

Before serving the *flammiche* pour a yolk of egg beaten with a little milk into the hole in the centre.

Quiche Lorraine

Quiche Lorraine is a wonderful dish which is usually served as a first course, but when you have eaten a large slice you will not want to eat anything else—for 10 minutes at least. I will describe in a moment the cream which is used to fill the *quiche*. At this stage you will need:

> 4 *ozs lean bacon,* 4 *ozs ham,* 6 *ozs flour,* 3 *ozs butter.*

While the bacon is cooking, put the flour, butter, 3 pinches of salt and a little water into a bowl and make a pastry, mixing with your finger tips. At first the paste will stick to your fingers, then it becomes drier and more elastic and comes away from the bowl. Leave it to rest while you prepare the cream for the filling.

> A good ¼ *pint milk,* ¼ *pint thick cream,* 2 *yolks of egg,*
> 1 *whole egg,* 1 *heaping tablespoon flour.*

Break the egg into a bowl, add the flour and the egg yolks and beat them with a wire whisk until the mixture is smooth. Add the cream and beat, and then the milk. You will have a smooth, fairly thin mixture. Season with a good pinch of salt and plenty of freshly-milled pepper. Beat again and the cream is ready.

47

The short crust, the bacon and the cream are prepared. Now you need nothing else but your culinary skill.

Roll the pastry thinly and line a large, buttered flan ring. Arrange the strips of bacon and ham in the bottom, pour the cream over them and put the *quiche* into a very hot oven (450° F. Gas 8).

After 15 minutes peep into the oven. The edge of the *quiche* is just beginning to brown. Ten minutes later the pastry is golden and the cream beginning to colour, but the centre is still liquid.

A further 10 minutes and the cream is rising to fill the mould and turning golden-brown. Five minutes more and you can test it with the point of a knife. If it does not stick to the knife the *quiche* is ready. Life it from the mould and carry it straight to the table. Follow each mouthful of *quiche* with a mouthful of hot *bouillon* and a sip of very cold white wine.

Quiche with Mussels.

This is an invention of my own, but don't be afraid. Make a *quiche* as I have just described, but instead of ham and bacon, use mussels prepared as described on p. 76, cooked and shelled. 1½ pints will be sufficient. To make the cream, use the liquor from the mussels instead of milk.

With this *quiche*, of course, you will not serve *bouillon*, but only chilled white wine.

Some Dishes made with Pancakes.

I learnt how to make pancakes in a small fishing port in Brittany from a professional *crépière*, Philomène Drougzalet. She had lived by selling pancakes ever since her husband and her two sons had been lost at sea. She made them kneeling in front of the hearth in the great chimney. When I asked why she did not sit down she replied that kneeling she could work and at the same time pray for the loved ones she had lost.

Poor Philomène Drougzalet! She sold her pancakes by the dozen and people took them home and warmed them in a frying pan with salt butter. Some sprinkled them with sugar and others ate them just as they were.

Italian *canneloni*, *kromeski* from Poland and *serniki*, which are eaten in all the Slav countries, are close relations, and each consists of a pancake wrapped round a filling.

Canneloni.

> 2 *eggs*, ½ *lb flour*, 1 *oz butter*.

Break the eggs into a medium-sized salad bowl. Add the flour and try to mix it with a wire whisk. You will not succeed, so add milk, a little at a time whisking as you go, until you have a smooth thin cream. Add ½ teaspoon of salt and mix well.

Wrap a walnut of butter in a piece of muslin. Heat an iron frying-pan and stroke it with the butter until this melts and smokes. Using the left hand, lift the pan from the fire and pour in 2 tablespoons of the batter, tipping the pan to spread it in all directions. Put the pan back on the fire. After half a minute, shake it. The pancake comes away from the surface. Toss it if you dare. If you haven't the knack or the courage, turn it with a slice. Count up to ten and slip the pancake on to a napkin. You will be able to make a dozen, perhaps thirteen, and that is a lucky number in Italy.

To make the filling use the following:

> 1 *lb spinach, cooked, a small cooked lamb's brain, grated Parmesan,* 1½ *ozs butter, a small tin of tomato purée.*

Mince the cooked lamb's brain and mix it with three times its volume of chopped, cooked spinach.

Melt 1½ ozs butter in a saucepan, add the brains and spinach, season with salt and pepper and stir over the fire until well mixed. Turn out onto a plate to cool.

Take a pancake and put 2 teaspoons of the filling onto the centre. Turn in the left and right sides so that their edges touch, then roll up the *canneloni*, moving your hands away from your body. The stuffing is wrapped safely in the middle and your *canneloni* made. Prepare the others in the same way.

Put the *canneloni* into a fireproof dish and cover them with tomato sauce made by adding hot water in which 1 oz of butter has been melted, to a small tin of tomato purée. Sprinkle the *canneloni* with grated cheese.

Put the dish into a moderate oven (about 350° F. Gas 4) for 20 minutes or until it is piping-hot and golden-brown on top. It will be a great success.

Kromeski.

This dish is often called *Kromeski à la Polonaise*. In Poland the dish itself is well known but the name *kromeski* is unknown, as so often happens when dishes go on their travels and adopt an alias.

Kromeski are like *canneloni*, but stuffed with meat and fried in butter. Cold boiled beef makes an excellent filling for them. Prepare pancakes as in the previous recipe. For the stuffing you will need:

> 10 *ozs cold boiled beef*, 1½ *ozs butter, a medium-sized onion,* 2 *eggs, a bunch of mixed herbs, breadcrumbs.*

To make the filling, chop the onion finely and simmer it in a small saucepan with very little water, for 20 minutes. Put ½ oz of the butter into a frying-pan, add the meat, minced, and the onion with its liquor which should have reduced to about 2 tablespoonfuls.

Season with salt, pepper and herbs. Stir the mixture over the fire and then turn it out on to a plate to cool. Add the yolk of egg and mix well.

Fill the pancakes in the same way as *canneloni* and egg-and-breadcrumb each in turn.

Melt the rest of the butter in a frying-pan and fry the *kromeski* on both sides. They should be served very hot with a cup of *bouillon*.

Serniki.

These are like *kromeski* filled with cottage cheese. They can be made very quickly using 12 pancakes and the following filling:

> 8 *ozs cottage cheese,* 1 *yolk of egg,* 2 *ozs caster sugar,* 2 *ozs currants,* 2 *ozs butter.*

Fill and fold the pancakes as if they were *canneloni*. Heat the butter in a frying-pan and arrange the *serniki* one beside the other. On a moderate fire brown first one side and then the other. Put them on a hot dish and serve sprinkled with caster sugar. They are really very good.

Pancakes with Ham.

This is an excellent way of using up the last scraps of a ham.

Make some pancakes as I have explained to you in the recipe for *canneloni*. For the filling take:

> 1½ *ozs butter,* 2 *level tablespoons flour,* ½ *pint milk,* 1 *egg yolk, minced ham.* (*You will need* 1 *oz butter for frying the pancakes.*)

Melt the butter in a saucepan and stir in the flour, mixing them well together over a gentle heat. Add, little by little, the milk, stirring over a low fire. Salt lightly and add pepper and an egg yolk. Stir in an equal quantity of minced ham. Let the mixture cool and it will become as thick as curd cheese.

Lay the pancakes before you, one by one, and put on each a roll of the ham mixture. Fold the edge of each pancake over at opposite sides and then roll it up in the other direction so that the filling is sealed in.

Make 1 oz of butter smoking hot and fry five of the filled pancakes, turning them as soon as they are golden-brown on one side. Fry the rest. Serve them immediately and enjoy the enthusiasm of your guests.

Friands.

Friands are small stuffed rolls of flaky pastry which all the *charcutiers* in France make, at least on Sundays. Looking back on my distant childhood they were the Sunday treat which stands out in my memory. Sunday was a special day on the Butte Montmartre. The housewives did not cook. They didn't think of dining in a restaurant either, but bought ready-made dishes or had their food cooked by the baker.

Punctually at half-past eleven on the rue des Abbesses and the rue Ravignan, one saw the errand boys hurrying along with their shining metal containers filled with cutlets in savoury sauce, sausages in batter, grilled black pudding and piping hot *friands*.

The richer families sent their eldest child to the baker's to fetch the leg of lamb they had taken on Saturday evening to be roasted next day. Watched by his envious playmates the child proudly bore the earthenware dish wrapped in a white cloth, from which escaped a savoury whiff of garlic and hot meat. A wonderful balancing feat was required to prevent the napkin from being stained with gravy.

The family sat down to table, savoured the *friands* and devoured the leg of lamb, then towards three o'clock the children went to play on the *Butte* at the edge of the fields of oats which grew where the busy rue Caulaincourt now runs. As they were wearing their Sunday clothes they were not allowed to paddle in the streams which flowed all about the Butte Montmartre of my childhood.

Last Sunday I tried to make some *friands* and I succeeded, so I shall tell you how to do it.

The pastry of which *friands* are made is an economical one, using half butter and half lard:

4 ozs lard, 4 ozs butter, 8 ozs flour.

Sieve the flour and salt into a basin. Add the water, a little at a time, mixing with your finger tips. The water is quickly absorbed by the flour to form a paste which sticks slightly to your fingers. Wrap the paste in a cloth. Now turn to the fat.

To make a success of this pastry the butter must be cold and very firm. Put the lard onto a board. Add the butter and mash them well together until they are completely blended. They should be quite firm. Using the back of a spoon, mould the fat into a round cake as wide as a saucer.

Now wrap the paste and, on a well-floured board, roll it out into a round about 12 inches across. Put the fat in the middle of it and fold over the edges of the paste so that they envelop the fat completely. It has disappeared for ever!

Wrap the paste up in a cloth once more and leave it in a cool place for 30 minutes. Then, on a floured board, roll it out once more until you have a round about 14 inches across. Fold the paste in three, and then in three in the other direction. Wrap it up and put it in a cool place once more. The paste has now had two rollings.

After 20 minutes repeat the process and at the end of another 20 minutes do it once more. The paste has now been folded in three 6 times and, if I am not mistaken, there will be seven hundred and twenty-nine very fine layers of paste, each separated by a fine layer of fat and a layer of air.

In the oven, the air will expand and separate the layers and you will have made puff pastry.

Roll out the pastry into an oblong about 13 by 16 inches and cut it into 12 pieces after drawing, with the point of a knife, 2 horizontal and 3 vertical lines. Now prepare the filling.

Filling.

4 ozs mushrooms, 1 oz butter, 6 ozs sausage meat.

Clean the mushrooms and chop them finely. Fry them in the butter until their juice has evaporated. Let them cool and then mix them together with the sausage meat. The filling is ready.

To prepare the *friands*, lay a small roll of filling on each rectangle of pastry, parallel with its shorter side, then roll it up as tightly as possible. Brush the edge with water, and lay the join downwards. Brush the top of the *friands* with yolk of egg and put them into a fireproof dish, and into an oven which you have heated to about 450° F. (Gas 8).

At the end of 10 minutes the sausage fat will have melted and run into the dish. The fat will probably be smoking. Peep into the oven. The *friands* have risen. Lower the heat a little and after 10 minutes more the *friands* will be ready, golden-brown, fluffy, admirable.

Take them out of the oven. You will be tempted to try one. It is exquisite, but you will burn your fingers and your tongue. Quick, a glass of white wine to the rescue.

These *friands* bring back all my childhood. Alas, the people I loved have vanished. Asphalte has covered the fields of the Butte Montmartre and the streams have disappeared beneath the pavements.

Knèfles a L'Alsacienne.

> 1 *lb flour, 2 eggs, a tumbler of milk (or a scant ½ pint).*

Break the eggs into a basin and sieve the flour onto them. Mix with a wooden spoon, adding the milk little by little, and beating until the mixture no longer sticks to the spoon.

Fill a large saucepan three-quarters full of water, well salted, and bring it to the boil. Dip a dessertspoon into the basin and scoop up a walnut of paste. Dip the spoon into the boiling water and knock it sharply on the edge of the saucepan so that the paste falls into the water. Do this again and again, without stopping, until you have used up all the mixture.

Detach the *knèfles* from the bottom of the pan. The water will come to the boil again and the *knèfles* will float to the top. Lower the heat so that the water, whilst boiling fast, does not pour over the edge of the saucepan. Boil for 10 minutes and pour the contents of the saucepan into a colander. The *knèfles* have doubled in size. Serve them covered with melted butter. They are very good.

Knèfles Paysanne.

> 1 *lb flour, 2 eggs, a good ¼ pint milk, 6 ozs fat bacon, 2 large onions, ½ oz butter.*

Make the *knèfles* as above and while they are boiling melt the bacon, cut in small pieces, in a frying-pan with a little butter. Chop the onions finely and toss them with the butter and bacon until they are golden-brown.

Put the *knèfles* into a hot dish and pour the onions and bacon over them, mixing them together. This is an economical and very satisfying dish.

Knèfles au Fromage.

Mix 6 ozs grated Gruyère cheese into the paste of which you make the *knèfles*. When they are ready to serve, pour melted butter over them and sprinkle them with crisp brown bread-crumbs.

Knèfles Gratinées.

> *Knèfles* (see p. 53). 2½ *ozs butter*, 6 *ozs Gruyère cheese.*

Put the *knèfles*, which you have made as before, into a hot fireproof dish and pour over them the butter, melted, and 4 ozs of the grated Gruyère cheese. Toss them very gently so that they do not break, and sprinkle over them the rest of the grated cheese.

Put them to brown under the grill or in the oven.

Knèfles a L'Italienne.

> *Knèfles* (see p. 53). 1 *oz butter, tomato sauce, grated Parmesan cheese.*

Prepare the *knèfles* as before and put them, well drained, into a hot dish. Pour over them 1 oz of melted butter and some thick, very hot tomato sauce. At table, top each helping with grated Parmesan cheese.

If your budget is a little strained, offer your guests a liberal helping of *knèfles* at the beginning of a meal. They will have very little appetite left, and this can be convenient.

Piroshki.

> 2 *eggs*, 20 *ozs flour*, 12 *ozs cooked meat*, 2 *large onions, a pinch of spice*, 3 *ozs butter.*

I have so often been asked for some way of using up cold meat as a change from the usual hash and so on. Thinking of food I had enjoyed upon my travels I hit upon *piroshki*, a dish which is eaten in all the Slav countries, though in each it goes by a different name.

Piroshki are tiny balls of cooked meat wrapped in paste, rather like *ravioli*, only bigger. They are poached for a few minutes then drained and served on a very hot dish, sprinkled with melted butter and crisp breadcrumbs.

To make the paste, break 2 eggs into a bowl and add a ½ tea-cup of water. Beat with a wire whisk and add 10 ozs of the flour, using at first the whisk and then your fingers. Add a little more flour and knead. The dough is sticky and rather unappetizing. Continue to knead and add more flour. That is better. The dough is now smooth.

Put the dough on a floured board and sprinkle it with flour. Knead it with both hands. The dough becomes firmer. Add more flour, kneading until the dough no longer sticks to your fingers. Now it is ready. Set it aside to rest.

Next prepare the filling. Mince the cold meat while the onions, chopped fine and just covered with water, are cooking on a low fire. After 15 minutes, almost all the water will have evaporated. Mix the onions with the meat. Season with salt and pepper and a pinch of spice. Add 1 oz of melted butter and let the mixture cool. When it is cold, make it into balls the size of a walnut.

Roll out one-third of the dough thinly to make a round of about 10 inches in diameter. Arrange six balls of meat across the upper part of the round, leaving about 1¼ inches between each. Fold the edge down over the balls so that they are completely covered. Using the side of your hand, firm down the paste between each ball and cut each one out with the rim of a sherry glass. Pinch the edges all round to seal the rims of the *piroshki*.

Continue in this way, using all the dough and all the filling and you will have about forty *piroshki*.

Boil 2 quarts of water, well salted, in a large saucepan. Drop the *piroshki* into the water, raise the heat until the water boils once more and leave them for 4 minutes. Then drain the *piroshki*, put them onto a hot dish and pour over them 2 ozs melted butter. Sprinkle them with crisp brown bread-crumbs and carry them to the table. Give four of your guests ten *piroshki*, taking care that they are well buttered. The experts eat them in one mouthful with a spoon. I break mine with a fork, but in any case they taste very good.

In Poland one would eat *piroshki* with a glass of brandy. In France one would choose a young burgundy.

Gnocchi.

Gnocchi can be made of flour, semolina or potatoes. Relations of this dish can be found in many countries—for instance, the *knèfles* of Alsace, which are more primitive than *gnocchi*; the Czechoslovak *galouchki*, which are more primitive still, and the *klouski* which they eat in Poland.

The Italian *gnocchi* are the most distinguished members of the family. They can be covered with all sorts of sauces such as cream, tomato or gravy. They can be browned in the oven or served freshly boiled. With a little imagination you can make so many different dishes starting with simple *gnocchi*.

Semolina Gnocchi.

> 6 *ozs coarse semolina,* ½ *pint milk,* 3 *ozs grated Gruyère cheese,* 2 *ozs grated Parmesan,* 2 *yolks of egg,* 2 *ozs butter, a small pinch nutmeg.*

Heat the milk in a medium-sized saucepan until it is boiling. Salt it lightly and add the nutmeg. Pour the semolina slowly into the boiling milk, beating all the time with a wire whisk. Stir over a low fire with a wooden spoon until the mixture is really thick. Continue for 5 or 6 minutes more over a very low heat. The grains of the semolina are now soft. Take the saucepan from the fire and mix in the grated Parmesan cheese. Cool for 2 minutes. Stir in the egg yolks and the mixture will turn a lovely golden colour.

Wet a wide shallow dish under the cold tap and pour the semolina mixture into it, spreading it out with a wooden spoon. Wet a large silver spoon with cold water and use it to firm down the mixture and smooth the surface. Put the dish in a cool place to stand for 6 hours.

Loosen the edges of the semolina from the dish, using the point of a knife, and turn it onto a board. With a buttered knife cut it into cubes about 1 inch across and put them into a fireproof dish, not allowing them to touch. Cover this layer with 2 ozs of the grated Gruyère cheese and dabs of butter. Cover them with another layer of semolina cubes, sprinkled with cheese and dotted with butter.

Now prepare a sauce with:

> 2 *ozs butter,* 1 *heaping tablespoon flour,* ½ *pint milk,*
> 2 *ozs grated Gruyère.*

Melt the butter in a thick saucepan and draw it off the fire. Sieve the flour into the pan and mix it carefully with the butter, using a wooden spoon. Return the pan to the fire for a moment or two so that the butter and flour mixture becomes a smooth shining paste. Warm the milk and stir it into the flour and butter. Season and add the Gruyère, stirring until it is melted.

Pour the sauce over the *gnocchi* and sprinkle with the rest of the Gruyère. Brown them for 15 minutes in a good oven (about 400° F. Gas 5).

Choux Pastry Gnocchi.

> 5 *ozs butter,* 4 *ozs flour,* ⅓ *pint water,* 3 *eggs,* 2 *ozs Parmesan,* 4 *ozs Gruyère.*

Put 2½ ozs of the butter, the water and 3 pinches of salt into a saucepan and heat them until the water boils. Remove the pan from the fire and pour the flour in all at once. Stir with a wooden spoon until the mixture is smooth. Put the saucepan back on a low fire. It forms a ball which gradually becomes shining like *mayonnaise,* which is beginning to curdle. When it begins to stick to the bottom of the saucepan, lift it off the fire.

One after the other, break the eggs and stir them into the mixture. Then add the Parmesan and beat it well in. Leave the paste to cool for 2 hours.

Now make the *gnocchi.* Boil a large saucepanful of water. Flour a board and cut the paste into strips. Roll these into sausages about ½ inch thick. Cut the sausages into pieces about ¾ inch long and drop them into the boiling water.

One can also form the *gnocchi* with a small teaspoon. They will be less regular in shape, but just as good to eat.

After 5 minutes, turn the *gnocchi* into a colander and pour cold water over them. Drain them well, and put them in layers in a fireproof dish, covering each layer with grated Gruyère and the rest of the butter in small dabs.

Put the dish into the oven for 10 to 15 minutes. The butter melts and the top becomes golden-brown. Carry them to the table. They are delicious—not to be recommended for those who are slimming, but one can always start slimming to-morrow.

Ramequins.

> 3 *ozs butter*, 4 *ozs flour*, ⅓ *pint water*, 3 *eggs*, 4 *ozs grated Gruyère*.

Make a *pâte à choux* as I have described in the preceding recipe, using Gruyère and no Parmesan.

Butter a baking sheet and, with the help of a teaspoon, arrange walnuts of paste, leaving room for them to expand.

Put them into a hot oven (about 420° F. Gas 6) for 20 minutes. They should be quite firm to the touch when you take them out. These make a good first course, served just as they are.

Pasta.

Most of us can remember, probably from school days, horrible dishes of yellowish, slippery, sticky macaroni which disgusted us for years. Then, one day, we tasted a dish of Italian spaghetti or noodles which showed quite plainly that it was not the dish but the cook which had been at fault.

What is the secret of success? First of all, *pasta* must be made of hard wheat with a low starch content. Then it must be cooked in plenty of water so that any surplus starch is removed, and only cooked just long enough to make it firm but not soft.

Different sorts of *pasta* vary slightly in texture, but as a general rule 18 minutes in lightly salted, fast-boiling water is sufficient for spaghetti and 12 minutes for noodles, *lasagne* and macaroni. As soon as they are done, remove the saucepan from the fire and let it stand for 2 minutes while the *pasta* swells. Drain the *pasta* in a colander for 10 seconds, then put it back into the saucepan or into a hot dish and serve it with various sauces.

People's capacity for *pasta* varies enormously, but if you are using it as a main dish about 3 ozs for each person will give a reasonable helping.

Spaghetti à L'Anglaise.

Prepare the spaghetti and bring it straight to table. Let each guest help himself to fresh butter and grated Parmesan, stirring them together in his plate.

If the spaghetti is of good quality, cooked to a turn and served very hot, this is a delicious dish.

Spaghetti with Tomato Sauce.

> 12 ozs spaghetti, 1 oz tinned tomato purée, 2 ozs butter, grated Parmesan or Gruyère.

Cook and drain the spaghetti and return it to the saucepan. Over a low fire stir in the tomato purée and butter. At table, sprinkle grated cheese over each helping.

Noodles with Mushrooms.

> 12 ozs noodles, 6 ozs mushrooms, 3½ ozs butter, grated Parmesan cheese.

Clean and slice the mushrooms and put them into a covered saucepan with 1½ ozs butter over a low fire. After 2 or 3 minutes lift the lid and allow the juice to evaporate. Season them with salt and set them aside.

Cook the noodles for 12 minutes in 4 pints of boiling salted water. Drain them well and mix them with the mushrooms and the rest of the butter. Serve on a hot dish and pass round a bowl of grated Parmesan cheese.

Nouilles à la Tchèque.

> ½ lb noodles, 2 ozs butter, 4 ozs chopped ham, 2 ozs butter, 2 beaten eggs, breadcrumbs.

Cook the noodles and mix them with the butter and chopped ham. Let them cool a little and stir in the beaten eggs. Butter a mould and sprinkle it with breadcrumbs. Pour in the noodles and put them in the oven for 45 minutes. Turn them out of the mould and serve very hot.

RICE DISHES

Adjem Pilaff.

Adjem pilaff is simply Turkish for Persian rice. It is an exquisite dish, very simple to prepare, and you can make it just as easily as I, who learnt to cook it on the banks of the Bosphorus.

The secret of a good *pilaff* is to keep the grains of rice separate and firm and delicately flavoured. I will explain how to do this. You will need:

2 large onions, 1 oz butter, 1 lb breast of lamb, cut in very small pieces and exactly *2 teacups unpolished Italian rice, a sprig of thyme, 2 bayleaves.*

Heat the butter in a heavy iron saucepan until it smokes, and add the lamb. While this is turning golden-brown, peel the onions and chop them finely. Stir the meat so that it does not burn and, after 8 to 10 minutes, pour the fat off into a bowl. You will need it later.

Add the onions and let them colour for 3 minutes or so. Season with salt and plenty of pepper and add exactly 3 cups of hot water. Perfume the broth with a sprig of thyme and the bayleaves and lower the heat. Simmer for nearly an hour, until the meat is done. Pour off the broth into a second bowl. Now you are going to cook the rice.

Put the fat from the lamb into a pan and heat it until it smokes. Pour in the rice, dry. Stir it well until it is glistening with fat, and leave it on the fire for 2 minutes, stirring all the time with a wooden spoon. Now add to it the broth which you have made up with water to *exactly* 3 cupfuls. Stir it all together.

Cover the pan and leave it on a very low fire for 18 minutes. Lift the lid. There is not a drop of liquid. The rice has absorbed it all. Taste it. The rice is done and no longer has a hard centre. But the grains of rice are still sticking slightly to one another. This is because they are enveloped in steam.

Leave the saucepan with the lid off on a very low heat for 10 minutes, lifting the rice frequently with a fork and shaking the pan to separate the grains. Now it is ready.

Warm the meat over a gentle heat. Mix it with the rice and serve the *pilaff* in a very hot dish on well-heated plates.

Why is it that the rice does not stick together? This is because the whole of the water has been absorbed by the rice and there is none left over to form a starchy paste between the grains.

Rice Salad.

½ lb rice, 4 ozs stoned black olives, 2 ozs anchovy fillets, a small cupful cooked peas, 3 tablespoons olive oil, ¾ table-spoonful vinegar, a sliced tomato.

Cook the rice in 6 pints of fast-boiling salted water. After 12 minutes test a grain. It will still be hard. Boil about 5 minutes more, testing from minute to minute.

The rice is ready. Pour the contents of the saucepan through a sieve and wash the rice under the cold tap. Drain it well and spread it out on a clean cloth.

When the rice is really cold, probably at the end of an hour, put it into a salad bowl with the olives and anchovy fillets, chopped in pieces, and the green peas.

Mix the olive oil and vinegar together with salt and pepper, and stir them into the rice with a light hand, so that the grains are not crushed. Decorate the dish with slices of tomato.

SEA FISH

From the earliest times fish has attracted the attention of the *gourmet* and the art of the cook. Juvenal, in his famous satire, tells how the Emperor Domitian assembled the Senate to decide how to cook his turbot—and this while the enemy were besieging Rome and on the point of forcing the gates. The Senate pronounced on this weighty question and the turbot was cooked with piquant sauce.

Gourmets have poured out floods of ink on the subject of the proper place for cheese in a menu. Some say it should be served before the pudding—some after. Each school of thought produces most convincing reasons, but they cannot come to an agreement.

All these arguments merely worry the people who fancy themselves as *gourmets* and prevent them from eating as they would like.

As to fish, everyone agrees that it must be served between the soup and the meat. The sacred position of fish before the meat course implies that one must eat fish *and* meat. Now such a meal, as any dietician will tell you, is far too rich in nitrogenous substances, since fish has just as much assimilable albumen as meat, and contains a great deal more phosphorus.

So in an effort to please everyone the fish course is reduced to a few miserable strips of flesh in a sauce which completely kills its flavour.

Fortunately, all the arts—cooking as much as sculpture, painting and interior decoration—have turned to simplicity. A main dish may just as well consist of fish as meat, and the cheaper fish have just as much nutritive value as the more expensive varieties. The art of cooking is to prepare simple and economical materials with such variety and skill that they delight the palate and whet the appetite.

Whiting.

At the beginning of the sixteenth century, when fish had to be brought to Paris from the sea in carts, drawn by galloping horses, the markets were stocked with truffled herrings, sardines, sour herrings, anchovies, salted salmon, salted eels and baskets of oysters. There were lampreys in *sauce Hippocras*, sturgeon, whales, mackerel, octopus, dabs, flounders, brill, plaice, fried oysters, scallops, crayfish, fresh salmon, turbot, red mullet, sea urchins, cockles, conger eels, sole, lobster, shrimps, cuttle-fish and crabs, besides salted hake, dried cod, mussels and young pike pickled with plenty of vinegar to make them more digestible.

Now, thanks to modern methods of transport and refrigeration fish reaches the market as fresh as it is caught, but we should search in vain for many of the varieties which delighted the heart of Rabelais.

Lampreys are rare; turbot too dear, and octopus is out of fashion. But we have marvellous whiting and this fish really deserves to return to favour. It has been despised because of its price, just like mackerel and herring. But what little masterpieces can be produced with these three fish which are hardly more expensive than new potatoes.

Supposing you have twenty minutes at your disposal and the choice of a beefsteak or a small whiting. You can grill the beefsteak or you can fry it in a pan, which comes to very much the same thing. As for the whiting, you can:

1. Boil it and eat it with melted butter.
2. Serve it with a *béchamel* sauce which you have prepared while it was boiling.
3. Poach it in white wine with shallots, mushrooms and butter, then sprinkle it with grated cheese and brown it under the grill.
4. Dip it in flour and fry it in butter, and you have *merlan meunière*.
5. Flour the whiting or dip it in batter, and deep-fry it in smoking hot oil.
6. Fillet the whiting and treat it in any of the above ways, which will give in each case a slightly different result.
7. Remove the skin and bone from the cooked fish and mix it with *béchamel* sauce and the yolk of two eggs. Fold in the beaten whites of the eggs and you will have a delicious fish *soufflé* ready for the oven.

I simply can't go on. It makes me too hungry.

Fried Whiting

Whiting dipped in batter and fried are very good. To make the batter for two whiting take:

> 1 *egg, 3½ ozs flour,* 1 *teaspoon baking powder.*

Put the flour, baking powder and egg into a bowl. Mix them with a wire whisk. You will not succeed for there is too much flour. Pour in milk or water, very gently. Beat with the whisk, crushing any lumps. Stop when the mixture has become a thick cream. Plunge a spoon into the batter. Lift it out. The cream is sticking to the spoon and this proves that it is not too thin. Salt it lightly and mix once again. If this batter is left to stand for an hour or more, it will be greatly improved.

Put the deep frying-pan containing oil on the fire. Take two soup plates and put some flour in one and batter in the other. Using a pair of scissors, cut the fins from the whiting, which you have washed and dried carefully. Dip them in the flour, shaking them to make sure that no more than necessary sticks to the fish, and plunge them in the batter. They emerge with a yellowish coating. Drop them into the smoking oil and lower the heat a little so that the outsides of the whiting do not cook more quickly than the centres. Fry for 5 or 6 minutes. The fish have scarcely coloured. Raise the heat. They rapidly become golden-brown. Lift them out with a perforated ladle. Drain them for a moment or two on some soft paper and put them on a hot dish. Sprinkle them with fine salt and decorate with slices of lemon.

This is a simple way of cooking a good dish.

Whiting in White Wine.

The dish which I am going to tell you about now is much more sophisticated than the fried whiting.

You must choose two fine fresh fish. Clean them, working through the gills so as not to cut open the stomach. Wash them carefully and snip off the fins with a pair of kitchen scissors. Using a sharp knife, cut down the middle of the back so as to expose the backbone. Cut through the backbone just below the head and above the tail. Detach it by lifting the flesh from the 'ribs' with the blade of a knife so that all the bones come away at once. Now your fish are ready and you will need besides:

5 *minced shallots, some finely chopped parsley,* 6 *ozs mushrooms cut in slices, white wine,* 2½ *ozs butter,* 1 *oz grated Gruyère cheese.*

Put the boned whiting into a flameproof dish and sprinkle them with the shallots, parsley and mushrooms. Season with salt and pepper and cover them with white wine.

Cook over a low fire for 8 to 10 minutes. The wine will have partly evaporated and the fish are cooked. Keep them warm and pour the liquid carefully into a small saucepan. Reduce it over the fire to about half a glassful.

Keep the saucepan on the lowest heat, stirring all the time while you add, bit by bit, the fresh butter. Be careful the sauce does not boil. As you stir, it will turn into a smooth yellow cream.

Spread this over the whiting. Sprinkle with grated Gruyère cheese and put the dish for a few minutes under the grill. The surface turns golden-brown.

Serve the whiting in the dish in which they have been cooked, with a glass of the same white wine which you used to make the sauce. This makes a charming harmony, the wine which you drink being subtly echoed in the flavour of the sauce.

Whiting à la Crème.

2 *filleted whiting,* 4 *minced shallots,* 6 *ozs mushrooms cut into fine slices,* ½ *bottle dry white wine,* 4 *ozs thick cream,* ½ *teaspoon flour,* 1 *oz grated Gruyère cheese.*

Arrange the fillets of fish in a flameproof dish with the shallots and mushrooms. Pour the white wine over them and season with salt and pepper. Poach over the fire for 15 minutes. Drain the wine carefully into a small saucepan and reduce it over the fire to half a glassful. Add the cream which you have mixed with the flour. Pour the sauce over the fish. Sprinkle it with grated Gruyère cheese.

Colin à la Basquaise.

3 *slices of codling* ¾ *to* 1-*inch thick,* ¼ *pint olive oil,* 2 *large onions,* 4 *slices of bread.*

Heat ⅛ pint of olive oil in a frying-pan until it smokes. Brown in this 2 good-sized onions, chopped very fine. When they are a rich mahogany brown add 2 or 3 tablespoons of water and heat until it boils. Season with salt and pepper and pour the mixture into an iron casserole. Lay the fish in the bottom of the casserole, put on the lid, and cook over a very slow fire for 20 minutes.

In the meantime, cut 3 slices of bread of the same thickness as the codling slices and trim off the crusts. Fry them in the rest of the oil and when they are golden-brown, arrange them in a deep dish. Put a slice of codling on each. Pour the sauce over them and await the congratulations of your guests.

Stuffed Herrings.

4 herrings, a shallot, parsley, 2 ozs butter.

Take four fine herrings with soft roes. Choose firm, shining fish with broad backs, their heads still red from the net which caught them. Clean them. Snip the backbone near the head and the tail and, using a knife to detach it from the flesh, lift it out.

Mince the roes with a shallot and a little parsley. Add a little melted butter, salt and pepper. Stuff the herrings with this mixture and wrap each one in oiled paper. Put them in a fireproof dish surrounded by some dabs of butter, and into a hot oven (about 400° F. Gas 6) for a bare half-hour. If the butter in the bottom of the dish looks like burning, add a very little white wine.

Maquereau à la Grècque.

4 mackerel, olive oil, 2 sprigs of thyme, 4 ozs black olives.

Clean the mackerel, cut off the fins, and put them into a fireproof dish, sprinkled with oil. Strip the leaves from a sprig of thyme and sprinkle them over the fish.

Bake the mackerel for 30 minutes, using a sprig of thyme to baste them with the oil from the dish. Ten minutes before serving, arrange the stoned black olives round the fish. With this Olympian dish drink a glass of strong white wine.

Salt Cod.

This fish is used in France on fast days and in Spain all the year round. *You* will probably have to look for it in Soho. To save time, buy fillets which have been skinned, and soak them in cold water for 24 hours to remove the salt.

To cook the fillets put them into a saucepan of cold water and, just as the water is about to boil, lower the heat. Leave the fish for 5 minutes in the almost boiling water, then lift it out and drain it. Now you can treat it in various ways. In all but the last of the following recipes the salt cod has been par-boiled in this way.

Morue à la Biscaïene.

> 1½ lbs filleted salt cod prepared as above, ½ lb onion, 2 cloves garlic, 2 ozs stale breadcrumbs, ⅛ pint olive oil, 1 teaspoon paprika, a trace of saffron, a pinch of cinnamon.

Peel the onions, cut them in rings and fry them a pale golden-brown in the oil. Lift them out of the pan, which you have drawn off the fire.

Into a small saucepan pour a ½ glass of the water in which the salt cod was cooked. Add the garlic, chopped very finely, and the paprika, saffron and cinnamon, and boil for 5 minutes.

Put the frying-pan back on the fire and heat the oil. In it brown the fish, cut in pieces. Add the breadcrumbs and let them colour a little. Add the onions and then pour into the frying-pan the fragrant contents of the small saucepan. Stir over the fire until the surplus liquid has evaporated. Adjust the seasoning to your taste and serve. When you eat this dish you can really imagine that you are in Spain.

Morue aux Epinards (Salt Cod with Spinach).

> 2 lbs spinach, 1½ lbs fillet of salt cod, soaked and then boiled as above, 4 ozs butter.

Wash the spinach and remove the thickest stalks. Plunge it into boiling water and cook for 10 minutes. Turn it into a colander to drain.

Melt 2 ozs of butter in a deep fireproof dish, add the spinach and salt it sparingly. Put the salt cod, cut in pieces, on top of the spinach and cover the pan until it is heated through.

Just before serving, pour the rest of the butter, melted, over the fish and sprinkle with paprika.

Morue au Riz (Salt Cod with Rice).

> ½ lb salt cod fillets, 3 onions, 2 cloves garlic, a breakfast cup unpolished rice, half a cup olive oil, 1 teaspoon paprika.

Soak the cod for 24 hours, dry it well and cut it in pieces. Brown them in the olive oil. Add the onions, sliced into rings. When they are coloured, add the garlic, finely chopped, and the rice. Stir over the fire until the rice becomes coated with oil and turns transluscent and just golden. Add 2 cups of hot water and the paprika. Leave the pan, covered, on a very low heat for 18 minutes. Life off the lid and shake the pan to loosen the rice which is now cooked but not quite dry. Leave it on a gentle heat for 10 minutes more, lifting the rice with a fork from time to time so that it does not stick to the bottom of the pan. Turn onto a hot dish and serve.

Petits Soldats de Pavie.

> 1 *lb fillet of salt cod which has been soaked for 24 hours,*
> ⅛ *pint olive oil,* 1 *egg,* 4 *ozs flour, fresh breadcrumbs.*

Cut the raw fish, which you have dried carefully, into small rectangles as equal in size as possible. Put into three different soup plates the flour, the egg beaten with a fork, and the breadcrumbs. Dip the pieces of fish into each of these in turn.

Heat the oil to smoking point and fry the pieces of fish for 3 minutes on each side. Serve them very hot sprinkled with a little salt and paprika. These 'little soldiers' can also be eaten cold.

Salad of Salt Cod with Eggs.

> 1 *lb fillet of salt cod soaked and parboiled,* 4 *eggs, olive oil,*
> *vinegar and paprika.*

Cut the cooked fish in pieces. Boil the eggs for 11 minutes, plunge them into cold water and, when they are cool, cut them in slices.

In a salad bowl mix the sliced egg and the pieces of fish very gently, so as not to break them. Dress them with olive oil and vinegar, salt if you wish, and paprika. Taste it. You will be charmed.

Bouillabaisse of Salt Cod.

In Marseilles I watched a fisherman making *bouillabaisse* with salt cod. First of all he dipped the fillets of *morue* five or six times into sea water and between each dipping he wrang them out in a cloth. Half an hour later he made a *bouillabaisse,*

using no other fish at all. To my amazement, it was excellent,
and not too salt. If you want to try this you will need:

> 1½ *lbs salt cod fillets, soaked for 24 hours, ⅛ pint olive oil,
> saffron, 4 cloves garlic, 2 large onions, 2 bayleaves, about
> ¼ lb stale bread.*

Cut the salt cod in pieces and put it into a heavy pan with
the oil and the garlic and onions, finely chopped. Stir over the
fire with a wooden spoon for 5 minutes. Add 2½ pints of cold
water and the bayleaves. Turn on full heat. The water boils.
Season it with plenty of freshly milled pepper and a good
pinch of saffron.

Boil the *bouillabaisse* hard for 12 minutes then test the fish
with a fork. When it is tender taste it and judge whether the
seasoning is sufficient.

Put the slices of stale bread into a tureen, three for each
person, and pour in the *bouillabaisse*. Serve this immediately,
with plenty of white wine—*vin de Cassis*, if you can get it.

Aïoli.

This is a complicated dish made with a mixture of salt cod
which has been soaked and boiled, vegetables and, if you like
them and can get them, snails which have been boiled in
water with a little onion. The whole is served with mayonnaise
very generously laced with garlic. The following mixture is
very good:

> 1 *lb fillet of salt cod*, 1 *lb new potatoes*, ½ *lb new carrots*,
> ¼ *lb new turnips.*

The salt cod must be soaked and boiled as I have described
on p. 66. The vegetables are boiled or steamed and then
sliced and allowed to cool. Now you must make the *aïoli*. For
this you will need:

> 3 *cloves garlic, a piece of stale bread, milk, 2 yolks of egg,
> about ¼ pint olive oil.*

Pound the garlic in a mortar or crush the chopped cloves of
garlic with a little salt beneath the blade of a large kitchen
knife. Squeeze the surplus moisture from a piece of stale bread
which you have soaked in milk. You should be left with a
lump about the size of a small egg. Mix this thoroughly with
the garlic. Add the yolks of egg and a good pinch of salt.
Using a whisk, stir in the oil, slowly at first, and faster as the

sauce becomes creamy, just as you would make a mayonnaise The breadcrumbs, however, will allow you to pour in the oil much more rapidly without fear of the sauce curdling. Put the sauce on one side.

Now arrange the fish in the middle of a dish and surround it with vegetables. Decorate it with some leaves of lettuce and add a few black olives. Make the dish look as tempting as possible and serve the *aïoli* in a separate bowl.

You may not finish all the vegetables and fish, but you will empty the bowl of *aïoli*. And you must drink with this a dry white wine, well chilled.

Skate—with or without Black Butter.

When one hears the word 'skate' one adds, almost by reflex action, the words 'black butter'. Why skate with black butter and not herring, whiting or mackerel with black butter?

One feels that this method of preparation is reserved for this ugly creature which always looks as if it had been dragged in the mud before being laid on the fishmonger's slab.

In fact, skate should be kept for a time before being cooked, and the fishermen say that it is very tough when fresh from the sea. I have, however, eaten very small skate which were just caught, and they were excellent.

For one reason or another, the grown-up skate always has to wait to be cooked and very often it gives off a smell of ammonia in consequence. The same thing applies to other members of the same family such as dog fish which is sold nowadays under the name of rock salmon.

So skate often smells of ammonia and chemists know that ammonia forms, together with acrolein, an insoluble and odourless compound. Acrolein is formed by the action of fat at a high temperature.

If therefore we sprinkle cooked skate with black butter which has been darkened by the action of heat we add enough acrolein to annihilate any possible smell of ammonia.

And that is why cooks, so often in advance of experts on hygiene, generally serve skate with black butter.

Skate with Black Butter.

> 2 *lbs skate*, 5 *ozs butter*, *vinegar*, *parsley minced very fine*,
> 1½ *ozs capers*, 1 *onion*, *a pinch of spice*, *a bayleaf*.

Put the skate into a saucepan full of cold water with plenty of salt. Add the onion, cut in four, the spice and the bayleaf. Simmer for 10 minutes.

During this time, prepare the *beurre noir*. Put all the butter into a frying-pan. It melts. Add the minced parsley. Hold it over the fire, tipping the pan gently to spread the heat.

The butter splutters. It is the water evaporating rather suddenly. The butter begins to smoke. Lower the flame a little. The butter turns golden, then brown, then pale mahogany. Lift the pan from the fire. Wait for 3 minutes. Add a teaspoon of vinegar and stir. Put the pan back on the fire and wait until it boils. Wait another minute. The butter is ready. Add a little pepper.

Lift the fish from the water and let it drain. *This is very important.* Put it on a hot dish. Sprinkle it with capers and the black butter.

Serve the fish and I guarantee that you will be scolded. Not enough butter . . . Next time, use double as much. It is dear, I grant you. As our old *concierge* said, when I was a boy of ten, "Skate is the death of butter".

Skate à la Vinaigrette.

If you find that butter is too expensive, prepare the skate in the same way, but using oil instead. It is excellent.

Skate with Cream.

Cook the skate as I have described, making sure when you buy it that the fish is fresh enough to be without any unpleasant smell.

Now make a sauce which is really quite economical. You will need a ladleful of the water in which the skate was cooked, which you have allowed to cool until it is tepid, and:

2 ozs butter, 2 teaspoons flour, ⅛ pint thick cream.

Mix the tepid water from the fish with the flour, using a wire whisk. Heat this until it begins to thicken. If it becomes too thick add some of the hot water from the fish. When the consistency is just right, stir in the cream. Boil for a moment.

Lift the fish from the saucepan and drain it carefully. Put it onto a hot dish. Cover it with the cream sauce. The black butter was better, but one must economize sometimes.

La Chaudrée.

At Rochefort in the Charente district I enjoyed one of the local dishes. The Poitevin Marshes are not in fact marshes, but an immense stretch of pastureland dapped with copses and veined by a network of small canals fed by the Niort branch of the River Sèvre. These canals are the only local high ways and the inhabitants move about them in flat black boats rowed by the stern, or punted. They glide silently beneath the branches of the trees on their way to the fields or to market; to take the children to school; to get married or to carry to the cemetery those who have died.

The marshes are a sort of green Venice where, instead of palaces there are great poplar trees, and the houses are replaced by the fantastic silhouettes of the ash trees.

This is the country of cognac and the finest butter in the world. The cooking is not remarkable for its originality, but it is succulent, though primitive. One of the best dishes, *la chaudrée*, is a ragout of fish and shell-fish cooked in white wine. For six people buy 3 lbs of mixed fish. You can choose any fish with firm flesh. You will need as well:

A bottle of white wine, 4 cloves garlic, 3 ozs butter.

Cut the fish into slices, removing the bones and skin. Pour a bottle of white wine into a saucepan and add pepper, salt, and garlic chopped fine and some minced parsley. Boil for 15 minutes with the lid off. The wine reduces and smells delicious. Throw in the fish and boil it for 10 minutes, then lower the heat and lift the fish into a deep dish. Stir the butter into the broth, bit by bit. The sauce becomes smooth and velvety. Be very careful that it does not boil. Pour it over the fish and serve.

Chaudrée should be eaten from a soup plate with a spoon.

Lobster with Mayonnaise.

From my window in a small Breton port I used to watch the red-sailed fishing boats returning with their catch. They were bringing in the lobsters and crawfish caught off the rocky coast of Brittany. Other, larger boats had been far away on the English side of the Channel. Their catch was so abundant that they sometimes wondered whether they would be able to sell it all.

So lobsters could be bought for a song, and I ate them every day, braving the threat of urticaria and, perhaps because I prepared them in a different way each day, there were no unpleasant consequences.

Really, though, one must admit that no complicated method of preparation is half as good as fresh-caught lobster simply boiled in sea water, cooled and served with mayonnaise.

Fot this, boil some sea water or well-salted tap water, in a large pot. Add pepper and sprigs of fennel. Plunge the live lobster into fast-boiling water so that its sufferings shall be as brief as possible, and after 1.5 minutes, draw the pot off the fire and let it stand for another 15 minutes. Lift out the lobster, allow it to cool and eat it with mayonnaise (p. 189).

Homard à l'Américaine.

This is a celebrated dish, but it offends a basic principle of taste. The sauce, which is too highly spiced and too rich in tomato and brandy, kills the delicate flavour of the lobster. With this reservation in mind one can eat it from time to time. Here is one of the many recipes which are used in the small restaurants in Brittany—a region which prides itself on being the home of this dish which, they say, should be called lobster *à l'amoricaine.*

> *A lobster, ¼ pint olive oil, white wine, a small tin of tomato purée, 6 shallots, black and cayenne pepper, a glass Madeira, a glass of cognac, 1 teaspoonful each of tarragon, chervil and parsley, stale bread, a dab of butter.*

Kill the lobster by plunging a sharp knife through its head. In this way it will die instantly. Remove the head and the intestine, which is the grey line running down through the tail meat. Cut the body in pieces leaving the shell on. Heat the oil in a saucepan and lay the lobster in it. Cover with white wine and add tomato purée, chopped shallots, some freshly-ground black pepper and as much cayenne as will lie on the very tip of a knife. Salt lightly, and boil for 15 minutes.

Pour in a large glass of Madeira, a glass of cognac and the chopped tarragon, chervil and parsley. Boil for 3 minutes more. The lobster is ready—almost. The sauce is a little too thin. Correct this by thickening it with a little stale bread and cooking for another 3 minutes.

Gratin de Homard.

This is a dish which I invented after giving a lecture on Dauphinois cooking at the Col de la Porte at the foot of the Grande Chartreuse. There I spent two hours in the kitchen helping to prepare a sensational dish for the next day—the *gratin d'écrivisses*. This is a dish which is far too expensive for everyday life. My own invention is not quite so good, but it is agreeable, and it is within your reach.

A large tin of lobster, white wine, a sprig of thyme, a little fennel, a trace of Cayenne, 2 ozs butter, 1 tablespoon flour, ¼ pint cream, grated Parmesan cheese.

Open a tin of lobster and drain off the juice. You will find that this has a pungent smell, but not much flavour. Pour it into a saucepan and add its own volume of white wine, a sprig of thyme, pepper and a little fennel, a trace of Cayenne pepper and *no salt*. Boil for 20 minutes with the lid off so that the liquid is reduced. Let it cool.

Make a white sauce by melting the butter and blending it with the flour over a low fire. Pour in the liquid you have prepared, a little at a time, stirring constantly. Mix in the cream and continue to stir over the fire. Let it boil and add the lobster meat cut in pieces. Heat again and taste, adding salt if necessary. Put the mixture into a fireproof dish and sprinkle it with grated Parmesan. Put it into the oven to brown.

The *gratin d'écrivisses* is made with crayfish and decorated with their heads, but you have no claws or tails and the lobster tin is hardly decorative. Never mind, serve it as it comes from the oven, golden-brown and steaming, with a glass of white wine which should not be too dry. And don't forget to drink to my health.

Langoustes à la Crème.

This dish can be made with imported crawfish tails which are good value, but not nearly so delicate in flavour or texture as fresh crawfish. You would need two tails weighing about 1 lb each.

2 crawfish weighing about 1½ lbs each, or 2 tails, 4 ozs butter, ½ teaspoon curry powder, a bottle of white wine, 1 tablespoon flour, 6 ozs double cream, a glass of Madeira.

Stab the crawfish through the back of the head with a sharp

knife and cut them in pieces crosswise, removing the heads and intestines.

Melt the butter and fry the pieces of crawfish until they are beginning to colour. Salt lightly and sprinkle with freshly-milled pepper and curry powder. Add a bottle of white wine.

Cover and boil for 20 minutes and draw the pan off the fire. Cool for a few minutes and then lift out the crawfish and remove the shells. The flesh is firm and fragrant. Now for the sauce:

> 1 *tablespoon flour*, 6 *ozs double cream, a large glass Madeira, a glass cognac*

Mix the flour with the cream and stir them into the liquid from the crawfish. Bring this to the boil. The sauce thickens. Enrich it with a glass of Madeira and a good glassful of cognac and boil for 3 minutes. Add the pieces of lobster and heat until the sauce begins to boil, then pour it into a deep dish. The crawfish should be served with rice which you have cooked for 20 minutes in one and a half times it's own volume of boiling salted water. This makes an excellent foil for the abundant creamy sauce.

Fill your glasses with the best white wine you can afford.

Mussels.

In Latin countries mussels have always been regarded both as a useful food and a delicacy.

Pliny praised the subtlety of these shell-fish and explained that the secret of their flavour consisted in growing them in water which was alternately salt and fresh. The Romans grew mussels in the estuaries and we do the same nowadays.

Mussels are grown on special timber frames at the mouth of rivers, but sometimes the water is polluted by sewage, so one should never eat them raw.

Many people avoid mussels for fear of poisoning, and their fears are not unfounded, though one must point out that mussel poisoning is rare and never very serious. It is not caused by the copper absorbed by mussels from ships' bottoms nor, as used to be thought, by the spawn of starfish which had got into the mussel shells. It is the result of a poison excreted at times by the livers of diseased mussels. If the stomach of a sufferer from mussel poisoning is artificially emptied, the symptoms disappear rapidly.

Mussels used to be prescribed for disorders of the liver,

stomach and intestine, and calcined mussels mixed with honey were used to make an ointment for the healing of wounds.

You must prepare your mussels carefully, since the water in which they are cooked is often used in the finished dish. They must be quite fresh and all the shells tightly closed. Scrape the shells with a short knife to remove the beard and any excrescences. If any shell is not quite closed tap it smartly with a knife. If it does not close at once the mussel is dead, and you must throw it away.

Wash the mussels in several bowls of water, moving them about all the time and draining them in a colander between each washing. The last water must be quite clean and without a trace of sand. If the mussels are to be served in the shell, the empty halves should be removed before they are brought to table. Don't forget to provide extra plates for the shells which are discarded as you eat.

Here, and in other chapters, I shall give you some recipes for mussels, and your imagination will discover many other ways of using these excellent shell-fish. I suggest that you try them with rice; with buttered noodles, or in an omelette.

Moules Marinières.

Put into a saucepan of cold water some freshly-milled pepper, two chopped shallots, a little parsley very finely chopped and 2 ozs of butter. Add 3 pints of mussels prepared as above. Cover and heat slowly. The mussels open, releasing their water. Boil for 5 minutes.

Serve the mussels in soup plates with the liquor in a sauce-boat. Soup plates piled with mussels, glasses filled with Chablis—this dish will rejoice your guests.

Moules à la Crème.

Prepare some *moules marinières* and put them into a deep dish. Add to the liquor in the saucepan ⅛ pint of thick cream mixed with a teaspoon of flour. Stir and boil for a moment. Pour it into a sauce-boat and hand it round with the mussels.

Moules Niçoises.

> 3 *pints mussels,* 1 *clove garlic, minced,* 2 *chopped shallots,*
> 2 *tablespoons olive oil, a pinch of saffron,* ½ *teaspoon flour,*
> ⅛ *pint of white wine.*

Put the garlic, shallots and olive oil into a saucepan. Add the mussels. They will open over the heat. Boil for 5 minutes and then lift them out and put them into a deep dish. Add a pinch of saffron to the liquid in the saucepan and let it boil.

Meanwhile, mix the flour and white wine and stir them into the sauce. Boil for a moment more, then empty the contents of the pan into a sauce-boat and carry it to table with the mussels. If you are lucky enough to have a bottle of white *vin de Cassis*, your happiness will be complete.

Moules à l'Espagnole.

Prepare some *moules niçoises* and add to the sauce a tablespoon of tinned tomato purée. Boil for 2 minutes and serve.

Fried Mussels.

Cook some *moules marinières*. Let them cool a little and take them out of their shells.

Make a light batter with 1 egg, 3½ ozs flour and a ½ glass of beer. Dip the mussels in this batter, which should be thick enough to coat them well, and throw them one by one into deep smoking-hot oil. In 3 minutes they will be crisp and golden-brown. Serve them with fried parsley.

Mussel Salad.

Prepare some *moules marinières* and let them stand until they are quite cold. Take them out of their shells and dress them with vinaigrette sauce which you have made by blending two-thirds of olive oil with one-third of vinegar mixed with chopped herbs. Parsley, chives, tarragon, capers and minced shallot with a trace of pickled gherkin make a very good mixture.

Cold *moules marinières* are also very good with mayonnaise.

Fricassée of Scallops.

In France, scallops are sold in their shells and one can see the poor things yawning with discomfort on the fishmonger's slab. It is always advisable to touch the back of a scallop with the tip of a knife. If the shell snaps shut on the blade this is a sign that the scallop is full of fight and in good health. If not, then it is past caring and should be rejected.

In England, the scallops are almost always ready cleaned and prepared by the fishmonger who should have carried out this test. All you have to watch is that the flesh is firm and not discoloured.

> 12 *scallops,* ½ *pint white wine,* 1 *oz butter,* ½ *teaspoon curry powder, a pinch of paprika,* 1 *glass Madeira,* 1 *glass cognac,* ⅛ *pint double cream,* 1 *heaping teaspoon flour.*

Using a sharp knife, detach the scallops from their shells and plunge them into cold water. Drain them. In a medium-sized saucepan bring the white wine to the boil. Add the scallops, butter, curry powder and paprika and season with pepper.

Poach over a low fire for 10 minutes. Add the Madeira and cognac and boil for 3–4 minutes more. Meanwhile mix a heaping teaspoon of flour with the cream. Stir this into the liquid in the saucepan and let it boil for a moment more.

Pour the fricassee into a dish and serve it surrounded with rice which you have prepared in the following way:

Melt 2 oz butter in a saucepan and put in a cupful of dry rice. Stir until the grains of rice are all shiny with butter, and then add 1½ cups of boiling water and season with salt. Cover the saucepan and let it boil for 20 minutes over a very low fire, stirring from time to time so that the rice does not stick. Test the rice to make sure that it is cooked, then pile it round the fricassee on a hot dish.

Scallops à l'Américaine.

> 12 *scallops,* 3 *tablespoons olive oil,* 3 *shallots chopped finely,* 2 *glasses white wine, a glass Madeira,* 2 *glasses cognac, a pinch of spice,* 2 *tablespoons tomato purée.*

Clean the scallops as before. Heat the oil in a saucepan. Into this put the scallops, shallots, white wine and a pinch of spice. Boil for 10 minutes and then add the Madeira and cognac. Instead of using cream and flour as in the previous recipe, stir in tomato purée.

Boil for 3 minutes. The scallops are ready. If the sauce should be too thin, add some breadcrumbs. Serve in a deep dish accompanied by some boiled noodles laced with plenty of butter.

Coquilles St. Jacques Gratinées.

Be sure to ask your fishmonger for at least six deep shells, unless you have these already in the house. Fishmongers sometimes give one the flat sides of the shell and these are quite useless as containers for a creamy mass of scallops.

Prepare a fricassee of scallops as above, cutting each scallop in three pieces. Add to the sauce 2 oz grated Parmesan cheese. Divide the mixture into six scallop shells, sprinkle with more Parmesan and brown them in the oven.

Coquilles St. Jacques à la Tomate.

Prepare a fricassee as in the previous recipe but flavour the sauce, which should be abundant, with tomato purée. Fill 6 scallop shells with the mixture and sprinkle them with breadcrumbs and grated Parmesan.

With all these scallop dishes serve a light Chablis, very dry and very well chilled.

FROGS, SNAILS, FRESHWATER FISH

Frogs and snails fill certain people with horror. If you are one of these I suggest that you adopt the system devised by the B.B.C. in their wonderful programme, Woman's Hour, when they are about to discuss a topic which might shock some of their listeners. Switch off if you don't want to listen, they say, and switch on again in so many minutes. In the same way I say to you, if you prefer to skip the subjects of frogs and snails, turn at once to p. 85.

The British used to refer to Frenchmen as 'frog-eaters' and they were quite right. This is one of our characteristics and not the least artistic of them. However, as long ago as 1893 Mr. M. C. Cooke in his book *Our Reptiles and Batrachians*, commented that the British were relaxing in their prejudices and that both Frenchmen and frogs were being better understood and appreciated. He reported that preserved frogs' legs were being regularly sold at some of the West End provision warehouses "packed in air-tight canisters, in the same manner as many other mysterious comestibles", and he described how he had summoned up his courage to test their edible qualities. To his surprise, he found them very agreeable.

Nowadays you can buy fresh frogs' legs, imported twice weekly from France, in Soho. These are sold by the dozen speared on a stick. One enterprising firm which imports frozen frogs' legs for the restaurants is planning to sell them, a dozen at a time, in a polythene bag. The cost of these will be about half that of the fresh. Tinned frogs' legs are also available, but they are more expensive than the frozen and the manager of the shop advises that the fresh or frozen ones are preferable in every way.

Edible frogs are found in Britain, though they are not believed to be native to the country. In 1837 a Mr. Berney went to Paris and brought back two hundred edible frogs and a great quantity of spawn which he deposited in the meadows of Morton in Lincolnshire. They did not like the meadows and left them for the ponds. In 1841 he imported another lot from

Brussels and in 1842 he brought thirteen hundred from St. Omer "in large hampers made like slave ships with plenty of tiers. These were movable and were covered with water-lily leaves stitched on to them, that the frogs might be comfortable and feel at home." The frogs were dispersed in the Fens and in Norfolk.

Since then edible frogs have been found in various parts of East Anglia. They differ from ordinary frogs in their larger size and their splendid voices, produced by the bladders at the corners of their mouths which distend when they croak. Edible frogs have distinct black markings and a light line running down the middle of their backs.

If you should feel the urge to catch these succulent little creatures, you can go out at night with a torch when, I am told, they stare quite motionless at the light, making no attempt to escape, and allow themselves to be picked up quite easily.

In France, they fish for frogs with a light cane and a hook baited with a scrap of red rag. With a small lead weight to give control, the bait is made to dance above the surface of the water amongst the reeds, and the frogs pounce on it eagerly. If you should take to fishing for frogs, don't torture the poor things, but end their misery at once by grasping them firmly by the back legs and tapping them smartly on the back of the head against your fishing-rod. This done, you snip across the lower half of the body with a pair of scissors, pull off the skin, cross the back legs and thread them onto a small stick.

There are various way of cooking frogs' legs, but I suggest that you disregard all those which do not respect their delicate flavour. Avoid complicated sauces. Use as flavouring only a few particles of garlic or shallot. Be prodigal with butter and parsley.

Grenouilles Sautées au Beurre.

This is the simplest way of preparing frogs.

> 2 *dozen pairs of frogs' legs, a scant 3 ozs butter, minced parsley, lemon.*

Melt half the butter in a frying-pan. When it is just smoking, put the frogs' legs into it. Shake the pan to prevent the butter from burning. The legs begin to colour. Turn them over so that they turn brown on the other side. Lower the heat and let them cook in all for about 10 minutes.

Put the rest of the butter into the pan. Dust them generously with parsley, and sprinkle with salt and the juice of a quarter of a lemon.

Serve them immediately in a hot dish, filling your glasses with well-chilled Chablis.

Fried Frogs' Legs.

> 2 *dozen pairs of frogs' legs*, 1 *egg, breadcrumbs made from stale white bread*, 2 *ozs butter, a lemon.*

Beat the egg with a fork. Dip the frogs' legs in it and then in the breadcrumbs which must be finely grated and quite white. Firm the breadcrumbs on to the flesh with the tips of your fingers.

Baked Frogs' Legs.

> 2 *dozen pairs of frogs' legs*, 4 *ozs white breadcrumbs*, 3½ *ozs butter*, 4 *shallots, a bouquet of parsley.*

Warm a fireproof dish. Arrange the frogs' legs in it without allowing them to overlap. Melt the butter and pour it into the dish. Strew the breadcrumbs, and the parsley and shallot, finely chopped, between the frogs. Sprinkle with salt and a little lemon juice. Put the dish into the oven for about 20 minutes at about 350° F.

When the top of the dish has turned golden-brown the frogs are ready. If the breadcrumbs have soaked up all the butter, add a little more at the last moment.

Grenouilles Sauce Poulette.

To make a *sauce poulette* begin by making *sauce suprême*, as I describe on p. 187. Besides this and 2 dozen pairs of frogs' legs you will need 1 oz of butter and 2 eggs.

Before adding the eggs to the sauce, set the saucepan on one side and melt the butter in a frying-pan. Fry the frogs' legs until they are nicely browned all over. Sprinkle them lightly with salt, and pour the unfinished sauce over the frogs' legs so that they are completely covered. Leave them for 5 minutes over a very low heat.

Now lift out the frogs and put them into a hot dish. Put 2 yolks of egg into a small saucepan and pour over them little by little, the hot sauce from the frying-pan, stirring all the time. Put the saucepan on a low fire. Go on stirring. The sauce thickens. It is just about to boil. Pour it over the frogs and sprinkle the dish with very finely chopped parsley.

Serve the frogs at once and with them, a bottle of Sauternes. Even rather a sweet wine suits this dish very well. I wish you a very good bottle.

Snails.

There is no doubt that people in England are becoming much more adventurous in their eating habits, and snails appear quite tame compared with the bumble bees, grasshoppers and chocolate-covered ants which I believe are selling well at some of the big stores. When I heard the other day of the London bus conductor who goes every week to Soho and takes home a dozen snails I felt that interest in new kinds of food was really becoming general.

Snails are fascinating creatures and not nearly so placid as their appearance would suggest. They devour our vegetable crops, so that it is only fair that we should devour them.

As far as gastronomy is concerned, there are several kinds of snails, but only two which are worth our attention:

1. The large, pale snail with shadowy markings known as the Roman snail, or *Helix Pomatia* to naturalists.

2. The little grey snail which is properly called *Helix Nemoralis*.

The Roman snail is a great traveller. You will find him on the plains, in the hills, amongst the vineyards, and so on. When you find one, search and you will always find another. Although they are harmaphrodites they go about in pairs.

The little grey snail is fond of stones. Look for him on rainy mornings at the foot of walls, especially those which face north or north-west.

Edible snails were introduced into Britain by the Romans and they are plentiful on the South Downs and on the Cornish headlands, where they were gathered by the crews of French coasting vessels.

Incidentally, tons of common garden snails used to be collected in Gloucestershire and sent to Bristol for the consumption of workers in the tobacco factories, whilst vanloads of snails travelled by train from Pembrokeshire to Bristol, where they were said to be enjoyed mainly by the glassblowers. I have no record of how these snails were cooked, but

I shall tell you how I would prepare the snails which we eat in France.

Supposing you had collected three or four dozen Roman snails or three hundred of the small grey ones which we called *petits gris*. What should you do with the good creatures? In the first case, don't shrink from the trouble involved, but serve the snails in their shells, after you have prepared them. In the second, serve the snails without their shells in a beautiful silver dish.

In either case you must let the snails fast. Put them into a bucket, a large pot, or a basket, but be sure that the vessel is firmly closed by a lid weighted down with stones. The lid must be perforated with small holes so that fresh air reaches the snails.

Let the snails fast for 48 hours. Lift the lid. It is a horrid sight. The volume of excrement seems almost as big as that of the snails. Empty the snails into another receptacle and fill it with cold water. The snails float. All the unwanted matter has remained on the walls of the first bucket which you clean immediately and fill with cold water.

Shake the snails well. Lift them out and put them back into the other bucket of fresh cold water. Change them round three times using fresh water each time and shaking them well. The snails are now clean.

Put a large pan half-full of water on the fire. Flavour it with *plenty* of salt and pepper, sliced onions, parsley stalks, thyme, bayleaf and fennel. The liquid boils. Throw in the snails. Poor things. They will do no more damage to the vegetation. Slime rises to the surface. The liquid begins to boil once more. It foams and is about to overflow. Watch carefully. Add 3 tablespoons of vinegar. The mucin coagulates on contact with the vinegar. The liquid no longer foams. Cover the pan and let it simmer for 3 hours.

Lift the shells out of the water with a straining spoon. Put them into a dish to cool. Take the snails out of the shells with a fine skewer. Rinse the shells with cold water and now comes the serious question . . . how to prepare them.

Escargots en Coquilles.

If you have 3 or 4 dozen large snails, prepare the classic butter.

> *A scant 6 ozs butter, a large bouquet of parsley, 4 large cloves of garlic.*

84

Chop the garlic and the parsley very finely. Add plenty of salt and pepper and, with a fork, mix them intimately with the butter.

Take each snail and, with your fingers remove the rolled-up appendage which contains the intestine. Put a snail back into each shell and fill it with savoury butter which you force in until it will hold no more.

Put them into a dish with the opening upwards so that the melted butter does not run out, and heat them in the oven. Three minutes before serving introduce into each shell with a medicine dropper, a teardrop of *marc* and put them back in the oven for another 3 minutes. Give a dozen snails to each person.

Escargots en Cassolette.

Suppose you have prepared and cooked 200 small grey snails and taken them out of their shells. Remove the intestines and put the snails into a fireproof dish. Make a savoury butter as before, using 4 ozs butter and a whole head of garlic besides plenty of parsley, pepper and salt.

Put the snails in a fireproof dish and dispose the butter round them. Sprinkle on top of them a large handful of grated stale bread. Put the dish in the oven for 10 minutes and add a small glass of *marc*.

Stir, and heat for 3 minutes more, then put the snails into a silver dish which you have previously warmed.

Serve them on hot plates and use a spoon so that you can drink the butter as you eat the snails.

With this, serve a little white wine from Anjou, well chilled.

Eels.

Do you know the mysterious story of the eels which are caught in the rivers and which, by the way, have absolutely nothing to do with congers, which are sometimes called sea eels? At a certain moment in their lives our freshwater eels get together in countless bands and travel to the sea. They cross the Atlantic, crawling to the depths of the ocean, and join the warm current of the Gulf Stream, but before reaching the coast of Mexico they stop in the Sargasso Sea. This strange sea is covered with floating weed. Here all the eels of the world meet to lay and fertilize their eggs. Then they die or disappear. The eggs hatch and the minute fry emerge. They grow a little and then cross the ocean and arrive in millions at the mouths of rivers in Europe and America. There, they are caught and massacred to make all sorts of delicious dishes like the *angulas* of Spain where baby eels, as fine as vermicelli, are baked in earthenware dishes with oil and garlic and eaten so hot that you need a wooden fork to avoid burning your mouth. Enough survive, however, to re-populate our rivers and spend there four or five years preparing for their nuptial journey to the Sargasso Sea.

The eels which do not return there are those which fall into a frying-pan or saucepan. Let us see what we can do to them.

Grilled Eel.

Fresh-caught eel is very good grilled. Choose a young eel weighing not more than 1½ lbs. Hang it by its head from a nail and slit the skin all round the neck. Using a rag with which to get a grip, pull off the skin. Clean the eel and cut it in pieces.

Grill the slices, if possible over a charcoal fire. Sprinkle them with salt and freshly milled pepper. With a glass of white wine this is a dish fit for a king.

Marinated Eel.

Prepare the eel as before and then marinate the pieces for several hours in a mixture of equal parts of water and vinegar perfumed with onion rings, thyme and bayleaf. Then drain them and grill them.

Anguille Maître d'Hôtel.

This is a good way of cooking older eels. These are inclined to be rather fat and in the frying-pan the surplus fat is melted out. It is not a dish which is generally appreciated, but I never tire of it.

Clean and skin the eel and cut it in pieces. (An easy way to remove the skin is to put the slices of eel into cold water and bring them to the boil. As soon as the water is boiling lift out the eel and the skin will come away very easily. You will also have removed some of the fat.)

Melt the butter in a frying-pan and fry the slices of eel for 15 minutes over a medium fire, turning them from time to time. When they are golden-brown, sprinkle them with salt and freshly-milled pepper and a little of the butter and fat from the pan. Dust them with the finest chopped parsley.

Jellied Eels.

> *2 young eels skinned and thinly sliced, 1 lb carrots, 1 lb turnips, 1 lb leeks and 2 onions, a small glass of port or Madeira, browning, mayonnaise or sauce vinaigrette.*

Boil the vegetables for 45 minutes in 1½ pints of water seasoned with salt and pepper. Remove the vegetables and put the eels into the stock. Poach them for 40 minutes with the lid on. Add a small glass of port or Madeira. Boil for 3 minutes more and add a few drops of browning. Pour into a deep dish and stand in a cool place until next day. The contents of the dish will have turned into a firm jelly. Detach the edges with the point of a knife and turn it onto a dish. The pieces of eel form a charming mosaic in their translucent setting.

Serve the jellied eels with mayonnaise (p. 189) or *sauce vinaigrette* (p. 119).

Stuffed Carp.

Wild carp are difficult to prepare as their scales are tough. They tend to have a muddy flavour. During the eighteenth century the monks in France were able, by careful selection, to breed a delicate variety called a mirror carp whose scales can easily be removed. Now these carp are mainly bred in Central Europe where they reach a weight of about 3 lbs in two years. From the breeding farms they are exported and kept in tanks ready for market. These tanks are so clean that the flesh of the fish never tastes of mud.

> *A carp weighing 3 lbs, 2 large onions, 4 rashers of bacon, 1 teaspoon flour, 2 ozs butter, burgundy, 8 ozs mushrooms, thyme.*

Remove the scales from the fish by scraping with a knife from the tail towards the head. Cut off the fins with a pair of scissors. Wash the fish and with a very sharp knife make an incision along the dorsal fin, taking care that the knife point touches the whole length of the backbone. Separate the flesh and, scraping along the backbone and the ribs, open up the fish so that it lies in front of you with the flesh uppermost. The backbone is attached to the dorsal fin. Cut across the head and the tail with your scissors and pull the backbone away. Now you can get at the stomach. You will find a huge roe. Put it on one side. Remove the guts. Wash the cavity, salt and pepper it and fill it with sliced raw onion. Leave it like this for 15 minutes.

Meanwhile prepare the stuffing. For this you will need:

> *6 ozs fat bacon chopped finely, 6 ozs mushrooms, 4 ozs chopped onion, 4 ozs stale breadcrumbs, 1½ ozs butter, thyme, a little milk, 1 egg.*

Soak the breadcrumbs in the milk and then squeeze them to remove the surplus moisture. Melt the butter in a frying-pan, add the bacon and 4 ozs of the mushrooms which you have chopped finely.

Raise the heat, and the juice of the mushrooms will begin to evaporate. Mix in the breadcrumbs using a fork. Add the roe and then the onion, stirring well over the fire. Season with salt and pepper and finely chopped thyme. Put the stuffing on a plate to cool and mix in the egg, which you have beaten.

Now return to the carp and remove the onions from the stomach, replacing them with the stuffing. Be careful not to fill the carp too full or it will burst during cooking. With a needle and thread sew up the back of the fish.

Put 2 rashers of bacon into a fireproof dish and then the carp. Sprinkle it with salt, top it with two more rashers of bacon and some dabs of butter. Put it in the oven for 15 minutes. The bacon has melted and the fish is beginning to brown.

Now pour into the dish a ½-bottle of Burgundy which you have heated to boiling point. Add the rest of the mushrooms cut in slices, and the onions which you removed from the stomach of the fish. Sprinkle a little more salt, pepper and thyme over it and bake for 45 minutes, basting frequently, sniffing the heavenly smell, admiring your beautiful dish, and adding more red wine as the liquid evaporates.

Mix 2 ozs of butter with a teaspoon of flour. Take the dish out of the oven and put the butter mixture in walnut-sized dabs into the dish. With great care stir the sauce with a spoon so that it thickens and becomes creamy. Carry the dish to table.

Find the end of the thread and draw it out. The boned fish can easily be sliced like a roast. Give each of your guests a slice of stuffed fish, mushrooms, sauce and a glass of Burgundy. Not a sound is to be heard, everyone is too absorbed in his food. Not even the sound of chewing, since the stuffed carp, free of all its bones, melts in one's mouth.

Carpe à la Juive.

This dish is a favourite amongst orthodox Jews who are not allowed to cook on the Sabbath, that is to say between sunset on Friday and the setting of the sun on Saturday evening.

A carp weighing about 3 lbs, 1 lb onions, 10 almonds, about 20 large raisins, ½ teaspoon spice, grated horse-radish.

Clean the carp and scrape off the scales, unless they are very fine. Snip off the fins and rub the fish with coarse salt, inside and out. Leave it for 30 minutes and then cut it in five slices, not counting the head and the tail.

Chop the onions and put them into a saucepan. Add the chopped almonds, the raisins, the fish, including the head and tail, plenty of salt and pepper and the spice. Just cover all this with cold water and bring it to the boil with the lid on. Skim, lower the heat and simmer for 1 hour.

Lift the pieces of fish delicately from the pan and arrange them on a deep dish in the shape of the whole carp. Pour over it the liquid from the pan and the onions and stand it overnight in a cool place.

Next morning the juice has turned to jelly and the dish looks very pretty. Serve it with grated horse-radish seasoned with vinegar to sharpen the flavour.

Carpe au Lard.

For this dish you will need:

A carp weighing about 2 lbs, sufficient rashers of bacon to cover the fish, 2 ozs butter, a bottle of very dry white wine.

Put the carp, which you have cleaned, and from which you have removed the scales and fins, onto a hot fireproof dish. Salt it lightly, sprinkle it with freshly-milled pepper and cover it with bacon. All round the fish put the butter in little pieces. Set the dish in a very hot oven (450° F. Gas 8).

After 10 minutes open the oven door and look at the fish. The bacon has melted and its fat is mixing with the melted butter. Five minutes later one can smell the hot butter and there is a faint sizzling noise. The butter is turning brown. It is about to burn. You must hurry. Pour a glass of white wine into the dish. It hisses and splutters furiously, then calm is restored. Baste the fish and close the oven door once more.

Every 5 minutes baste the fish, adding wine as it evaporates. The carp becomes a beautiful golden-brown. Its skin is crackling.

After 40 minutes in the oven the fish is ready. Set it between two bottles of dry white wine (*vin d'Alsace* would be my choice). The flesh of the fish with its creamy, fragrant juice will melt in your mouth.

Brochet au Beurre Blanc.

To cook a pike is simple. To make *beurre blanc* is thought to be very difficult. Don't believe it. I learnt how to make this sauce at Nantes, which is its home, and I shall tell you the secret.

To make this dish for four people you will need a pike weighing not less than 2 lbs, otherwise the proportion of bones to flesh is too great. You will also need:

$\frac{1}{2}$ *lb salt butter, 4 shallots, 1 tablespoon vinegar.*

Peel the shallots and chop them finely. Put them into a small heavy saucepan with thick sides—a copper pan if you are lucky enough to possess one. Add the vinegar and 2 tablespoons of cold water. Boil them over a low fire until the liquid has almost evaporated, then draw the saucepan off the fire, stir in 2 tablespoons of cold water and forget about it for the moment.

Now you must cook the pike. Make a *court-bouillon* by boiling for an hour in water which you have salted and acidulated with vinegar, all the herbs of Saint John that is to say:

onion, parsley, thyme, bayleaf, pepper, and so on.

Ten minutes before the hour is up, add half a dozen peppercorns. Strain the *court-bouillon* and let it cool.

Poach the pike for 20 minutes in this liquid. While it is cooking make the *beurre blanc*. Divide the butter into ten pieces. Put your small saucepan back onto a very low fire and warm the liquid in it. Add a piece of butter which will melt very slowly. Stir with a wire whisk. Add a second piece of butter which, as it melts, will mix with the water and the shallot so that it becomes white and creamy. Continue over the gentlest heat to whisk in the butter bit by bit. Stir for another minute and the sauce thickens. Your *beurre blanc* is ready. It is the consistency of thin ·hollandaise sauce. Put it into a warmed sauce-boat.

Lift the pike out of the water and lay it on a dish with a folded napkin beneath it. Garnish it with some leaves of lettuce and carry it to the table. It will be received with a gasp of admiration. But wait till your guests taste the *beurre blanc*!

Roast Shad.

> *A shad weighing 3 lbs, 4 ozs butter, 3 shallots, thyme, ½ glass white wine, 3 ozs thick cream, ½ teaspoon flour.*

Most people prefer sea fish to freshwater fish. They have less bones and are simpler to eat. The sea fish are more varied and provide a greater choice of dishes and they are far easier to obtain. There are, however, some tasty river fish, and I should like to tell you about a delicious roast shad which I ate in the Loire Valley not far from Orléans.

Shad is one of the handsomest of the freshwater fish and its tiny scales sparkle with all the colours of the rainbow. However, the joy of admiring it must give way to the pleasure of eating it, so if you can find a shad weighing 3 lbs, scrape off the scales and remove the fins, using a pair of scissors. Heat your oven to about 350° F. (Gas 4).

Dot the bottom of a fireproof dish with 2 ozs of butter and lay the shad in it. Spread over the fish, using a broad-bladed knife, another 2 ozs of butter. Whilst you are making these preparations, the oven has been heating.

Put the shad in oven for 20 minutes. The shad is turning golden-brown and the butter is sizzling in the dish. Baste the fish and close the oven again. Wait for 5 minutes and look once more. The fish has become an even more beautiful colour. Sprinkle it with fine salt. Twenty-five minutes have now passed.

Strew the bottom of the dish with the shallots, chopped very finely, and a sprinkling of thyme. Then pour in a glass of white wine which you have previously brought to the boil. Every 5 minutes baste the fish with this fragrant blend of wine and butter. Forty minutes after the dish entered the oven, lift it out and put it on a gentle heat. You will find that the sauce is not very abundant. Add a ½-glass of boiling water, tipping the dish slightly so that you can stir it in.

Now complete the sauce. In a little bowl, mix the cream with the flour. Stir into this some of the sauce from the fish, then pour the contents of the bowl into the dish and mix carefully. Baste the fish with the sauce. It begins to boil. Carry the fish straight to the table and fill your glasses with the same white wine which you used for the sauce.

This dish should be followed by a *platée de pommes* which you will find on p. 202.

Shad with Sorrel.

> *A shad weighing 2 lbs, ½ pint thick cream, 2 lbs sorrel, 2½ ozs butter.*

Wash and scrape the shad and snip off the fins with the kitchen scissors. Put the fish into a fireproof dish and pour a little less than half the cream over it. Sprinkle with salt and a few turns of pepper from the mill and put it into a hot oven (425° F. Gas 7). Let the surface brown and then moisten it with all but 2 tablespoons of the cream that is left. Lower the heat and continue to baste the fish from time to time with the cream, which will have become buttery. The liquid will turn slowly to a caramel. In 1 hour the fish will be done.

Meanwhile, prepare a sorrel purée as I describe on p. 178. Serve the shad on a hot dish surrounded by sorrel and bathed in the buttery sauce in which it has cooked, and to which you have added the rest of the cream.

Grey Mullet with Cucumbers.

> *A grey mullet weighing about 2 lbs, 2 cucumbers, mayonnaise made with 1 egg, and lemon instead of vinegar, 2½ ozs thick cream, 2 ozs black olives, slices of lemon, lettuce leaves for garnish.*

Make a *court-bouillon* as I described in the recipe for *brochet au beurre blanc* on p. 90, and into it put the grey mullet which you have cleaned and washed very carefully. Cover the fish with a cloth, so that even if it floats on the surface it will keep moist.

Put the fish kettle on the fire and bring it to the boil again and poach the mullet for 25 minutes. Lift the fish out of the water and slip it onto a dish. It should stand in a cool place for 6 hours.

Meanwhile, peel the cucumbers and cut them in paper-thin slices. Sprinkle them with salt and put them in a salad bowl beneath a plate with a weight on top. After 4 hours drain off the juice of the cucumbers. Make a mayonnaise with 1 egg

and lemon juice instead of vinegar. Mix it with the cream and
a little more pepper. Dress the cucumbers with this sauce and
arrange them round the fish. Decorate it with shining black
olives and crisp slices of lemon, and at each end of the dish a
plume of lettuce leaves.

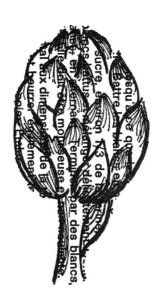

MEAT

How to make the best of your Meat.

It is not easy to cook a piece of meat to perfection. So many factors have to be taken into account—whether the meat is to be rare or well done; the size and type of your cut; the animal from which it comes, and goodness knows what else.

Let us say right away that only tender cuts of really good quality should be served underdone. For this, cooking time must be short and the temperature in the centre of the meat should not rise above 140° F. The meat will be rosy, juice-filled and tender because it was tender to start with.

Cuts from parts of the body which have had to work very hard during the life of the animal must be cooked for a long time so that the meat is subjected to a process of pre-digestion. The pepsin which is formed during slow cooking dissolves in the liquid in which the meat is cooked and makes the meat tender. If the liquid is restricted, it will form a gravy. If it is abundant the result will be a broth.

There are various ways of improving the flavour of meat dishes. Generally, these consist in the addition of onions, garlic, spice, herbs and so on, to the liquid.

One can go further and introduce various flavours into the meat itself. Leg of mutton with garlic is a classic example. There are methods which are more complicated such as the use of stuffings.

I am going to tell you about a dish of which I am particularly fond—*bœuf à la houssarde*. It consists of a piece of beef interspersed with layers of savoury stuffing and cooked very slowly in a casserole.

Bœuf à la Houssarde.

> 2½ *lbs rump steak or roll of silverside, 6 rashers fat bacon, 2 ozs butter, 1 medium-sized onion, 4 ozs sliced mushrooms, a glass white wine, a glass Madeira, stuffing (see below), lettuce leaves for garnish.*

Choose a piece of beef weighing 2½ lbs as near the shape of a cube as possible. If you can afford it, buy rump steak. If not, then ask for roll of silverside. Get the butcher to cut the meat so that it forms 12 slices, still joined at the base.

Now make a stuffing with:

> *5 ozs white breadcrumbs, 2 medium-sized onions, 3 ozs minced calf's liver, 4 ozs mushrooms, 1 egg, 2 ozs butter, ½ teaspoon spice, a little milk.*

Soak the breadcrumbs in the milk and squeeze them to remove the surplus liquid.

Clean the mushrooms carefully and chop them very finely. Mince the onions. Heat the mushrooms in melted butter until their moisture has evaporated, then add the breadcrumbs, onions and liver. Season with salt, spice and a sprinkling of thyme. Mix well with a wooden spoon and taste. Add some more salt and pepper and set the stuffing to cool on a plate. Add the yolk of egg and mix well. You will now have a soft, fragrant mixture.

Spread the stuffing between the slices of meat, reserving a little of it. Wrap the meat in a slice or two of fat bacon, tying the stuffed meat with string which should not be too tight, or the stuffing will be squeezed out.

Melt 2 ozs butter in an iron casserole and put in the meat. Raise the heat. The bacon melts and the meat begins to brown. Turn it so that it browns all over, then add the onion, finely chopped, the mushrooms and a glass of white wine. When the liquid is boiling, lower the heat and put on the lid. Simmer for 4 hours adding, when necessary, a little hot water.

Five minutes before serving, stir in the rest of the stuffing and a glass of Madeira. While the meat is cooking prepare a good potato purée or some rice.

When the meat is ready, lift it onto a hot dish and take off the string. Garnish the dish with some leaves of lettuce, just to delight your eyes.

The sauce, which is very copious, must be served separately. It is child's play to carve this joint as each slice, with its coating of savoury stuffing, has only to be detached from the next with the point of a knife. Serve with this dish your best red wine.

Bœuf à la Ficelle

To make this dish all you need is a piece of top rump steak weighing between 1½ and 2 lbs, a large saucepan of well-salted water boiling on the fire, and a piece of string.

Get the butcher to give you a piece of rump steak as nearly cube-shaped as possible and to tie it securely in shape.

Now fix a piece of string to the meat. Lift it up, and the meat swings slowly on its string like an incense burner. Look at your watch and take careful note of the time. Plunge the meat into the saucepan and tie the string to the handle in such a way that the meat is suspended in the water without touching the bottom. Put on the lid and wait. The water will have gone off the boil for a moment, but as the heat is intense it soon boils once more.

But, you will say, surely this is not the way to make a stew? You are quite right, but you are making a *bœuf à la ficelle*. When you make a stew you want the meat to be edible whilst the gravy is rich and savoury. For this reason you put the meat into cold water and raise the temperature very slowly so that after long, slow cooking the goodness is drawn out of the meat.

But now you are in a hurry and you want to prepare the meat so that it conserves all its juices. For this reason you must seal it by plunging it straight into boiling, salted water. You must allow 15 minutes' cooking time for every pound of meat, so look at your watch carefully.

When the meat is almost ready, prepare a hot dish and some watercress and see that your salt mill is ready on the table. Lift the beef from the saucepan and remove the string. The meat is grey outside and not very appetising. At this moment you may feel a little depressed. But don't worry. Take a very sharp knife and slice into the beef. Inside, it is rosy and tender and the gravy pours into your plate. No roast could be quite like this.

Give each of your guests a thick slice of meat, some water-cress and a piece of French bread. A couple of turns with the salt mill and you are ready to eat.

Entrecôte.

Entrecôte, in England, is usually cut from the eye of the sirloin or the upper fillet. It should be veined finely with fat which melts during cooking so that the meat remains tender and full of flavour. Rump steak can be substituted. In this case, after it is grilled, rub it over lightly with butter, or top it with creamed butter when it is served.

One of the most delicious ways to prepare an entrecôte is to grill it over a charcoal fire, but since very few households are equipped with charcoal you can grill it in the ordinary way.

First, I shall tell you about a red wine sauce which is excellent with steak and afterwards, how to cook the steak in a frying-pan in case you have no grill.

Red Wine Sauce.

Since an entrecôte needs barely 15 minutes to cook and should be eaten immediately, prepare your sauce first of all. You will need:

1½ ozs butter, ½ teaspoon flour, a medium-sized onion, 4 shallots, 4 ozs mushrooms, 3 ozs bone marrow, 1½ large glasses Burgundy.

Peel the onions and shallots and chop them finely. Now clean the mushrooms and, without peeling them, cut them in slices.

Melt half the butter in a medium-sized heavy saucepan. Add the onions and shallots and raise the heat so that the moisture evaporates and they turn a pale mahogany colour. Add the mushrooms and cover the pan for 2 minutes. Take off the lid and let the juice evaporate. Add the wine and cover the pan once more. Season with salt and a trace of pepper. Taste the sauce. It is very good but too thin.

In a small bowl mix the rest of the butter into the flour. Divide the resulting mass into four and, with a wooden spoon, stir each piece into the sauce when the one before has melted. The sauce bubbles quietly and becomes creamy.

Cut the marrow into four pieces and lay them on top of the sauce. Cover the pan and leave it over the very lowest heat while you grill the steak. During this time the marrow will cook in the sauce.

Fried Entrecôte.

If you have no grill you can cook the entrecôte in a frying-pan. First of all, open the window, otherwise the kitchen will be filled with smoke. Melt a walnut of butter in a heavy frying-pan. When it smokes, put in the steak and make your fire blazing hot. Glance at your watch. Your entrecôte, if it is about ¾-inch thick, should be cooked in about 12 minutes. At the end of 5 minutes lift the steak with a fork and look at the underneath. It should be almost burnt on the outside. Turn it over and wait again for 5 or 6 minutes, sniffing the delicious smell of the steak and the sizzling butter.

With a sharp knife make a cut at the side of the meat. If it is too rare for your taste, lower the heat and wait for 3 or 4 minutes more. Sprinkle with fine salt and put it onto a hot dish with a piece of butter on top.

Using a spoon and fork, lift the rounds of marrow delicately from the red wine sauce and lay them on the steak. Pour the sauce into a gravy boat and carry it all to the table.

Divide the entrecôte into four and give a piece, topped with a slice of marrow, to each person, with a generous helping of sauce and a glass of Burgundy.

The Cheaper Cuts of Beef.

Not everyone can afford fillet of beef. In any case, I pity those who eat it every day. The meat is rather flabby and the flavour not outstanding. As for the price, the least said the better.

For roasting one can use top rump or even *la tranche*. (A cut from the buttock. There is no exact equivalent of this to be found in the English butchers' shops.) These cuts, juicy and full of flavour, make my mouth water, but their price, more reasonable than that of fillet, is still very high.

You can buy the cheaper cuts from the neck or forequarter and these, carefully cut, will make excellent dishes which have the advantage of being more economical.

Here are three recipes each made with 1½ lbs of beef. My butcher gave me forequarter when I told him that I was going to make a *bœuf bourguignon* and this was satisfactory for the purpose. You will get excellent results with roll of silverside, top rump or topside of beef.

Bœuf Bourguignon.

> 1½ *lbs beef* (*see above*), ½ *lb onions*, ½ *bottle red wine*, 2 *ozs butter*, 3 *ozs back pork fat*, 3 *ozs bacon rinds*, 1 *teaspoon flour*, *thyme and a bayleaf.*

Heat a very small knob of butter and the bacon, cut in dice. When the fat has run out of the bacon add the meat, cut into pieces, and brown it on all sides. Then brown the onions, season with salt and pepper, pour in the red wine and add the bacon rinds cut into small pieces. Cover the casserole and simmer it on a very low fire for 3 hours. Test the meat. It is done.

Work the butter into the flour and then drop it, a little at a time, into the gravy, stirring constantly. The gravy becomes thick and smooth. If you want to be extravagant, add a small glass of cognac and heat for 5 minutes more. This is delicious and deserves to be accompanied by your best Burgundy.

Bœuf Mariné à la Crème.

This dish is very economical but has all the glamour of *haute cuisine.*

> 1½ *lbs forequarter of beef,* 4 *ozs fat bacon,* 1 *oz butter,* ¼ *pint thick cream,* 1 *tablespoon flour,* 1 *lb beetroot,* 1 *tablespoon vinegar.*

Cut the beef into pieces and marinade it in the following mixture for 48 hours:

> 3 *glasses water,* 2 *tablespoons wine vinegar,* ½ *lb chopped onions,* 2 *cloves garlic, crushed with salt, thyme, a bayleaf.*

Melt the bacon, cut into small pieces, with a walnut of butter. Take the meat out of the marinade, dry it with a cloth and brown it slowly in the butter and bacon fat. Add the onions from the marinade and let them colour. This will be a slow business as they have been soaked.

Meanwhile, boil the marinade with the garlic and herbs until it has reduced a little. Pour this boiling liquid onto the meat and cover with a lid. Simmer for 3 hours, adding water if necessary.

In a small bowl mix ¼-pint of thick cream with a tablespoon of flour. Stir this into the liquid round the meat and let it boil for a minute. Try accompanying this dish with 1 lb of beetroot which you have cooked in the oven, chopped roughly, and sautéd in butter. After you have salted the beetroot, sprinkle it with a tablespoon of vinegar.

Spanish Stew.

> 1½ *lbs neck of beef,* ½ *lb onions,* 2 *cloves garlic,* 2 *tablespoons olive oil,* 3 *ozs thick tomato purée,* 2 *large green peppers.*

Heat the oil to smoking point in a heavy saucepan and add the meat cut in pieces. Let it brown, add the onions sliced, and when these have browned, season with salt and pepper and just cover the meat with water. Chop the garlic with some salt and crush it to a cream under the blade of a large kitchen knife. Stir this and the tomato into the liquid in the pan. Add the peppers, cut in pieces after the pips have been removed. Simmer for 3 hours with the lid on and then taste. It is very good. If you prefer, you can use butter for this dish instead of olive oil.

Hochepot.

Spoken by a Frenchman, "*Le Hochepot et le Goulache*" reminds one of the title of a fable by La Fontaine. If La Fontaine linked the fox with the crow it was because these two very different animals had found something in common—a cheese.

Now there is little in common between the *hochepot*, which comes from Flanders and the goulash which is a native of Hungary, except that both of them are extraordinarily simple to prepare.

Hochepot consists of a piece of beef boiled in very little water with plenty of vegetables. It is a *pot-au-feu* without much gravy, but a *pot-au-feu* of rather a special kind since it is enhanced by a pig's ear and some country sausage. It is a heavy dish and one that you should make in cold weather.

> 1½ *lbs flank of beef*, 1½ *lbs pig's head with the ear*, ¾ *lb uncooked, coarse sausage such as the* saucisse de Toulouse *which you can find in Soho and in many big stores*, 2 *ozs lard*, 10 *ozs carrots*, 10 *ozs turnips*, 4 *leeks and a white cabbage*, ½ *teaspoon spice.*

Heat the lard to smoking-point in a frying-pan and brown the meat all over. Put it into a casserole with the pig's head and the carrots, turnips and leeks, washed and cut in slices. Cut the cabbage in four and add this with a sprinkling of salt and the spice. Bring this to the boil and leave it to simmer for 2 hours. Look from time to time to see if there is enough liquid, adding if necessary half a glass of water.

At the end of 2 hours add the sausage and cook for 1 hour more, making 3 hours in all. The *hochepot* is now ready.

Lift the meat, pig's head and sausage onto a large dish, using a perforated ladle. Slice them and serve each guest, pouring over their helping half a ladleful of steaming broth, rich, thick and fragrant. A few turns of the salt mill, mustard and a glass of beer complete their contentment.

Goulash.

> 2 *lbs roll of silverside,* 1 *lb onions,* 4 *ozs fat pork,* 1 *oz butter,* 1 *teaspoon paprika,* ¼ *pint thick cream.*

Cut the meat in pieces. Peel the onions and chop them finely and never use less, please note, than one pound of onions to two pounds of meat. Melt the butter in a thick saucepan and add the pork, cut in cubes. When it has melted a little put half the meat in the bottom of the casserole, sprinkle with salt and cover it with half the onions. Sprinkle with the paprika and arrange the rest of your ingredients in layers in the same order. Pour over them 2 glasses of hot water. Cover the saucepan and bring it to the boil. Let it simmer for 3 hours. At the end of this time the onion has melted to a thick purée. Add the cream and let it boil for a moment.

Serve the goulash with boiled potatoes. It will set your mouth on fire but you can put out the blaze with a glass of rough red wine.

Remains of Boiled Beef.

Bouillon made by the lengthy simmering of the cheaper cuts of beef such as brisket or aitch bone is quite delicious, but unless good use can be made of the meat which remains, it is rather an extravagance.

Here are five recipes which will transform the dreary cold meat and allow you to enjoy your *bouillon* with a good conscience.

Boiled Beef with Date Sauce.

This is a dish from Ancient Rome. I found the recipe in a cookery book by Apicius and I think you will enjoy making it.

> 10 *dates,* 10 *almonds, a bunch of parsley,* 1 *shallot,* 2 *tablespoons vinegar, freshly ground pepper,* 1 *tablespoon olive oil.*

Stone the dates and chop them very finely, using a sharp knife. Plunge the almonds for a minute into boiling water and remove their skins. Dry them, and fry them golden-brown in a lightly oiled pan. Chop them very finely.

Your bunch of parsley should be a generous one, about the size of a bunch of violets. Strip off the leaves and chop them finely and the shallots too. Put the dates, almonds, parsley and shallots into a small saucepan and add a tablespoon of olive oil. Stir and heat for 3 minutes. Add the water, vinegar and a little salt, and boil for 10 minutes with the lid off. Add plenty of freshly-milled pepper and let the sauce reduce by about a quarter.

While the sauce is cooking, cut your cold beef into slices and arrange them in a hot dish. Cover them with sauce. Now taste this two-thousand-year-old dish. It is rather strange, but has an unexpected charm.

Boiled Beef with Horse-Radish Sauce.

Warm up the boiled beef in some of its own broth and make a sauce with the following:

> 1 *oz butter*, 1 *tablespoon flour*, ½ *pint broth*, 2 *tablespoons thick cream*, 2 *tablespoons grated horse-radish*.

Melt the butter in a small saucepan and blend it with the flour. Stirring all the time, add the broth and raise the heat. The sauce boils and thickens. Add a little more salt and the cream. Mix well, and boil for 10 seconds. Stir in the horse-radish for which you have used rather a coarse grater, and boil for a moment more. The sauce is ready and only needs to be poured over the beef which you have cut in slices.

Your very dull boiled beef has become a dish with a personality of its own.

If you are unable to buy horse-radish, try using raw turnip instead. It makes an interesting substitute.

Sauté Beef with Hard-boiled Eggs.

> *Cold beef*, 2 *shallots*, 3 *tablespoons white wine*, 2½ *ozs butter*, *parsley*.

This is a dish which you can prepare in a quarter of an hour. Put the eggs into boiling water and let them boil for 12 minutes. Meanwhile, heat 1½ ozs of butter in a frying-pan until it smokes. Mince the shallots finely and cut the meat in cubes. Put the meat and shallots into the frying-pan with the white wine, salt and pepper. Raise the heat. The wine will evaporate completely. Add the rest of the butter and lower the heat.

The eggs are ready. Plunge them into cold water. Peel them and chop them finely. Mix them with the contents of the frying-pan and serve very hot sprinkled with chopped parsley.

French Rissoles.

Cold beef, chopped onions, spice, 1½ ozs butter.

Mince some cold beef. Simmer the onions with a little water for 15 minutes, keeping the lid on the pan. Mix the onions and meat and season with salt, a pinch of spice and some freshly-milled pepper. Heat 1½ ozs butter in a frying-pan and stir the mince mixture in this for 5 minutes, then put it on a plate to cool.

Make a paste using:

6 ozs flour, 3 ozs butter, 4 tablespoons water, ½ teaspoon salt.

Mix the ingredients to a smooth paste, using your finger tips. Roll it out on a floured board to the thickness of a penny. Cut out about fourteen pieces two inches square.

On each square put a small spoonful of mince. Wet the borders and fold them into triangles, pinching with floured finger tips to seal them. Fry the rissoles in deep fat and drain them on soft paper.

Serve them with a cup of *bouillon* and a glass of Marsala. A little of your mince mixture will probably be left over. With this you can make the following dish:

Boiled Beef Pâté.

Mix a beaten egg with the mince mixture left from the preceding recipe. Put it into a small fireproof dish and sprinkle it with grated Gruyère cheese. Bake it in a hot oven for 15 minutes. This frugal pâté is very good accompanied by a glass of Chablis, or simply spread on hot buttered toast.

Lamb and Mutton.

Nowadays one hears very little about mutton. The shops are full of lamb, but lamb of such generous proportions that one feels that they must belong to the teenage group, if not older. In the strict gastronomical sense, a lamb should never have tasted any other food but its mother's milk, and in France and Italy one can buy lamb which is so tender that it melts in your mouth. The simpler the preparation of this delicate meat the better.

The next two recipes can well be made with the lamb which you will find at your local butcher's.

Blanquette d'Agneau.

> *2 lbs shoulder of lamb, ½ lb carrots, ½ lb turnips, 3 leeks, 6 small onions, 2 cloves garlic, 4 ozs mushrooms, 3 yolks of egg, 2½ ozs butter, 1½ tablespoons flour.*

Cut the meat into ten or twelve pieces, leaving it on the bone. Put them into a basin of cold water for 2 hours to blanch. Lift out the meat and put it in an enamel saucepan, covered with salted cold water. Bring it to the boil, skim and add the onions, crushed garlic, carrots, turnips and leeks, washed and sliced. There should be just enough water to cover.

Put the lid on and when the water is boiling once more, turn down the heat and simmer for an hour. Try the meat. It should be done. Remove the carrots, turnips and leeks. Put the meat and onions into a dish and the broth into a bowl. Now wash and dry your saucepan and put it back on the fire.

Melt the butter and work the flour into it with a wooden spoon. Stirring all the time over the fire, add the warm broth, little by little. Beat with a wire whisk. The liquid boils and the sauce thickens. Add the mushroons, sliced, and the meat. Cook for 10 minutes.

Put the yolks of egg into a bowl. Add a little of the sauce and mix with a wire whisk. Take your saucepan from the fire and let it cool for five minutes. Add the diluted egg yolks and mix well. Put the pan back on a very low fire, stirring it gently. The sauce becomes thicker. Be very careful not to let it boil or the eggs will curdle. Serve the *blanquette* with a glass of Graves.

Pilaff of Lamb.

> *About 2 lbs shoulder of lamb, ½ lb onions, 1 cup rice, 2½ ozs butter, thyme.*

Heat 1 oz butter in an iron casserole and add the shoulder of lamb, cut in pieces, and the onions, each cut in four. When they are beautifully browned, add 3 teacups of hot water, salt, pepper and a sprinkling of thyme. Cover the pan and simmer for 1 hour. Lift out the meat, which is done, and pour the broth into a bowl. Wash the casserole and put it back on the fire. Melt the rest of the butter and toss the rice in it for 3 minutes until it is all buttery. Measure exactly 3 cupfuls of broth, using the same cup in which you measured the rice and making up the quantity with water if necessary. Pour it over the rice. Cover the casserole and let it cook over a low fire for 15 minutes. By this time, the rice will have absorbed all the liquid.

Take off the lid and stir the rice with a gentle lifting movement. The grains will be quite separate. Mix in the meat, taking care not to squash the rice. Warm over a low fire with the lid on for 5 minutes. Take off the lid and shake the pot. Warm it for 10 minutes more on a very gentle heat so that the rice is completely dry.

Serve on very hot plates with red wine—Côtes du Rhône, if possible.

Boiled Leg of Lamb.

As a change, half a leg of lamb can very easily be boiled. Ask the butcher to cover it with caul fat and tie it together.

Plunge the lamb into fast-boiling water which you have salted and perfumed with thyme. Keep the fire very hot until boiling is re-established. Then cover the saucepan and let it simmer for 15 minutes for each pound of meat.

Serve the lamb surrounded by watercress and accompanied by a purée of turnips sharpened with some capers. Sitting on the dish the lamb will look grey and a little sad, but when it is cut, the slices are rosy and running with delicious juice.

Two Economical Dishes.

From time to time, and especially towards the end of the month, one is apt to go through a domestic crisis and feel the need for economy. But that does not mean that one cannot eat well. There is no necessity to use the most expensive materials to produce good food.

If you cook with love, understanding the taste of the people for whom you are cooking and sincerely trying to please them, be sure that you will produce excellent meals.

Here are two dishes which are as tasty as they are economical.

Haut de Côtelette aux Haricots.

1 lb scrag end of neck of lamb, ¾ lb haricot beans, 6 ozs fat bacon rind, 2 ozs back pork fat, 1 oz butter, 2 onions, 1 clove garlic, 2 sprigs thyme, a bayleaf, a glass white wine.

You will need a certain courage to ask the butcher for scrag end of neck of lamb. I have tried and I had to put up with the contemptuous glance of the butcher's assistant. Naturally, he prefers more prosperous clients, but never mind. You will need a little more courage to try and persuade the shop assistant to slice your fat bacon rind into small pieces. If, after all this, they weigh your 2 ozs of back pork fat rather generously, that is all a triumph and will improve your dish.

The haricot beans which you buy for this dish should be of the best quality, and insisting on this will help to restore your morale. The beans must be carefully picked over to remove any small stones and so on. Soak them overnight in cold water. Be sure that they stand in a cool place.

Whilst you are preparing the beans, put the bacon rind into a small saucepan and cover it with water. Simmer for at least 2 hours, adding more water as necessary.

Next morning, melt the butter in an iron casserole and arrange the meat in it. Raise the heat and brown the meat all over. Add the onions, chopped small, and the garlic crushed with a little salt beneath the blade of a large kitchen knife. It is beginning to smell good. Add a little more salt.

Cover the meat with boiling water. Add the haricot beans and see that there is enough water to allow them to float comfortably on the surface.

The bacon rind which you cooked the evening before will have turned to a solid jelly. Add this to your casserole with freshly-milled pepper, the bayleaf and the white wine. Raise the heat until the contents of the casserole are boiling, and then let it simmer over a very low fire for about 1½ hours, stirring from time to time so that nothing sticks to the bottom. At this point, if you wish, you can break off the preparation of this dish and complete it just before serving.

Cut the fat pork in small pieces and melt it in a frying-pan with a small piece of butter. When the fat has all run out and the pieces of bacon are beginning to dry, pour the contents of the frying-pan into the casserole. Stir well, and correct the seasoning. Lift the casserole by its ears and carry it to the table.

This dish reminds one of a *cassoulet*, though it lacks the goose and the sausage.

Haut de Côtelette Pané.

> *2 lbs boned scrag end of neck of lamb, soup vegetables, egg, breadcrumbs, oil or lard for frying.*

This dish arises from one of those happy combinations whereby you can cook your meat and enhance its flavour, whilst adding richness to a soup.

Make a good vegetable soup using potatoes, cabbage, beans and so on. Ask your butcher to fold 2 lbs of boned scrag end of neck of lamb in three and tie it with a string. Put this into the soup for an hour, whilst it is simmering. Lift out the meat and, whilst it is still warm, remove any gristle and then put it over-night between two plates or boards with a heavy weight on top.

Next morning your meat will be a solid block which you can cut easily with a knife. Cut it in pieces as long and thick as two fingers.

Egg and breadcrumb the fingers and fry them in smoking oil or lard. Sprinkle them with fine salt and enjoy them with a glass of light red wine.

Shashlik.

> 1½ *lbs fillet of lamb, 3 Spanish onions, melted butter, vinegar.*

To make real *shashlik* takes days of preparation, but quite a pleasant imitation can be made by cutting a slice of fillet of lamb into pieces weighing about one ounce each. Soak these for 6 hours in vinegar to which you have added a generous quantity of onion rings.

Just before cooking lift the meat from the marinade and dry the pieces on a cloth. Thread them onto spits (steel knitting needles make quite a useful substitute), brush them with melted butter and put them under a hot grill for 5 or 6 minutes. Sprinkle them with salt, and serve with the onion rings from the marinade.

As this is a Georgian dish one should really drink with it a Caucasian wine, but ordinary red wine will do very well instead.

Kebabs with Bacon.

This dish resembles *shashlik*, though its flavour is quite different. Cut some fillet of mutton in pieces and thread them on spits with a small slice of bacon between each. Use a sprig of thyme to brush the fillets with hot oil. This should be done several times during the 5–6 minutes which it will take to cook the *kebabs* under a hot grill.

Sprinkle the *kebabs* with salt, and serve. Your braver guests will eat them with their fingers.

Kebabs are delicious grilled over a picnic fire. Split rolls and, opening them as if they were oysters, grip the sizzling meat and draw out the skewer. A sprinkling of cumin seed, and you can imagine that you are in a *souk* in Morocco.

Tourte au Mouton.

One Sunday I asked some friends to a simple lunch in the country—roast leg of mutton, green peas, Camembert and a cascade of cherries, followed by coffee and Kirsch.

The leg of mutton was roasting on a spit in front of a charcoal fire just below my bedroom window. This window, wreathed in vines, framed the head and shoulders of my wife, in wrapt contemplation of the scene below. "Is it love," I enquired, "which makes you follow my movements so devotedly?" "No," she replied, "I am enjoying the smell of the mutton."

The mutton was as delicious as its smell, and in the evening all that was left was a pound or so of scrappy meat clinging to the bone. We took it back to Paris.

Next day the telephone rang. Two friends were arriving for dinner that night. Something must be done with the mutton bone, but what? This is what I did, and if you follow me carefully you will have both the pleasure of preparing it and the joy of eating it.

Make some pastry as I described in the recipe for onion tart (p. 46), using half as much again of each ingredient. Now make your *tourte* using:

> 1 *lb cold mutton or lamb*, ¾ *lb sausage meat*, 3 *ozs butter*,
> *a sprinkling of thyme, a small glass cognac*, 1 *yolk of egg*,
> *a little milk*.

Cut the meat in the thinnest possible slices. Gather up all the scraps, chop them as finely as you can, and mix them with the sausage meat.

Take two-thirds of the pastry and roll it out about ⅛-inch thick. Line with it a buttered pie dish, allowing the pastry to hang about an inch over the edge of the dish. Arrange half the sausage meat in the bottom of the pie and sprinkle it with a little thyme. Then put a layer of sliced meat, sprinkled with salt, pepper and cognac. Dot this layer with dabs of butter. Arrange a second layer of sausage and sliced meat, seasoned as before, dotted with butter and sprinkled with cognac.

Roll out the pastry which is left and lay it as a lid over the top of the pie dish, leaving a small hole in the middle. Roll the hanging edges of the lower pastry over the lid to make a festooned border, and brush it all over with yolk of egg mixed with a little milk.

Put the *tourte* into a hot oven (about 425° F. Gas 7). In 10 minutes it will begin to colour. Lower the heat to about 350° F. (Gas 4) and bake for 40 minutes. A delicious smell of thyme and cognac seeps out of the hole in the centre of the pie—and of garlic too, if you had slipped a clove or two into the knuckle of the leg of mutton, when you roasted it.

At the last moment pour a little melted butter into the hole which is the source of this glorious smell, and eat the *tourte* with a glass of Beaujolais. The conversation will die down as your guests enjoy your triumph.

Pigeons Moscovites.

Take the best leaves from a fine white cabbage and soak them in boiling water for 10 minutes. Refresh them under the cold tap and put them to dry on a clean cloth. Now make a stuffing with:

> *½ lb boned shoulder lamb, 2½ ozs rice, 3 ozs back pork fat, 2 onions, 2 cloves garlic, 2½ ozs butter, 1 egg, 2½ ozs thick cream, a small glass Madeira, 1 teaspoon flour.*

Cook the rice in a large saucepan of boiling, salted water. After 15 minutes strain off the water and wash away the surplus starch under the cold tap.

Mince the lamb and the pork fat. Melt half the butter in a frying-pan and add the onion and the garlic, chopped finely. Let them brown and add the minced meat and fry for 5 minutes. Season with salt and pepper, add the rice, mix well together, and lift the pan off the fire. Let the mixture cool, and beat in the yolk of egg.

On each cabbage leaf arrange a little heap of stuffing and fold the leaf round it as neatly as you can, tucking in the ends and rolling and tying the pigeon with thread.

Melt the rest of the butter in an iron casserole. Brown the pigeons all over and add a little water. Cover the pan and simmer for 1 hour. Add the Madeira and cook for another 5 minutes. Meanwhile, mix the flour and the cream in a little bowl and then stir them into the liquid surrounding the pigeons, scraping every last scrap from the bowl. Let the sauce come to the boil once more and then carry your casserole to table. In spite of being a Russian dish it will enjoy the company of a bottle of Saint Emilion.

Escalopes de Veau Poêlées.

The name 'escalope' is derived from the same source as the word scalpel and means, simply, something which has been cut. An escalope is, therefore, a thin slice of meat taken from some fleshy part, and can consist of beef, turkey or any other meat. However, an escalope of veal is the most usual. Its texture allows of rapid cooking and it is the prototype of the dish which is prepared rapidly though not necessarily without art. On the theme of escalopes one can create endless variations, some of which are small gastronomic symphonies. For the moment, let us deal with the simplest of all.

Buy 2 thin escalopes of veal. All you will need to prepare them is some butter and a little flour.

Melt 1 oz of butter in a frying-pan, being careful not to let it burn. Meanwhile, dip your escalopes in flour, tapping them gently so that no surplus sticks to them. Lay the escalopes in the hot butter. As soon as you see that the lower surfaces are turning brown and that the juice from the meat is beginning to moisten the flour on the upper surfaces, turn the escalopes and let the other side brown. Sprinkle them with salt and lower the heat so that it can penetrate to the centre of the meat without burning the outside. Ten minutes in all should be enough to cook your escalopes perfectly. Catch them on the point of a fork and lift them onto a hot dish.

In the frying-pan you will have some caramel known as the glaze. Dissolve this in a little boiling water. Let it simmer for a minute and pour it over the meat.

This is the simplest way of preparing escalopes. One can vary this with all sorts of garnishes and flavours.

Escalopes of Veal with Olives.

In *Cooking in Ten Minutes* I told you how to prepare escalopes of veal with green olives. You can do the same thing with black ones. Prepare the escalopes as before then, as soon as you have turned them, add 4 ozs of stoned black or green olives. These will heat through and form part of the sauce.

Escalopes Vénitiennes.

> 3 escalopes of veal, 2½ ozs butter, 3 slices cooked ham, 1 lb pumpkin, 4 ozs grated Gruyére cheese.

Peel the pumpkin and cut it into cubes. Melt 1 oz of butter in a saucepan and add the pumpkin and a very little water. Cook for 10 minutes, add salt and pepper and mash the pulp with a fork. Stir in half the cheese.

Prepare the escalopes as I have just described. Lay the ham in a fireproof dish and cover each slice with an escalope. Top with the pumpkin purée sprinkled with grated cheese and dabs of butter. Brown your escalopes in the oven or under the grill.

Paupiettes.

Paupiettes are pieces of meat stuffed, rolled and tied with string. They are cooked in a savoury sauce. The origin of the name is probably Italian and they are said to have been brought to France by the cooks in the train of Marie de Medici on her marriage to Henry of Navarre. The French often called them *alouettes* and sometimes just 'birds' and they certainly look rather like tiny headless chickens.

> 4 escalopes of veal as large as possible, but cut very thin, 4 small thin slices of cooked ham, ½ lb onions, stale bread, a little milk, thyme, 3 ozs butter, white wine.

Chop a medium-sized onion, cover it with cold water, bring it to the boil and simmer for 4 or 5 minutes, then drain. Mix the onion with a piece of stale bread the size of an egg which you have previously soaked in milk and squeezed to remove the surplus moisture. Season lightly with salt and pepper and 2 teaspoons thyme. Mix well with a fork.

Melt 1 oz of butter in a frying-pan. Add the onions and bread and stir over the fire for 3 minutes. The stuffing is now ready.

On each of the escalopes spread a slice of ham and a good

spoonful of stuffing. Roll the *paupiettes* up and tie them, without squeezing or the stuffing will escape.

Melt 2 ozs butter in an iron casserole and brown the *paupiettes* all over, scraping loose any stuffing which sticks to the bottom of the pan. They will take a little time to brown as your fire must not be too hot. Now surround the *paupiettes* with chopped onion which will fairly quickly turn a light mahogany brown. Pour a glass of white wine into the casserole, cover it and cook over a low fire for an hour, turning the *paupiettes* from time to time and adding wine if necessary.

This dish needs plenty of sauce, so add some water and then stir in the remains of your stuffing. Mix it carefully. After 5 minutes more the sauce will have thickened. All you have to do is to serve your *paupiettes* surrounded by their fragrant savoury sauce. They are so tempting that you will want to eat all four. But I must warn you that this is not a cheap dish.

If you want to eat your fill and still have some money for a bottle of wine, make your *paupiettes* from roll of silverside of beef, leaving out the ham and adding a few mushrooms to the stuffing.

Messicani.

These are tiny *paupiettes* of veal without stuffing. They are cooked in a few minutes and eaten in a few seconds. This dish should be made from the *noix* of veal, a cut which corresponds to the topside of leg in beef, but if your butcher cannot supply this, a piece from the top of the knuckle or from the shoulder can be used as a substitute.

> 1 *lb veal, 6 ozs sliced ham, a small bunch of thyme, 2 ozs butter.*

Slice the veal as thinly as possible, using a very sharp knife. Each of your slices should be not more than $\frac{1}{4}$-inch thick and about the size of the palm of your hand. On each of the slices lay a rather smaller, very thin slice of ham and a few leaves of thyme. Roll them up and secure each of them with a wooden toothpick. You will have about twelve *paupiettes*.

Melt the butter in an iron casserole and arrange the rolls of meat in the bottom. Heat for 5 minutes. Turn them and sprinkle with a little salt and pepper. Put them onto a hot dish and serve two to each of your guests after they have eaten a generous plate of spaghetti with tomato sauce and cheese. A few leaves of salad and some fresh fruit, and your meal is complete.

Médaillons de Veau.

We are going to make our *médaillons* with minced meat, but don't be disappointed. My instinctive reaction against minced meat dates from the time when large joints were the fashion and there was always cold meat to be used up, disguised in more or less appetizing forms.

Now one buys fresh minced meat, or minces it at home, but as it is ground up finely, odd pieces and less expensive cuts can be used and the price is much more reasonable than that of a similar quality bought in the piece.

> 1 *lb minced veal, 3 ozs stale bread, milk, 1 tablespoon cream, yolk of 1 egg, flour, 1 oz butter.*

Soak the bread in milk and squeeze out the surplus moisture. Mix the bread with the meat and add salt, pepper, the cream and the yolk of egg.

Stir well until the mixture is smooth, and divide it into twelve portions, each the size of a small egg. On a floured board form these into round cakes about an inch high and as nearly equal in size as possible.

Melt a good ounce of butter in a frying-pan and when it is smoking fry six of the *médaillons*, which you have dipped in flour, first on one side until they are golden-brown and then on the other. Melt a little more butter and fry the other six *médaillons*. Now they are ready and you can serve them in various ways.

Médaillons au Citron.

Make your *médaillons* as described in the previous recipe and put them onto a hot dish. Stir half a glass of water into the glaze which is left in the frying-pan. This will make a sauce with a pleasant colour, but it won't have a great deal of flavour. Add the juice of half a lemon and some pieces of thinnest lemon peel cut with a razor-sharp knife. Boil for a ½-minute, then pour the sauce over the *médaillons* and garnish each one with a quarter-slice of lemon. Serve them with creamy mashed potatoes.

Médaillons à la Crème.

Make the *médaillons* as before and keep them hot on a dish. Stir half a glass of water into the frying-pan in which they have cooked and add 2½ ozs of thick cream which you have stirred with ½-teaspoon of flour. Boil the sauce for a moment and serve the *médaillons* covered with this and topped with mushroom caps which you have sautéd for a few minutes in butter.

Médaillons à la Russe.

Arrange the *médaillons* on a silver dish, and round them heaps of vegetables in contrasting colours—peas, carrots, noodles, .lettuce leaves dressed with cream, and beetroot tossed in hot butter and sprinkled with vinegar. Hand round a sauce-boat of melted butter and let each guest sprinkle it over his *médaillons*. It is simple . . . and it is exquisite.

Blanquette de Veau.

> 1½ *lbs boned shoulder of veal,* 1 *lb carrots,* 1 *lb turnips,*
> 2 *leeks,* ½ *lb onions, thyme,* 1 *bayleaf,* 4 *ozs mushrooms,*
> 2½ *ozs thick cream,* 2 *ozs butter,* 1 *oz flour.*

Cut the meat in pieces, put it into a heavy saucepan and salt and pepper it lightly. Cover the meat with cold water and bring it to the boil. Skim, and add the carrots, turnips and leeks, cleaned and cut in pieces. Simmer for a few minutes, skimming all the time. Add the onions, peeled but left whole, and the thyme and bayleaf. Simmer with the lid on for another hour.

Test the meat with a fork to see whether it is done, and when it is ready lift it out and keep it hot. Strain the contents of the saucepan.

Melt the butter and mix it with the flour over a low fire, taking care that it does not brown. Add the warm broth a little at a time, stirring it in with a wire whisk. The sauce will thicken. Let it boil for a moment or two, adding just enough liquid to make it like thin cream.

Clean and slice the mushrooms and throw them into the boiling sauce. Let it boil for a minute or two more, then add the meat and onions and stir in the cream. Let it boil for half a minute and serve on a very hot dish. Don't add lemon juice if you are going to drink red wine with this dish.

Veau Marengo.

> 1½ *lbs shoulder of veal,* 1½ *tablespoons olive oil,* 1 *oz butter,* ½ *lb mushrooms,* 2 *ozs tomato purée,* 1 *oz flour.*

Put the butter and oil into an iron saucepan on a good heat and when they are just smoking add the meat. Keep the pieces of meat moving on a hot fire until they have turned mahogany brown. Add the onions, peeled and chopped, and let them colour. Season with salt and pepper and sprinkle with the flour, stirring all the time until this forms a brown *roux*. Work tepid water into the *roux* until the sauce just covers the meat and then add the tomato purée. Let the sauce come to the boil and then simmer on a very low fire for 1 hour.

Add the mushrooms, cleaned and cut in slices and cook for another 10 minutes. Your veal is ready. Drink with this a glass of red *vin ordinaire*.

Pork Chops with Rhubarb.

> 3 *pork chops, a bundle of rhubarb,* 1 *oz butter,* 2 *lumps of sugar.*

Wipe and trim a bundle of rhubarb and cut the stalks into pieces just over an inch long. Put them into a saucepan with cold water, bring it to the boil and drain it off immediately. The rhubarb is limp, almost shapeless, but it will have lost some of its acid. Return it to the saucepan with 1 oz of butter and 2 lumps of sugar. Cook it for 10 minutes.

Fry three good-sized fat pork chops until they are well cooked and golden-brown. Put them on a hot dish while you heat the rhubarb in the pan in which the chops have fried, mixing it with the juice from the meat and the caramel in the bottom of the pan. Serve the chops surrounded with rhubarb purée. This is a very good dish.

Pork Chops with Green Peppers.

> 2 *pork chops,* 1 *oz lard,* 2 *green peppers.*

Split the peppers lengthwise and remove the seeds and the stalks. Slice them crosswise.

Melt a small piece of lard in a frying-pan over a hot fire and fry two fine pork chops for about 5 minutes, until the underside is golden brown and the fat is running out. Turn the chops and fry them for another 5 minutes so that the other side browns. They look beautiful, but they are not yet cooked through. Another 10 minutes with the heat lowered, and you can sprinkle them with salt and put them on a hot dish in the oven to keep warm.

Now lower the heat and toss the peppers into the hot fat. They will lose their beautiful colour, shrivel and become brownish. Salt the peppers and keep stirring them. At the end of 10 minutes the peppers will be done. Arrange these round the chops and your dish is ready for the table. In your place I should tuck my napkin under my chin and anticipate some moments of real pleasure.

Stuffed Cabbage.

After All Saints Day, when the melancholy chrysanthemums are fading slowly on the tombstones in the French cemeteries and, but for the carrots, the vegetable stalls in the market are almost colourless, one's eye is caught by the huge, firm globes of the cabbages, waxy white and palest green. Here is a dish which does honour to this splendid vegetable.

Buy a white cabbage, not too big or too close in texture, and strip off the outer leaves so that you have a smooth white globe. Now make the stuffing using:

> $\frac{1}{2}$ *lb lean pork*, $\frac{1}{4}$ *lb cooked ham*, 4 *ozs back pork fat*,
> $\frac{1}{4}$ *lb sliced bacon*, $\frac{1}{2}$ *lb chestnuts, a small bunch of parsley*,
> 1 *egg*, 2 *ozs butter*.

Mince all the meat and pork fat together. Peel the chestnuts, using a sharp knife, and plunge them into boiling water for 5 minutes and then for a moment into cold water. The brown inner skin will come away easily. Boil the skinned chestnuts for 20 minutes and mince them together with the parsley. Mix with the minced meat and add salt, pepper and the egg, stirring well.

Now return to your cabbage. Plunge it into boiling water for 10 minutes and then into cold water, and leave it for 15 minutes. Drain, and then separate the leaves delicately, filling the spaces between each with stuffing. Arrange the leaves so that the cabbage regains as nearly as possible its original shape and tie a piece of string round its 'Equator'. Cover the top with rashers of bacon and secure the whole creation with more string.

Arrange the butter in dabs on the bottom of a fireproof dish and stand the cabbage in the middle. Put it in a medium oven (350° F. Gas 4) for about 1½ hours, basting from time to time with the fat in the dish to which you add, towards the end of the cooking time, a little white wine. If the cabbage shows any sign of burning, cover it with foil or buttered greaseproof paper.

Serve the cabbage straight from the oven with a glass of Beaujolais.

Brains.

It is a common fallacy that brains are particularly suitable for invalids and young children. It is true that they contain nourishment in concentrated form, but in the course of many experiments I have been able to produce the artificial digestion of all the edible animal tissues with the exception of brains.

There is no reason, however, why people in good health should not enjoy brains. Their texture is smooth and indescribable, so that they afford our palates a sensation which is rather tactile than one of taste.

Since brains have no very pronounced flavour, one must season them with skill and a certain restraint.

As to which kind of brains to buy, they are all equally good, though sheep's brains being smaller and therefore suitable for single portions, are more attractive than those of calf, ox or pig.

Cervelle au Beurre Noir.

An ox brain, 1 teaspoon chopped parsley, ½ teaspoon vinegar.

Suppose you buy an ox brain. Wash it in running water and remove carefully the membrane and any clots of blood. Plunge the brain into a saucepan of boiling water to which you have added a tablespoonful of vinegar. After 15 minutes lift out the brain and put it into a basin of cold water beneath the running tap.

When it is quite cold, cut the brain into thick slices and drain them well. Meanwhile, heat 4 ozs of butter until it has stopped sizzling and turned pale brown. Be very careful not to heat the butter beyond this stage as it will break down into substances which are extremely indigestible.

Draw the pan off the heat and wait at least 3 minutes. Add

a teaspoon of parsley which you have chopped, wrapped in a piece of muslin, held for a moment or two under the running cold tap and shaken as dry as possible.

The butter sizzles violently and the parsley becomes as brown as the butter. Draw the pan off the fire once more and after 3 minutes add a ½-teaspoonful of vinegar. If you did not allow this slight cooling the butter would splutter in all directions.

Put the pan back on a low fire and heat it once more. The vinegar begins to boil. Turn the slices of brain in the *beurre noir* and serve them on a hot dish. With them drink a good Sauternes which, as you know, is a little sweet.

Cervelle en Papillotes.

An ox brain, 6 ozs sliced ham, 2 ozs butter.

Cook the ox brain as before and cut it in slices. Salt and pepper them. Cut some slices of ham the same size as the brains and spread them with soft butter.

Sandwich the pieces of brain between slices of buttered ham and put each sandwich on a round of buttered greaseproof paper large enough to fold over and roll together at the edges. Arrange them all on a buttered fireproof dish and bake in the oven for 20 minutes.

What a charming surprise for your guests! Each has his own *papillotte* which he unwraps and enjoys.

Croquettes de Cervelle.

An ox brain, breadcrumbs, milk, 2 eggs, nutmeg, flour, 2 ozs butter, a lemon.

Chop a cold cooked ox brain and mix it with half its own volume of breadcrumbs which have been soaked in milk and squeezed to remove the surplus moisture. Add a yolk of egg, some salt and a grating of nutmeg.

Make the mixture into small cakes and dip them in flour, beaten yolk of egg and breadcrumbs, in turn.

Melt 2 ozs of butter in a frying-pan and brown the *croquettes* on both sides. Serve them on a hot dish garnished with slices of lemon, and drink white wine—naturally.

Calf's Head.

Calf's head is a very pleasant dish. I know what you will say—that it has no flavour of its own; that it depends on the sauce which accompanies it; that it has no nutritive value.

Don't be too sure of all this. There is plenty of nourishment in calf's head, and for certain people it is even too rich in certain substances which encourage rheumatism.

It can be prepared in many different ways, some simple and some complicated, and it is not the latter which are necessarily the best.

Calf's Head Vinaigrette.

Buy half a calf's head, white and fresh and neatly prepared. Have it boned, rolled and tied. Like this it will be much easier to manage. Now you have a coice of two ways of cooking. It may be steamed, in which case it will keep a neat shape, but its appearance will be less appetizing as the flesh will turn grey.

If you boil the calf's head the flavour will not be so good, but it will be beautifully white, especially if you add flour to the water in which it is boiled.

To boil calf's head, heat some water in a saucepan and as soon as it is tepid, plunge the head into the water, bring it to the boil and after a moment or two, drain off the water. Repeat the operation so that you will have blanched your calf's head twice. (In the case of steaming you should also carry out this preliminary operation.)

Now bring 5 pints of water to the boil and stir into it a heaping tablespoon of flour which you have mixed to a cream with cold water. Stir, and add cooking salt, a bayleaf, a sprig of thyme and a peeled onion. Submerge the calf's head beneath the water and bring it to the boil once again. Skim, cover, and simmer for 1½ hours. The calf's head is cooked, neither too firm nor too soft.

Serve it hot with a sauce-boat filled with *vinaigrette sauce* which you have made by mixing two-thirds of oil to one-third of vinegar and adding chopped tarragon and the yolks of 2 hard-boiled eggs mashed with a fork. Salt and pepper the sauce to please your taste.

Tête de Veau Madrilène.

I ate this dish in Madrid and it charmed me, so I shall tell you about it.

> *A boiled calf's head, 2½ ozs concentrated tomato purée, a clove of garlic, 1 tablespoon oil, 1½ ozs capers, 4 stoned black olives.*

Heat in a saucepan the tomato purée, thinned to a syrupy consistency with water. Add the garlic finely chopped, the oil, capers and black olives. Salt and pepper liberally and cook for about 20 minutes on a low fire.

Put the boiled calf's head, cut into large pieces, into a saucepan and cover it with the sauce. Heat it through.

Prepare as many hard-boiled eggs as you have guests. Peel them and cut them in half and arrange them round the dish on which you serve the calf's head. This dish demands a strong red wine, preferably from the Roussillon.

Tête de Veau Panée.

> *1 lb boned calf's head, flour, egg, breadcrumbs, oil for frying.*

Cook the calf's head and, whilst it is still tepid, cut it into flat pieces. Dip these in flour, beaten egg and breadcrumbs in turn. Deep-fry them in oil for about 4 minutes and drain them on soft paper. Sprinkle with salt and serve with rounds of lemon. Try this, it is really rather good.

Calf's Feet in Jelly.

> *2 calf's feet, 1 lb mixed vegetables, the white of an egg, 3 tablespoons oil, 1 tablespoon vinegar, parsley, chives, capers, chervil and tarragon if possible, a small onion, lemon peel.*

Buy two calf's feet and ask the butcher to cut them in pieces. See if you can persuade your greengrocer to sell you a pound of mixed vegetables—carrots, turnips, leeks and onions. You may be lucky.

Put the pieces of calf's foot into a saucepan and cover them with cold water. Salt and bring to the boil. Skim, and add the vegetables, cleaned and cut in pieces. Simmer with the lid on for 3 hours. Pour the whole thing through a sieve, being careful to save all the broth. The bones can easily be detached from the flesh. Remove them and the vegetables, leaving only the eatable pieces of meat.

Colour the broth lightly. This can be done by sprinkling a slice of onion or tomato with sugar and letting it brown in a pan or on top of an electric cooking plate and stirring it into the broth. Instead of this you can also use a little browning.

Pour the broth into a saucepan and, while it is still tepid, stir in the white of an egg. Bring it to the boil. The white of egg will coagulate and fall to the bottom, clarifying the broth. Strain it through a muslin.

Put the pieces of calf's feet into a mould and pour the broth over them. Leave them in a cool place overnight. Turn out the jelly and serve it with a vinaigrette sauce made with two-thirds of oil to one-third of vinegar, plenty of freshly-milled pepper and salt and a generous amount of chopped parsley, chives, capers, chervil, tarragon, minced onion and lemon peel.

Kidneys.

Meyerbeer is said to have eaten kidneys at every meal and many people who could not name the composer of one of his operas know that scrambled eggs mixed with kidneys are called *œufs Meyerbeer*. Happy the genius who, just by associating with a frying-pan, can ensure that his name will go down to posterity, at least in the form of something to eat.

As for me, who am no genius, I only ask your attention for a few minutes while I tell you how to prepare kidneys. First of all, which kind shall you buy?

Calf's kidney is too expensive for my budget. Ox kidney is the one for me, and pig's kidney for those who like it. I do not, as it exudes too much water in the frying-pan and this juice has an unpleasant smell. As for sheep's kidneys, they are ridiculously small and you need four for each person. In the end, they are just as expensive as calf's kidney.

Rognon de Bœuf Saignant.

For four people buy a medium-sized ox kidney. Ask the butcher to remove the membrane as well as the piece of fat at the centre, but do not have it cut up. Carry it home just as it is. Besides the kidney you will need:

2½ ozs butter, some very finely chopped parsley and a little watercress.

Cut the kidney in thick slices along its length. It should make six or eight. Each of the slices should be at least ¾-inch thick.

Melt 1 oz of butter in a frying-pan. When the butter is smoking, put the kidneys into the pan and raise the heat. The underneath of each slice browns rapidly. Wait 3 minutes and turn the slices. Cook for about 4 minutes after turning (7 or 8 minutes in all).

While the kidney is cooking melt the butter in a small saucepan and add the parsley. Put the slices of kidney onto a hot dish and sprinkle them with salt, freshly-milled pepper and the parsley butter. Garnish the dish with watercress. The crimson juice of the kidneys mixes with the butter in the dish to make a delicious gravy. With the kidneys I drink a finger of Bourgueil, which is a red wine from the Loire valley.

Kidney's à la Poêle.

> 1 *lb calf's kidney*, 4 *ozs mushrooms*, 2 *ozs butter, a small glass of brandy.*

Get the butcher, if he is amiable, to cut the kidney into pieces the size of a walnut.

Wash and drain the mushrooms and slice them finely. Bring the butter to smoking point in a frying-pan and toss in the pieces of kidney. They will pale and turn almost white. Shake the pan continually and add the mushrooms. As these will exude water, increase the heat so that it will evaporate almost completely. Sprinkle with salt and freshly-milled black pepper.

Six minutes have passed and there is hardly any sauce left in the pan. Add the cognac, stir and taste. The raw flavour of the cognac spoils the sauce. Let it cook for another minute. Now it is better. Two more minutes, and it is delicious.

Arrange the kidney in a hot dish and serve it with a glass of red wine. My choice would be *vin de Cahors* from the Lot. This is the blackest of all the wines of France.

Kidneys à la Crème.

Prepare this dish in exactly the same way as the previous recipe, with butter and cognac, then just as you are about to lift it from the fire stir in ⅛-pint of thick cream which you have mixed with a ½-teaspoon of mustard.

Let the sauce bubble for ten seconds and taste it. It is divine.

This is *haute cuisine* in ten minutes. Think of me while you are enjoying it.

Liver—but not Calf's Liver.

Once upon a time, many years ago, a slave called Æsop was ordered by his master Xanthus to prepare a meal with the finest food in the world. The feast consisted entirely of dishes made with tongue.

On being told to produce a meal using the worst food that he could find Æsop once more served tongue and only tongue.

For tongues, according to Æsop, were both the best and the worst things in the world. Certainly in Ancient Greece the tongue was of supreme inportance, for the destiny of the nation hung on the words spoken at the Agora.

In our day other organs enjoy a more considerable reputation since medicine has demonstrated their importance. Amongst the first of these is the liver.

The liver regulates the supply of sugar in our organism and sugar is the fuel for our living motor. The liver secretes bile; adjusts the intake of iron in our systems; arrests the poisons which come from the intestine and transforms insoluble uric acid into easily eliminated urea. The liver has many other properties which are suspected, though not yet fully understood, by the doctors.

When a learned American named Whipple discovered that calf's liver would cure anaemia the pharmaceutical factories rushed to buy up calf's liver at fancy prices. Since then it has become a rich man's dish.

So for those of my readers who are not millionaires I am going to describe some very good dishes which can be made with sheep's, pig's or ox liver.

Ox Liver Baked.

> 2 *lbs ox liver larded (if possible by the butcher), a thick slice of fat bacon,* 1 *oz butter,* ¼-*pint of thick cream,* ½-*teaspoon flour.*

Arrange the liver into a deep fireproof dish or baking tin. Cover it with the fat bacon and surround it with dabs of butter. Put it into a very hot oven (450° F. Gas 8). The butter melts, the bacon sizzles and the liver begins to colour. Baste frequently, and when the liver is golden-brown sprinkle it with a very little salt and pepper.

Turn the liver so that it colours on all sides, then pour a little hot water into the dish, cover it with some greaseproof paper and bake for 30 minutes more.

Now add half the cream. It melts and turns buttery. Baste well and after another 30 minutes take the dish out of the oven and pour the sauce, which is not very abundant, into a small saucepan, making up the required quantity with boiling water.

When the sauce is boiling, add the rest of the cream into which you have stirred a ½-teaspoonful of flour. Let the sauce boil for a moment, then pour it over the hot liver and serve.

Brochettes of Sheep's Liver.

> 1 *lb sheep's liver cut into fairly thick slices*, 6 *ozs bacon, a little olive oil, watercress.*

Cut each slice of liver into four pieces. You should have about sixteen in all. Cut the bacon into corresponding pieces and thread them, alternately with the liver, onto four small skewers or pieces of galvanized wire five or six inches long. Brush each *brochette* with oil and grill for 7–8 minutes, turning them once.

Arrange the skewers on a hot dish, sprinkle with salt and pepper and garnish with watercress.

The Transformation of a Ham Bone.

Even the most perfect ham—or perhaps the perfect ham quickest of all—will reach a stage when it is no more than an ungainly bone covered with scrappy pink flesh from which no more smooth slices can be cut. You will probably have kept some of the fat which you cut off so as to give leaner slices to those who preferred them.

This ham bone, far from being a melancholy remainder is still a treasure. With a sharp knife pare off long strips of meat and then shave off all the scraps, keeping these separate. Besides the *Nouilles à la Tchèque* which I described on p. 59, you can turn these into the following excellent dishes:

Ham Flakes.

For this dish you will need a deep frying-pan and a batter made with these materials:

> 1 *egg*, 2½ *ozs flour, a little beer.*

Break the egg into a small basin. Add the flour and mix with a fork. Thin the mixture with beer, beating until it has the consistency of a smooth cream.

Dip one of the strips of ham into the batter. It should emerge smoothly coated. Coat each of the strips delicately with batter and drop them all into smoking hot fat. In 2 minutes they are crisp. Put them on a hot dish, and enjoy them with salt, pepper and a glass of white wine.

Pancakes Stuffed with Ham.

Mince the scraps of ham and mix them with an equal quantity of thick Béchamel sauce made with the following:

> ¾ *oz flour*, ¾ *oz butter, a glass of milk*, 1 *yolk of egg.*

Melt the butter and sieve in the flour. Mix well over a gentle heat and then stir in the milk, little by little. Boil for 10 seconds, salt and pepper lightly. Remove the pan from the fire and stir in the yolk of egg and then the ham. Let the mixture cool and thicken.

To make the batter use:

> 1 *egg*, 4 *ozs plain flour, a cup of milk*, 1 *oz butter.*

Mix the flour and egg and beat in the milk so that you have a thin cream without any lumps. Let it stand for 30 minutes. Add a pinch of salt.

Wrap the butter in a piece of muslin and rub it round a heated frying-pan until it is smoking. Lift the pan from the fire and pour in a large spoonful of batter, tilting the pan so that the mixture spreads in every direction. Return the pan to the fire for 20 seconds and toss the pancake. Twenty seconds more and it is done. Lay it and its successors—about twelve in all—-on a clean napkin.

Put a small cylinder of the ham mixture onto each pancake. Turn in the edges, left and right, and then roll them up so that the stuffing is tucked completely in.

Put 1½ ozs butter into a frying-pan and make it smoking hot. Fry half the rolls at a time, over a moderate fire, turning them so that they are golden-brown all over. Keep them hot and fry the rest. Serve immediately and enjoy your success.

Flageolets with Ham.

Now there is only the fat which you have saved and the bare bone of the ham, but you can still prepare an excellent and satisfying dish. You will need:

> ½ *oz butter*, 1 *lb flageolets of the best quality, a handful of chervil.*

Saw the hambone in two and put it into a saucepan half filled with water. Add the flageolets and simmer gently for 1½ hours until the water is absorbed and the flageolets cooked.

Cut the ham fat in pieces and let it melt and turn golden-brown with the butter, then pour this over the beans and add the chervil, finely chopped. Taste, and add salt if necessary. You have a dish for at least six people. All that is left of your ham is the bone—and the memory.

POULTRY & GAME

Poule au Pot.

This is one way of making a boiling fowl into an excellent dish, which, besides providing a large number of helpings, will also give you a quantity of very savoury broth. It should be accompanied by some carefully cooked rice and a cream sauce flavoured with curry.

> *A boiling fowl, 2 lbs flank of beef, ½ lb carrots, ½ lb turnips, 2 large leeks, 2 or 3 whole dried red peppers (these are very hot so go carefully the first time), 2 sausages, smoked if possible.*

Put the beef into a heavy iron pan with 6 pints of salted water. Bring it slowly to the boil and skim very carefully. Add the fresh vegetables sliced, and the peppers whole. Simmer for 4 hours so gently that the bubbles just break the surface. Lift out the meat and vegetables and set them aside.

It is not easy to gauge just how long to cook a boiling fowl, so it is a wise precaution to tie the bird round with string, leaving a loose end attached to the handle of the pot. Like this you can lift if out after 1 hour and test the flesh gently with a fork.

When the fowl has been simmering quietly for about 30 minutes drop the sausages into the broth. A quarter of an hour before it is ready to serve, return the meat and vegetables to the pot so that they heat through thoroughly. Meanwhile, prepare the rice and the sauce.

The Rice.

> *2 ozs butter, a cupful of curry rice.*

Melt the butter in a heavy frying-pan and pour in the rice which you have not washed. Let it heat for 2 minutes so that it is all shiny with butter, being careful that it does not stick or burn.

Pour the hot broth over the rice and bring it to the boil. Cover the pan and regulate the heat so that the liquid is just simmering. After 20 minutes uncover the pan and shake it well. The rice is cooked and all the grains are separate. Leave it over a very low heat, uncovered, while you make the sauce.

The Sauce.

> 2 ozs butter, 2 tablespoons flour, 1 cupful broth, 1 teaspoon curry, 3½ ozs thick cream.

Melt the butter and sieve the flour into it. Work them together until you have a shiny, golden paste, then stir in a cupful of broth which you have allowed to cool a little, and the curry. Cook over a low fire for 10 minutes and add the cream. Heat it once more. The sauce is ready.

Now put the casserole with the chicken in the middle of the table and a soup plate in front of each guest. Help them to broth which can be made even more delicious by a sprinkling of grated Parmesan or Gruyère cheese.

Using the same deep plates, if you wish to eat in the true peasant manner and incidentally save yourself some trouble, serve for each guest a piece of chicken, a slice of beef, a round of sausage with vegetables. Pour the creamy, golden sauce over the chicken and flank it with a pile of rice.

Poulet Tamara.

Georgia is a legendary country beyond the Caucasus where the women are said to be the most beautiful in the world. Its legends have inspired many Russian writers and musicians and even given rise to a famous dish, *poulet Tamara.*

According to a story denied by some Georgians, the country was ruled in the twelfth century by Tamara, a queen of rare beauty who, having cast out her drunken husband, the Muscovite prince, Bogolubski, decided to drive her lover, the poet Rousthaveli, author of the marvellous poem 'The Leopard Skin', mad with jealousy. To inflame the passions of the wretched man she took lovers at random, welcoming them in her castle on a crag above the Georgian highway over the Caucasus, and preparing with her own hands the principal dish of the banquet she offered them. The chance lover was overwhelmed with wine and caresses. Next morning he was hurled to his death over a precipice which one can see to this day.

The dish which Tamara enjoyed so much is perhaps better known than the legend and I shall tell you how to make it. If you decide to try I can promise you a completely novel gastronomic sensation.

A plump roasting chicken, ½ lb onions, 1 lb peeled walnuts, ½ glass vinegar, 3 ozs butter, 6 yolks of egg, ½ lb carrots, ½ lb turnips, 2 large leeks, thyme, 2 bayleaves, 2 cloves, 2 cloves of garlic, a large pinch of cinnamon.

Put the chicken into a heavy iron casserole with the carrots, onions and leeks, cut in pieces, the herbs and spices and 3½ pints water. Boil with the lid on for 30 minutes. Lift out the chicken and let it cool slightly. Rub it all over with about one-third of the butter and roast it in the oven for 30 minutes.

Whilst the chicken is roasting make the sauce. Reduce the broth over a hot fire until you have about 1¾ pints of liquid, then strain it.

Heat the rest of the butter in a frying-pan and melt the finely-chopped onions and garlic until they are a pale golden-brown. Remove the pan from the fire.

Pound the nuts to a paste adding a teaspoon of broth from time to time. Mix the nuts with the onions and stir in the broth and then the vinegar over the fire, being careful that the sauce does not boil.

Beat the egg yolks in a bowl and stir in the sauce a little at a time. Return it to the casserole and warm it very carefully until it thickens, taking great care that the sauce does not boil or it will curdle. Adjust the seasoning with salt and a little freshly-milled pepper.

Cut the chicken in pieces and arrange them in a deep dish. Pour the sauce over them and let them cool overnight. Invite some Georgian *emigrés*, if you happen to know any, and listen to nostalgic stories of their unhappy country.

Poulet Flambé à l'Estragon.

A chicken weighing a good 2 lbs, 3 ozs bacon, 2 ozs butter, a glass of white wine, a sherry-glassful of brandy, a bunch of tarragon, 2 shallots, ¼ lb mushrooms, ½ teaspoon paprika.

Cut the chicken in pieces.

Melt the diced bacon in an iron casserole with half the butter. Raise the heat and brown the pieces of chicken all over. Add the minced shallot and, 2 minutes later, the white wine and the mushrooms finely chopped. Sprinkle with about thirty of the tarragon leaves. Cover the casserole and simmer for 25 minutes.

Lift the lid and add the paprika, then allow the liquid to evaporate a little. Warm the brandy in a small saucepan, shaking the pan briskly, set it alight and pour it over the chicken. Add a ½-glass of boiling water, 20 more tarragon leaves and the rest of the butter.

Taste the sauce. It will probably be salt enough because of the bacon. There is not a great quantity of sauce but the flesh of the chicken is perfumed with tarragon and the dish is just as it should be.

Le Poulet Canaille.

The use of garlic can be traced back to the beginnings of Western civilization. Almost five thousand years ago Cheops, when he was building the pyramid at Gizeh, supplemented the rations of the slaves with a large quantity of garlic—or so Heredotus tells us.

The Egyptians loved garlic so much that they began to worship it as a divinity and its use was forbidden by the priests. Only the Hebrews, in bondage in Egypt, failed to obey the law. They went on eating garlic, and they still use a great deal in their ritual cooking. The Romans tended to look down on garlic as the food of the plebs.

Garlic was used as a specific against the plague. It was the active principle in an ancient remedy called the Vinegar of the Four Thieves, invented by four ruffians who, in 1726, during the plague, were able to rob the houses of the dead and dying in Marseilles thanks to the protection of their own medicine. When they were caught, they gladly exchanged the formula for a free pardon.

In the South of France they still eat garlic in quantities, and the recipe which I shall give you now is an example. Garlic is creeping into the English home, and you can now buy it at any good greengrocer's. If this recipe for *poulet canaille* is too strong for you, cut down the garlic. Next time you will probably be braver. It is a taste which grows rapidly.

A chicken, 1½ ozs butter, 4 tablespoons olive oil, 30 cloves of garlic, 10 shallots, dry white wine.

Buy a plump little chicken and cut it into eight pieces. Melt the butter in an iron casserole. Add the oil and heat until it is smoking. Arrange the chicken in the bottom of the casserole and brown the pieces on one side over a moderate fire so that the fat does not burn. Turn the pieces and brown them on the other side.

Now listen carefully. In case you are wondering whether there was a mis-print in the quantity of garlic for this dish, I will make it quite clear by saying that I mean twice 15. These must not be peeled but put into the casserole with their skins on, together with the shallots, finely chopped. Leave them for 10 minutes, so that the skins are just coloured.

Salt and pepper copiously, and add a glass of dry white wine. Put on the lid and simmer for 30 minutes. The chicken is cooked. Uncover the casserole and raise the heat so that the wine evaporates completely and the chicken browns once more.

Set the casserole on the table. There is no juice left in it. Everyone receives a portion of chicken and 6 cloves of browned garlic.

Eat some chicken and then put a clove of garlic into your mouth. Bite it and the inside will slip out. It is exquisite. Spit the skin discreetly onto your fork and slip it onto the rim of your plate. You can repeat this pleasure five times more, sipping as you do so a very dry white wine.

Poulet à la Crème.

A chicken weighing about 3 lbs, 2 ozs butter, ½ lb mushrooms, 3 medium-sized onions, 3½ ozs thick cream, ½ teaspoon flour.

Melt the butter in a heavy iron casserole and brown the chicken all over on a moderate fire so that the butter does not burn. Some time will pass before the chicken is a lovely mahogany colour but it smells so good as it sizzles in the butter that one loses all sense of time.

Salt the chicken and add the onions chopped finely. They in their turn will colour.

Meanwhile wash the mushrooms without peeling them and cut them in slices. Put them into the casserole with half a small glassful of water and cover. Turn the chicken from time to time and after 35 minutes on a moderate fire test the flesh with a fork. It should be done.

Mix the cream and the flour and pour them into the juice from the chicken. Bring to the boil and the sauce thickens.

Rinse out the cream bowl with a little sauce and taste. It is just right.

Serve the chicken with its sauce very hot on a deep dish, and wait for the compliments of your guests.

Coq au Vin.

The good king Henry IV of France wanted each of his subjects to have a chicken in the pot on Sundays. May his good intentions be fulfilled in Paradise! We have certainly not reached that stage yet.

Chickens vary tremendously in size and quality. Some have a beautiful full figure, their curves enhanced by a taut, snowy skin. These should be roasted, basting frequently with their own fat mixed with the melted butter which you have rubbed over the breast. There is no better dish than a superb roast chicken.

Birds of more modest proportions shrink in the dry heat of the oven whereas, cooked in a casserole, they keep their shape and even swell in the damp heat.

For the following dish, which is very old and very French, leave the most expensive chickens aside and choose one weighing about 3 lbs (which is within my price range). You will also need:

> *2½ ozs butter, 2½ ozs bacon, ¼ lb mushrooms, 2 medium-sized onions, a sprig of thyme, a bottle of inexpensive Burgundy, a small glass of brandy, ½ teaspoon flour.*

Joint the chicken and brown the pieces in a heavy iron casserole in which you have melted the diced bacon in half the butter. Add the onions sliced in four and let them turn golden-brown. Salt and pepper lightly. Add the sliced mushrooms and the thyme and pour in the whole bottle of wine.

Leave the pot uncovered on a very hot fire so that the liquid boils rapidly and reduces in volume. At the same time the wine colours the flesh of the chicken.

When you have about a wineglass and a half of liquid lower the heat, put on the lid and simmer for 20 minutes more. Test the chicken with a fork to see if it is done.

Mix the flour into the rest of the butter, thinning it with 2 tablespoonfuls of liquid from the chicken. Stir it into the wine sauce together with the brandy and simmer for 5 minutes more. Taste and correct the seasoning.

Carry the casserole to the table and fill your guests' glasses with the same wine which you have used to make the sauce for the *Coq au Vin*.

Ducks and Ducklings.

A duckling is a young duck, but at just what moment does he shed his down and begin to look with a more appreciative eye at his young female companions? Modern ducks raised by the new-fangled methods mature at about ten weeks, and from this moment their tender flesh becomes progressively tougher. A good duck is certainly not to be despised, but it needs careful treatment and longer cooking. In general it is wiser to roast the ducklings and choose a slower method of cooking the ducks.

Caneton à l'Orange.

A duckling, 4 oranges, 1 oz butter, ½ glass of dry white wine.

Peel two of the oranges and separate the segments, removing any pith. Pack them inside the bird, closing the entrance (which during the lifetime of the duckling was, of course, an exit) with thread or a small skewer.

Melt the butter in an iron casserole and brown the duckling all over. Spoon away three-quarters of the fat which it exudes and pour over it the juice of two more oranges and the white wine. Add the rest of one of the oranges very finely chopped and plenty of freshly-milled pepper. Simmer for 45 minutes.

Test the flesh with the points of a fork. If they penetrate easily the duckling is cooked. The juice is not very abundant, so add a little boiling water and bring to the boil once more, stirring well.

This dish will just serve four people. It is popular now and owes a great deal of its popularity just to fashion. To my mind the next dish is better.

Caneton aux Cervelas.

A duckling, 3 Cervelas sausages,[1] *2 ozs bacon, 1 oz butter, a small sprig of thyme, ½ glass white wine.*

---

[1] Cervelas sausages are not easy to find in this country but Italian *cotecchino* which is obtainable in Soho, may be used as a substitute. Many delicatessen shops sell a boiling sausage—often made by Poles—which is quite suitable for this dish.

Peel the sausages, slice them and put them into the duckling with the leaves of the thyme. Close the aperture with thread. In an iron casserole melt the butter and brown the duckling, adding the bacon, diced. Pour in the white wine but avoid both salt and pepper at this stage, since the bacon is salt and the sausage well seasoned. Cover the casserole and simmer from 30–45 minutes.

Taste the sauce and adjust the seasoning.

Now sit down and enjoy the duckling with, of course, a bottle of good Burgundy.

Canard aux Navets.

This dish takes some time to prepare and it may well be made the day beforehand and warmed before the meal. You can use an old duck, but you must be sure to have the head left on. I shall explain why when I describe the dish. Besides the duck you will need:

> 2 *lbs young turnips,* 4 *ozs of breadcrumbs, a cup of milk,*
> 3 *shallots,* 2½ *ozs butter, a yolk of egg,* 1 *tablespoon flour,*
> *marjoram or a little thyme.*

Cut off the head of the duck and then separate the neck, rolling off the skin and putting it on one side. Cut the duck into eight pieces.

Mince the liver and heart and mix them with the breadcrumbs which you have soaked in milk and squeezed to drain away the surplus moisture. Add the shallots minced, two dessertspoons of melted butter and the yolk of egg. Fill the skin of the neck with this mixture and tie it at both ends. You have made a sort of sausage.

Melt the rest of the butter in a heavy iron casserole and brown the pieces of duck. This will take some time. Remove half the fat from the pan and sprinkle the joints of duck with flour. Add a glass of water, salt and pepper, the stuffed neck of the duck and the chopped marjoram or thyme.

Cover the casserole and simmer for 30 minutes. Add the turnips, peeled and cut in pieces. Cover once more and simmer for three-quarters of an hour. Now try the meat and if the flesh is not tender continue cooking until you are satisfied, testing fairly frequently.

This dish, to my mind, is actually better when it is prepared a day in advance.

Goose.

There is an old traditional saying that a goose is too big for one and not enough for two. Nowadays this particular problem does not worry us, but the goose remains a deceptive bird. With all its feathers on it looks enormous and in the oven it is still plump and comfortable, but when you come to carve it you wonder with consternation whether there will ever be enough for the six people who are impatiently waiting. However, though everyone helps themselves with delight very few have a second helping, since the meat and the sauce and the accompaniments are so rich. So your goose is sufficient after all, and your worry quite unnecessary.

Roast Goose with Apples and Cervelas Sausage.

> *A goose, 4 sharp apples of good quality, 4 Cervelas sausages,[1] 1 oz butter.*

Your goose is before you, plump and trussed and waiting to be stuffed. Peel and core the apples which must be fine specimens with a good flavour, and divide each into eight pieces. Skin the sausages, cut them in slices 2–3 inches thick and mix them with the apples, salt and pepper. Stuff the goose and sew up the aperture with coarse thread.

Rub the breast of the goose with butter and put it in a very hot oven (about 450° F. Gas 8). Cooking time will vary from 45 minutes to 2 hours according to the size and age of the bird, and you will have to explore the flesh delicately with the point of a fork to decide whether it is done.

As the butter melts the breast of the goose begins to brown. Sprinkle it with salt, and lower the heat of the oven so that it does not burn. The fat in the tin is also in danger of burning, so pour into it a glass of cold water.

When the goose is done, skim off as much of the liquid fat as possible. What remains in the tin will make your sauce. It is a wise precaution to carve the goose in the kitchen as it is a messy operation and you may need the help of your fingers. In France the goose is cut into joints arranged round a pile of apple and sausage stuffing.

Far from being insufficient, your goose will leave your guests comfortably filled and dozing in their armchairs. It may even happen, as it did to *me* the other day, that they are too com-

[1] See note on p. 133.

fortable to leave and stay on to supper. If you suspect that this is likely to happen, face the emergency in advance and prepare the soup which I describe on p. 30. In fact, if you are prudent, you will lay in a stock of barley, carrots, turnips, leeks and onions at the same time that you buy the goose.

The giblets and any remains of goose will make an excellent addition, minced and seasoned, to a white risotto p. 232. The fat from the goose and any remains of meat will also make the following delicious dish.

Goose and Cabbage.

> 2 *small white cabbages, fat from a roast goose, and any remains of the meat.*

Choose small, tender, snow-white cabbages, wash them and cut them in four, removing the stalk. Now slice the quarters finely using a very sharp kitchen knife and wash once more. Throw the cabbage into a saucepan of boiling water and cook for 5 minutes. Drain off the water and put the cabbage into a heavy iron casserole with the fat from the goose. Simmer gently with the lid on for 2 hours, then add the goose meat which you have saved, and cover everything with the bones which you will later throw away.

After an hour correct the seasoning and the dish is ready to serve. It is simple, but extremely good.

Goose fat should never be thrown away. It is especially useful for frying potatoes.

Ragoût of Goose with Apples.

This is a heavy dish and better eaten in cold weather. In France one can buy separate pieces of goose by weight. Two pounds should be enough for four people, so if you buy a whole goose you can work out the proportions of the recipe accordingly.

> 1 *lb cooking apples to every pound of goose.*

Melt a little goose fat in a heavy iron casserole and brown the goose which you have cut into pieces. Turn the pieces constantly until the skin is crisp and golden. Drain off the fat, sprinkle the meat with salt, add the sliced apples, and cover. Five minutes later the apples are beginning to soften and the smell is delicious. Stir them with a fork, cover and leave on a low fire for a good hour.

Now test the meat and you will find that it is tender and lifts easily from the bone. The goose is ready but the surplus fat must still be skimmed off with care. Serve it in a hot dish. The apples have melted into a smooth purée and the ragoût is fragrant.

Rabbit with Turnips.

This dish comes from Normandy. Choose a young rabbit so that the flesh is tender. Besides this you will need:

> 2 *ozs butter*, 6 *ozs onion, half a bottle of dry cider,* 1½ *lbs young turnips.*

Cut the rabbit in pieces and brown these, in a heavy iron casserole, in smoking hot butter. It is wisest to do them half at a time so that you have room to turn them on all sides.

Add the sliced onions, sprinkled with salt and pepper, and let them turn golden-brown. Now pour in half a bottle of dry cider, cover the casserole and simmer for a quarter of an hour.

Put the turnips, which you have washed, peeled and cut in pieces, into the casserole and cook for three quarters of an hour more with the lid on.

Taste, correct the seasoning and serve the rabbit with glasses of sparkling cider.

Roast Rabbit with Cream.

> *The back of a rabbit,* 2 *ozs butter,* ¼ *pint thick cream,* 2 *glasses white wine,* 2 *yolks of eggs,* ½ *lb small new onions.*

Butter the rabbit, put it in a fireproof dish and into a hot oven (about 440° F. Gas 7). The butter melts and the rabbit begins to colour. Baste it, using besides the melted butter nearly half the cream.

Arrange the whole onions round the rabbit and when they are slightly coloured pour in the white wine. Baste from time to time. After 45 minutes the rabbit should be done.

Take the dish out of the oven and pour the sauce into a small saucepan, adding the rest of the cream. Heat it on a very low fire until it thickens.

Cut the rabbit in pieces, put them onto a hot dish and pour the sauce over them.

Rabbit with Mustard.

The back of a rabbit, a small pot of French mustard, 4 ozs butter, 2 glasses of brandy.

Spread the contents of your pot of mustard over the rabbit. Roast it in a good oven (400° F. Gas 5), basting right from the beginning with melted butter. The rabbit will cook quickly and you must watch that the butter does not burn. To prevent this add a little water.

After 45 minutes take the rabbit out of the oven and pour the brandy into the hot dish. Set it on fire, and carry the dish to table. With this excellent rabbit drink a bottle of light Beaujolais.

Some things you should remember about Game.

Certain people—and happily extremely few—are unable to eat game without suffering from disagreeable skin eruptions, attacks of rheumatism, and so on. Others enjoy game for years and then, quite suddenly, after eating a delicious jugged hare, almost die of poisoning. What is the explanation?

The first group is allergic to game in the same way that sufferers from hay fever are allergic to pollen; the second, victims of an accident, having eaten game which was not high but putrid. The difference is not, as some people believe, a question of degree, but of a quite separate process.

The bodies of animals which die in the woods do not putrefy but dry up and mummify without producing any disagreeable smell. This is the result of bacteria found in the intestines which invade the whole body after death. The bodies of domestic animals, on the other hand, are invaded by microbes from outside and decompose, producing a violent poison called ptomaine. Everything touched by man and civilization is soiled by these microbes which are very rare in woods and open country.

If game has been cleanly killed and the skin, except for small shot holes, is intact, it will merely become high and have no offensive smell. If the flesh is torn or the intestines are drawn with soiled hands the harmful microbes will cause putrefaction and it will become poisonous. For this reason, once game is killed it should not be touched but hung, out of reach of flies, until it is tender and gamy.

The length of time for which game should be hung varies according to the weather, the age of the game and the taste of the individual, but as a rough guide, if you can pull out the feathers above the tail with ease, then the bird is ready. If you are one of those people who likes their game very high, then wait a day or two more.

The improvement in texture and flavour which is produced by hanging can be achieved by soaking the meat of a red deer, hare, etc., in a bath of acid liquid, since acidity hinders decay. This is the principle of the marinade which is spiced and acidulated with wine or vinegar. A process of auto-digestion is set up and the meat becomes tender and absorbs the flavour of the liquid.

Once you understand the processes I have described it becomes clear that to be perfectly safe from food poisoning you should avoid any game which you have not seen in its own fur or feathers and which you meet for the first time on your plate. Stick to those creatures whose bodies you have inspected and which have been hung under your watchful eye.

Civet of Hare.

To make a good civet of hare the animal should be hung for four or five days but unless, as I have just explained, you are sure that it has been cleanly killed and properly prepared, it is better to eat the hare quickly.

A civet is a noble dish and to enjoy it to the full use your two best bottles of red wine—one for the cooking and the other to accompany it at table. Besides the hare and the wine you will use the following ingredients:

> 4 *level tablespoons flour,* 1 *large onion,* 1 *clove of garlic, a bouquet of parsley and a bouquet of thyme,* 6 *ozs cultivated mushrooms,* 4 *ozs mild fat bacon,* 2 *ozs butter.*

Skin the hare and clean it. Collect carefully any clots of blood and put them into a cup together with the liver which you have removed with your fingers. Then with the point of a very sharp knife strip away the whitish tissues which cover the back and the legs, otherwise the meat will be tough when it is cooked.

Separate the hare into joints and, with the help of a strong knife and a wooden mallet cut the back into pieces.

Chop the bacon and put it, with the butter, into a large iron casserole over a good fire. The butter melts and the bacon too.

Arrange the pieces of meat in the bottom of the casserole. Their rosy colour turns to grey and they begin to brown on the outside. Ten minutes have passed.

Add the minced onions and garlic and cook for another 5 minutes, then sprinkle in the whole of the flour. Keep the pieces of hare moving over the fire for 5 minutes more so that they are well coated with flour, then add the bouquets of thyme and parsley and pour in the bottle of red wine. Season with salt and pepper.

Cover the casserole and let it boil briskly. Part of the wine evaporates and the sauce thickens. Now is the moment to put in the sliced mushrooms and lower the heat.

Ideas about the length of time a civet should cook vary considerably. Some say 3 hours and some 5. Personally I don't wait for the meat to become a purée and after 2 hours, when the meat is beginning to come away from the bone, I consider that the hare is done. But the civet is not yet finished.

Put the liver and blood through a mincing machine followed by a little breadcrumb so that no scrap of it is wasted. Pour 2 small glasses of cognac into a saucepan and let it boil for 5 minutes. Now add the liver mixture and boil for 1 minute more, stirring all the time. Stir this into the civet and let it boil for another minute.

Put the civet into a deep dish, fill your glasses with red wine, and enjoy the expressions on the faces of your guests. How I wish I were a millionaire and could make a civet with Chambertin!

Hare à la Royale.

This is a famous dish. If you do not consider it worthy of being called royal, you must excuse me, but in any case, try it. You will need plenty of patience, two good friends as guests, two bottles of Burgundy and:

> *A hare, 2 large rashers of bacon, 20 cloves of garlic, 40 shallots, ½-glass wine vinegar, 2 ozs butter, a small glass of brandy, a sprig of thyme, 2 bayleaves.*

Hang the hare for only 4 days. Skin and draw it and use only the saddle and back legs for this dish. Mince the garlic and shallots.

Melt the butter in a heavy iron casserole, lay a rasher of bacon in the bottom and then the hare, with the second rasher of bacon on top. Add the garlic, shallots, bayleaves, thyme and cloves. Season with salt and pepper and pour into the casserole the vinegar and one of your bottles of Burgundy. Cook over a slow fire for 3 hours. Some of the wine will evaporate.

Meanwhile, mince the hare's liver, lungs and any clots of blood and add them to the casserole at the end of the first 3 hours' cooking together with half a bottle more Burgundy.

After 3 more hours you will find that the meat has detached itself completely from the bones. Lift these out, using two forks. In the bottom of the casserole you have a savoury, shapeless mass. Sprinkle it with a glass of cognac, warm it for 5 minutes more. Transfer it very carefully to a piping hot dish and carry it to table.

In front of each person put a glass of your best Burgundy, a very hot plate, a piece of bread and a spoon. That is all. *Lièvre à la Royale* is eaten simply with a spoon—and with reverence.

Hare with Beetroot.

For this dish you will need the saddle and back legs of a plump hare, which should be carefully separated from the rest. The other pieces will make a *civet* prepared according to the recipe which follows. Besides the hare you will need:

> 2 *thick rashers of bacon,* ⅓ *pint of double cream,* 1½ *lb cooked beetroot,* 3½ *ozs butter,* ¼ *teaspoon flour.*

Marinade.

> ½ *bottle white wine,* 2 *tablespoons wine vinegar, a medium-sized onion, a bouquet of thyme,* 4–5 *peppercorns,* 4 *juniper berries,* 2 *tablespoons olive oil.*

Boil all the ingredients for the marinade together for half an hour and cool. When they are thoroughly cold add the oil and then soak the back of the hare for 24 hours.

Lift out the hare and dry it. Put it on a board and, using the blade of a strong knife and a wooden mallet, make a number of incisions on the inside of the backbone so that at table you will be able to divide the joint into neat pieces of equal size. Whilst you are preparing and cooking the hare, let the marinade bubble in a small saucepan so that it reduces and thickens.

Lay the hare in a fireproof dish with one slice of bacon beneath and one on top. Put it in a very hot oven (440°–480° F. Gas 8–9). I warn you that in 20 minutes your hare must be done, so the heat must be fierce in order that it shall brown in the time.

When the hare has been in the oven for 10 minutes sprinkle it with salt and pour over it two-thirds of the cream diluted with a little of the boiling marinade.

Whilst the hare is cooking peel and chop the beetroot finely, and warm it in the butter which you have melted in a frying-pan. Season with salt and a tablespoon of vinegar. As you stir the beetroot it turns a brilliant ruby red. Now it is ready.

When the hare has been in the oven for 20 minutes it is ready. The meat is underdone and the cream has turned buttery. Mix the caramel in the bottom of the dish with a good glassful of boiling, thickened marinade and spoon it once or twice over the hare. Lift the hare onto a hot dish.

Now pour the sauce into a small pan and add the rest of the cream which you have mixed with a ½-teaspoon of flour. Let it boil for a moment, stirring all the time. Now try it. It is delicious.

The hare is ready on the dish. Pile the beetroot round it, put the sauce into your best sauce-boat, carry it to the table and enjoy your success.

You may object that this is an expensive dish—the best part of a hare, a third of a pint of cream and a half a bottle of wine. So it is, unless like me you have a friend who supplies you with hares. I wish you the same good fortune.

Terrine of Hare.

I hate shooting, but I love a good shot because, unless they have a deep freeze of their own, these charming people distribute their bag amongst their friends and I have even had as many as three hares hanging by my kitchen window to the surprise and admiration of my neighbours.

If you are faced with such a glut and are determined not to weary your family by repeating the same recipe, however good, here is a dish which will give you considerable trouble to prepare, but which is quite excellent.

You will need the following:

> 1½ *lbs lean pork*, ¾ *lb back pork fat*, 10 *ozs bacon*, 5 *ozs bacon-rinds and trimmings, a glass of cognac, thyme, a clove of garlic.*

Skin and clean the hare and joint it. Using a very sharp, pointed knife, separate the meat from the bones and cut it into thin strips, making each as long as possible. Sprinkle these with salt, half the cognac, and a little dried thyme.

With the point of the knife scratch off any meat which may be clinging to the carcass. Put the scraps of hare, together with the pork, which you have cut into small pieces, the liver, lungs, kidney and any clots of blood, through the mincer. You will have a nice quantity of farce. Season this with salt, pepper, the rest of the cognac and a little more thyme.

Rub the inside of a terrine, or a small earthenware casserole, with garlic and line it with rashers of bacon. Spread it with alternate layers of farce and meat, finishing with a layer of farce topped with a rasher of bacon. Put the lid on the terrine, sealing it with a paste made of flour and water.

Now stand the terrine in a bain-marie and let the water boil on top of the stove for 15 minutes. (You can use for this any receptacle which is strong enough to resist the heat of the stove and big enough to surround the terrine with an inch or two of water.) Meanwhile heat the oven to about 320° F. (Gas 3), and put the hare to cook for three hours. From time to time add some hot water to the bain-marie as it evaporates.

Whilst the terrine is cooking cover the bones of the hare and the bacon rinds and trimmings with cold water and simmer them, seasoned with salt, pepper and thyme, for 2½ hours, covered with a lid. Strain the broth into a bowl. When cold, it will make a good jelly.

Take the terrine from the oven and let it cool for half an hour, then lift the lid. It is not a very encouraging sight but don't worry. Fit into your casserole a plate or small board and, on top of this a small bowl containing a couple of pounds weight.

After 2 hours remove the weight, melt the jelly and pour it over the terrine, cover it with a lid and put it in a cool place for 24 hours.

You will be impatient to try your terrine. Perhaps you have invited the friend who shot the hare and perhaps, if he realizes the immense amount of trouble you have taken to prepare it, he will bring a bottle of really good red wine to wash it down!

Haunch of Wild Boar.

A very charming and generous person who had been listening to my lectures on cooking over the Paris Radio sent me, one day, a haunch of young and tender wild boar. This is royal fare and I must own that I had never in my life eaten it. I had once eaten the meat of an elderly boar, during the First World War. And this reminds me of a story which I must tell you since it will show what a tremendous part suggestion plays in our perceptions of taste.

It was wartime, and I was in charge of the mess for our ambulance group. I did my best to prepare a ragoût of wild boar. Its arrival at table was a triumph, quickly followed by hoots of derision. I was accused of having served ragoût of beef. The reason for my failure was that I had omitted to marinade the meat. Protests were useless. My comrades would not be convinced.

But I had my revenge. Two days later I marinaded some fillet of beef and served it with a well-spiced sauce. My comrades found the 'wild boar' admirable.

Moral: you must always marinade venison, roe deer or wild boar if you wish to avoid being called an imposter, and to be sure that the meat has the flavour which is believed to be that of game.

But how did this habit of marinading game arise? This is a problem of bacteriology which I will explain to you.

At the moment when wild animals are killed after being hunted, they are exhausted. Their flesh is charged with acids produced as a result of fatigue. After death, the flesh, upon contact with these acids, coagulates, toughens and becomes uneatable. The meat must be allowed to 'hang' and become tender. This meat, however, has been soiled by the hands which cut it up. It is polluted with the microbes of putrefaction. If we were to hang this meat in the open air it would be invaded by microbes and putrefy rapidly.

To check this decomposition we only need to soak the meat in an acid liquid—white wine or water acidulated with vinegar. The meat will then undergo a process of auto-digestion which will make it tender, but it will not putrefy, since the harmful bacteria are hindered from developing in an acid environment.

To return to my haunch of young wild boar, I soaked this for 3 days in a marinade consisting of 1¾ pints of dry white wine and 6 tablespoons vinegar.

To this liquid I added all the herbs and spices which I could find in my kitchen: onions cut in rings, crushed garlic, thyme, bayleaf, savoury, fennel, basil, peppercorns, spice. My larder was fragrant for three days.

Now I was ready to cook the haunch of wild boar. I lifted it out of the marinade, dried it and laid it on a large slice of bacon. Then I sprinkled it with salt and covered it with another thick slice and put it into a very hot oven (about 440° F. Gas 8). My haunch of wild boar weighed about 2 lbs and I decided to leave it in the oven for about 45 minutes.

In the meantime, I boiled the marinade with all its herbs and spices until it had reduced to little less than 1 pint. I tasted it. The liquid was highly flavoured and very acid.

After 30 minutes in the oven the bacon had melted and shrivelled up. The surface of the boar was a beautiful brown. In the bottom of the dish there was a thick coating of caramel and juice from the meat. I dissolved this in the boiling marinade and basted the meat with it.

After 45 minutes I took the dish out of the oven and transferred the haunch of wild boar to my best china dish which I had heated, and surrounded it with boiled potatoes. The gravy I poured into a small saucepan, making it up to nearly a pint with boiling water, which I used to remove the last of the juice from the dish in which the meat had roasted.

In a small bowl I mixed 1 teaspoonful of flour with 3½ ozs of thick cream, thinned this with a little of the hot liquid, and then poured it back into the saucepan. I stirred, let it boil for a second, tasted and then added some freshly-milled pepper.

I served my beautiful haunch of wild boar with the potatoes and its gravy, adding for those who liked it, a bowl of gooseberry jelly.

Then came the moment to carve the joint. It was rare, juicy, fragrant. . . . I was content.

But supposing I hadn't a haunch of young wild boar, what would I do? Buy a small leg of mutton and marinade it. Treat it exactly as I have described and I should believe that I was eating wild boar, especially if I washed it down with plenty of old Burgundy.

VEGETABLES

Artichokes.

The larger artichokes are delicious steamed or boiled and eaten with melted butter or Hollandaise sauce, or cold with sauce vinaigrette. They also provide the *fonds d'artichauts* which are the basis of various excellent dishes.

For the following recipes choose tender, young artichokes and green ones rather than those with a purple tint.

Artichauts à la Juive.

> 6 *small artichokes*, 2 *tablespoons olive oil*, 1 *teaspoon sugar.*

Trim off the stem of the artichokes and cut an inch off the tip of the leaves. You will see the 'choke' in the centre. Remove this carefully with the tip of a rounded knife. Wash the artichokes and put them in a saucepan with enough water to cover. Season with salt and pepper, add the olive oil and sugar and bring them to the boil.

Simmer for 30 minutes with the lid on, then uncover the pan and raise the heat. The water evaporates completely, the oil begins to sputter and the sugar forms a film of caramel on the leaves.

Lift the pan from the fire, let it cool, and serve the artichokes sprinkled with a little lemon juice.

Artichauts Sautés à la Crème.

> 4 *small artichokes*, 2 *large onions*, 3 *ozs butter*, ¼ *pint thick cream.*

Prepare the artichokes as before, cut them in quarters and throw them into boiling salted water for ten minutes. Take them out and let them cool.

Melt the butter in a frying-pan and sauté the artichokes for 5 minutes. Add the onions chopped finely and let them and the artichokes turn golden-brown. Season with salt and pepper and lower the fire. In another 5 minutes they are cooked.

Pour the cream into the pan and let it boil for ½-minute. Turn the artichokes into a hot dish and dust them with freshly-milled pepper.

Artichauts à la Barigoule.

Prepare 6 young artichokes as before, but leave them whole. Sprinkle the hollows from which you have taken the 'chokes' with lemon juice and fill them with a farce which you make mixing the following:

> 4 *ozs minced ham,* 4 *ozs chopped onion,* 2 *small egg-cups crisp breadcrumbs which have been soaked in milk and squeezed dry,* 1 *oz melted butter,* 6 *rashers of bacon,* 1 *glass white wine, thick tomato sauce.*

Wrap a rasher of bacon round each stuffed artichoke, tying it in place with string. Choose a flameproof dish which has a lid. Melt the butter and arrange the artichokes in it. When the bacon begins to cook, pour in the white wine and dust with salt and pepper. Put on the lid and simmer very gently for 1 hour. Add a little thick tomato sauce, stirring it carefully into the juice in the dish. Cook for 5 minutes more, then remove the strings and any hard bits of bacon.

It is rather a complicated dish, but it is *grande cuisine*.

Artichauts à la Grèque.

I learned to make *artichauts à la grèque* many years ago in the course of a prolonged journey in the Middle East. From the quay at Piraeus I watched the steamer which had brought me sail away on its course to the Black Sea whilst I remained, for a time at least, in the land of Homer.

Then I turned. The Acropolis was before me. From a distance the Parthenon seemed quite new, pure white beneath the blue sky. Suddenly I was transported from the world of books and legends to that of reality. The whole of Ancient Greece lay before me.

If I had been a Renan I might have recited a prayer worthy of the beauty of the Acropolis. As it was, I could only remain mute and, as a devoted pilgrim, ascend the sacred hill on foot, disdaining the railway and the horses which were offered to me.

I stayed the whole afternoon amidst the burning stones and contemplated the deserted landscape before me, but my stomach recalled me to reality. I had to return to the town and I had to eat.

On the Acropolis, not far from the Parthenon, there was a small restaurant famous for its artichokes. Every day a little donkey carried a load of them to the city and every day people flocked to the restaurant to enjoy them. They even said that King George, *incognito*, sometimes came to eat them on the bare table with its oil stains.

I arrived and sat down on a wooden bench. Immediately, the proprietress called the woman who served as cook and waitress too. "Aphrodite! Aphrodite!" She appeared, but what a disappointment. Aphrodite was blind in one eye and had a limp. She was more than sixty. Venus had aged.

She brought me three artichokes and some broad beans glistening with oil and a glass of *resinata*, a wine prepared, it seems, with a sort of resin. The artichokes were incomparable. The proprietress allowed me to watch Aphrodite and I shall tell you just what she did. If you wish to copy her you will need:

> 8 *small artichokes*, 10 *ozs onions chopped very fine, a glass of olive oil*, 1 *lb freshly-shelled broad beans, chopped parsley and chervil.*

Trim the artichokes as in the previous recipes and rub the hollow where the 'choke' has been with lemon juice to prevent its turning black. Fill the hollows with minced onions, parsley and chervil and put the artichokes into a flameproof dish, just covering them with cold water. Sprinkle them with salt and pepper, add the broad beans and the rest of the minced onion, and cover the dish. Let it simmer on top of the stove until the beans are cooked and you can easily detach the leaves of the artichoke. This will take at least half an hour.

Take the lid off the dish and let it boil on a hot fire until all the water has evaporated and the oil is beginning to splutter. Now lift it off the fire and stand it to cool for an hour or two, and try to restrain your impatience. The moment will soon come when you can enjoy your cold artichokes and dream. For me they recall sunset and the hard wooden bench of the little inn. Spread beneath me I see Piraeus and the Bay of Salamis, the Temple of Theseus and Hymettus veiled in violet. In the far distance, merging into the rosy sky, Pantelikon catches the last rosy glow of the setting sun.

Asparagus.

Asparagus came to us from Asia. They were known to the Romans since Pliny wrote that the asparagus of Ravenna each weighed a third of a pound, though one must not forget that the Roman pound was only about thirteen ounces.

Before this, in the distant past, the Romans called the tender tips of all green vegetables asparagus and it was only later that the name was used as we use it now.

Rabelais, in his immortal work, made asparagus grow after having sown crushed rams' horns and watered them well. The result was the best asparagus in the world—except for those of Ravenna, he added. Besides 'those of Ravenna' there are the blue asparagus of Holland, the violet of Ulm and the green of Paris and finally those of Argenteuil, though one wonders where they are grown since Argenteuil is bristling with factory chimneys, which thrust menacingly at the sky.

Besides its gastronomic qualities, asparagus has medicinal virtues. It is a powerful diuretic. The root is used for the celebrated Syrup of Five Roots which is made of asparagus, smallage, fennel, parsley and butcher's broom.

Asparagus may be either steamed or boiled. I prefer the former method as so often, when boiling, the heads fall off before the stems are cooked. However, if you have no steamer you are obliged to boil them, and you must just be a little more careful.

Cut all the asparagus to the same length, removing the woody ends with a sharp knife. If the asparagus are large and firm spread a cloth on the table before you and scrape each stem from below the head in the direction of the root. When you have scraped all the asparagus, put it to soak in cold water for a few minutes.

Tie the asparagus in a bundle. Tape is useful for this as it does not cut the stems. Put the asparagus into fast-boiling, salted water and cover the pan. The time of cooking will depend on the age and size of the asparagus, but after 12 minutes lift the lid and test the white part of the stems with a fork. If the tips of the fork penetrate easily they are done and should be lifted out, drained and eaten as soon as possible. During the last few minutes of cooking prepare the melted butter or sauce to accompany the asparagus.

Asparagus with Melted Butter.

You can serve asparagus hot with lightly-salted melted butter. It tastes good, but the butter doesn't stick to the asparagus sufficiently. To be honest, it is a little disappointing. I prefer:

Asperges à la Polonaise.

Boil your asparagus as before, being very careful to take them from the water the moment that the heads are cooked and the stems just soft, and this usually takes from 12 to 14 minutes from the moment when the water returns to the boil.

Serve them with melted butter, but this time add to every 3 ounces of butter 1½ teaspoons of fine white breadcrumbs. The bread swells in the melted butter and forms a mixture which sticks to the asparagus stems. We have already made some progress.

Asperges à la Flamande.

Hot asparagus once more, served with melted butter which you have treated in rather a special way. Mash the yolk of a hard boiled egg with a fork and add to it, little by little, 3½ ozs melted butter, very hot, stirring all the time. You will have a creamy sauce, slightly fluid, which will blend admirably with your asparagus.

Asperges Hollandaise.

While the asparagus are cooking prepare a hollandaise sauce which can be quickly made, using:

3½ ozs butter, 2 yolks of egg, 1 tablespoon water.

Put all the ingredients except butter into a small pan with a little salt. Choose another pan big enough to surround the smaller pan with 2–3 inches of water. Set it to boil on the stove. Holding the smaller pan in the water, beat the eggs with a fork until they just thicken. Lift out the saucepan and stir in a piece of butter the size of a hazelnut. It melts and then stiffens as the mixture cools. Return the little pan to the boiling water, stirring all the time, and add another nut of butter. Continue stirring, adding small pieces of butter, lifting the pan as you do so until all your butter is used up. Lifting the pan is very important as it prevents the sauce from becoming too hot. If this happens, the egg will curdle and instead of a sauce you will have some very dubious looking scrambled egg.

If you are careful to follow this simple procedure, your sauce will be admirable, smooth and golden. Close your eyes as you taste it. Hollandaise sauce is the supreme essence of gastronomy. It offers every satisfaction to the palate: flavour, perfume, velvety smoothness—a caress. But enough of poetry. Unless you serve the asparagus at once the sauce will get cold.

Asperges au Gratin.

Boil the asparagus and drain them carefully. Lay them in a dish with all the points the same way and pour over the tips 3½ ozs of cream which you have salted and heated in a small saucepan.

Sprinkle the tips of the asparagus with a mixture of grated Parmesan and Gruyère cheese. Cover the stems with buttered paper. Put the dish into a very hot oven (450° F. Gas 8) or under the grill. In 4 minutes the surface is golden-brown.

Put the dish before your guests who will be delighted. It really looks most attractive. Serve with the asparagus a sauce-boat of cream, hot and slightly salted. . . . Between ourselves, I find that the cheese is almost superfluous.

Aubergines.

Aubergines were first mentioned in the writings of Arab doctors. The first of these, Avicenne, who lived in the tenth century believed that aubergines were responsible for cancer, leprosy and epilepsy.

Ibn Massout, another Arab doctor, recommended a curious and rather tedious method of preparing this charming vegetable. He advised that it should be washed, slit and filled with coarse salt, then soaked in cold water for 10 hours. After this, it should be boiled for a few minutes and cooked in fat, together with mutton, goat or chicken meat.

One could also, he suggested, season aubergines with sweet almond oil, vinegar and *garum*, which was a liquid prepared from certain kinds of fish.

In the fifteenth century the aubergine became known in France, but did not make its appearance in the markets of Paris until it was introduced in 1825 by Monsieur Decouflé, a greengrocer of the rue de la Santé, who specialized in *primeurs*.

I am going to describe some aubergine dishes which I collected here and there during my travels in the near East.

Aubergines à l'Orientale.

This is a dish which I ate in the Constantinople of many years ago, whilst the muezzins called from their minarets and stray dogs and men lay sleeping in the streets at night, driven out of doors by the heat of the houses. From time to time the muted cries of the sellers of grapes and yoghurt, wandering amongst the sleepers, disturbed for a moment their rest. All this has changed, but when I think that I have seen it with my own eyes, I feel as if I were a hundred years old.

The Arabian Nights atmosphere of the Middle East may be disappearing but the secrets of its cookery remain, and you can make *aubergines à l'orientale* if you follow my instructions and use:

> 4 *aubergines*, ⅜ *pint olive oil*, 10 *ozs onions*, 1 *lb tomatoes made into a purée*, 3½ *ozs breadcrumbs*, *curry powder*, 6 *ozs black olives*.

Plunge the aubergines in boiling water for 10 minutes and then into cold water. When they are cold, cut them in half lengthwise, remove the seeds and scoop out as much of the pulp as you can whilst preserving the skin intact.

Put the hollowed aubergines into a saucepan and pour over them two-thirds of the oil. Sprinkle them with salt and pepper and cook them over a very low fire for 45 minutes.

Meanwhile cook the onions, chopped finely, with very little water. When they are tender add the tomato purée, breadcrumbs, and the pulp from the aubergines and put them in a frying-pan. Stir in the rest of the olive oil, salt, pepper, and a pinch of curry powder. Taste. You may need a hint more pepper. Cook over a gentle heat for 20 minutes.

Lift the aubergines carefully from the saucepan and arrange them in a deep dish. Fill each one with the farce you have prepared and sprinkle them with the rest of the oil from the frying-pan. Surround the aubergines with a circle of stoned, black olives and set them to cool. This dish should stand for 8–10 hours before it is served.

Fried Aubergines.

 3 *aubergines, milk, flour, oil for frying, a lemon.*

Wipe the aubergines with a damp cloth. They really are the most magnificent vegetables, lustrous as Chinese bronzes. With a sharp knife cut them in lengthwise slices about a quarter of an inch thick. Dip each slice in milk and then in a plate of flour, firming it in place with your finger-tips.

Bring the oil to smoking point in a deep frying-pan and fry them until they are golden-brown. As they are done, pile the slices on a hot dish and sprinkle them with salt.

Put a halved lemon on the table and let each guest sprinkle a few drops of the juice over his aubergine slices, and follow this with a turn or two of the white pepper mill.

Grilled Aubergines.

 2 *aubergines,* 6 *ozs breadcrumbs,* 1 *yolk of egg, olive oil,*
 2 *cloves garlic,* 1 *teaspoon lemon juice.*

Cut the aubergines into thin lengthwise slices and spread them with a paste made by pounding together the bread-crumbs, egg, finely-minced garlic, lemon juice and enough oil to bind.

Grill the slices for 5–6 minutes, then turn them, spread the other side with savoury paste, grill once more and serve them on a very hot dish. It is very good, but I must own that it tastes more of garlic than aubergine.

Aubergines with Onions.

English cooks, if they think of aubergines at all, usually regard them as a vegetable to be eaten hot, and preferably stuffed or stewed. In the Eastern Mediterranean cold dishes are a necessity during the heat of summer. Here are some excellent aubergine dishes which can be prepared in the morning and eaten, chilled, in the evening.

 2 *medium-sized aubergines,* ¼ *pint olive oil,* 1 *lb onions.*

Plunge the aubergines in boiling water for 10 minutes without peeling them. They will soften slightly. Lift them out and put them under the cold tap. When they are quite cold, cut them in slices about ¾-inch thick.

Heat the oil in a frying-pan until it is smoking. Tip in the rounds of aubergine and fry them for about 10 minutes or until they are mahogany-coloured. Lift them out with a slice and arrange them on a dish, sprinkling them with salt and pepper.

Peel the onions, cut them in rings and fry them in the hot oil which is left in the pan. The onion rings must be well coloured and this will take about 10 minutes, stirring all the time.

Arrange a small heap of onion rings on each slice of aubergine, salt and pepper once more, and sprinkle them with the last drops of oil from the pan. Let the dish cool and serve it thoroughly chilled.

Aubergines à la Grècque.

> 4 *small aubergines,* ¼ *pint olive oil,* 1 *lb tomatoes,* ½ *lb onions, a piece of stale bread.*

Plunge the aubergines in boiling water for 10 minutes. Let them cool. Slice them in half lengthwise and scoop out the seeds. Using a silver teaspoon and great delicacy remove as much of the flesh as you can without breaking the blackish skin.

Now, even more difficult, put the emptied skins of the aubergines into a saucepan which contains rather more than half the olive oil and cook them gently for 20 minutes.

Arrange the hollow skins on a dish. They are slightly deformed, but never mind. Whilst they are cooling prepare the stuffing.

Cut the tomatoes in pieces and simmer them with very little water. When they are soft, rub them through a sieve. Put the rest of the olive oil into a saucepan with the tomato purée and the pulp of the aubergines. Add the onions, chopped finely. Cook for 15 minutes and add a piece of stale bread the size of an egg, which you have soaked in water. Stir the mixture a fork, add plenty of salt and pepper and, if you wish, a little more olive oil. You will now have a very thick purée.

With aid of a spoon, fill the aubergines with the farce which is still warm. This will help to restore their figures. Pour over them any oil which remains in the pan and cool for 1 hour or more.

Serve well chilled with a dusting of chopped parsley, and fill your glasses with very dry, very cold white wine.

Aubergine Caviar.

> 2 *aubergines, a little olive oil,* 1 *tablespoon each of finely chopped parsley, chervil and tarragon, a small onion.*

Put the aubergines into a fireproof dish with very little water and olive oil. Bake them for 35 minutes in a moderate oven (350° F. Gas 4). Test them with a fork or, if you are brave enough, the tip of your finger. When they are soft, they are ready. Plunge the aubergines into cold water and a miracle occurs. The skin comes away easily.

Mash the pulp and mix it with the minced herbs, salt, plenty of pepper and enough oil to make a smooth paste. Put this in small individual dishes and chill them. Eat the 'caviar' with slices of black bread as hors d'oeuvres. This calls for a glass of vodka or schnapps.

Caponata Sicilienne.

> 3 *aubergines, a head of celery,* 1 *lb sweet red peppers,* 12 *ozs tomatoes,* ¼ *pint olive oil.*

Slice the aubergines. Wash the heart of the celery and cut it in pieces. Cut the tomatoes in quarters, remove the pips and slice what is left. Remove the seeds from the peppers and cut them in slices.

Put all the vegetables in a flameproof dish. Add the olive oil, salt and pepper. Cover the dish and let it cook on a very low fire for 1 hour. Take off the lid and let the moisture evaporate. When the oil begins to splutter, lift the dish from the fire and stand it in a very cool place.

This dish, well chilled, makes an excellent substitute for soup in hot weather.

Batavian Endive with Onions.

This recipe was sent me by one of my readers and it has become a favourite of mine.

> 1 *oz butter,* 2 *medium-sized onions,* ¼ *pint double cream, a teaspoon vinegar, a large Batavian endive.*

Take a large saucepan which should be of enamel or copper, not aluminium. Make the butter smoking-hot and add the onions cut crosswise in rings. The onions turn golden and the rings separate and gradually become a rich brown.

Stir in the cream, vinegar, salt and pepper, heating all the time. As soon as the cream begins to boil, lift the pan off the fire and put into it the white leaves of a fine Batavian endive which you have washed and dried carefully.

Mix the leaves in the sauce as you would an ordinary salad and turn them straight into a salad bowl which you have heated with boiling water.

This should be eaten at the end of a meal, just before the cheese. The delicate impact of sensations of taste, temperature and texture is indescribable. Try it.

Beetroot.

The beet is a curious vegetable. First of all, it suffers from a bad press. Already, towards the fourth century, Oribase, physician to the Emperor Julian, spoke very ill of it. However later, by a natural reaction, it was considered a universal panacea, and believed to cure putrid fevers and scurvy.

The beet really 'arrived' the day that Margraff, in 1740, discovered that its root contained sugar. From that day sugar no longer had to be imported and the cultivation of sugar-beet became extensive.

The beet, or *Beta vulgaris*, to give it its Latin name, is therefore cultivated mainly for the production of sugar, but the beet family includes a yellow root which is excellent for animal fodder, and the beetroot which puts in a timid appearance on our tables. This unfortunate vegetable is known to most people only as the duller part of a salad.

In the Northern countries, however, where the choice of vegetables is far more limited, beetroot appears in a number of more exciting forms.

In Russia, raw beetroot is cut into fine strips, lightly salted and allowed to ferment like sauerkraut. This transforms it into a slightly sour vegetable which can be cooked in a number of ways. In this country beetroot is generally sold ready-cooked, so we shall use this for the recipes which follow.

First, a word of warning: see that your beetroot is very dark red—almost black—and refuse the coarse, pinkish roots. Choose those roots which are as long and slender as possible.

Cold Beetroot with Cream.

$\frac{1}{2}$ lb cooked beetroot, $\frac{1}{4}$ pint thick cream, 2 small teaspoons French mustard, 1 teaspoon vinegar.

Mix the cream, mustard and vinegar in a bowl with a little salt.

Shave the beetroot into fine slices and arrange them in a dish, salting them lightly. Sprinkle them with a very little vinegar and pour the seasoned cream over them. Let them stand for 1 hour and then serve as hors d'oeuvres.

Hot Beetroot with Cream.

> 1 *lb beetroot which has been cooked, if possible, in the oven,*
> 2 *ozs butter,* 2 *teaspoons vinegar,* ⅛ *pint thick cream.*

Chop the beetroot finely. Melt the butter in a frying-pan and heat the beetroot in it, stirring with a wooden spoon. Salt, and add the vinegar. The beetroot turns brilliant ruby red. Add the cream, stir well, and heat for three minutes.

This is very good with game or fried pork chops.

Beetroot with Horse-Radish.

> 1 *lb cooked beetroot, horse-radish,* 3 *tablespoons vinegar.*

Cut the beetroot in cubes. Grate a root of horse-radish. This is a most unpleasant task and I can assure you that it will make you cry—more even than peeling onions.

You will now have a white, rather dry pulp. Add 3 table-spoons of water and the same quantity of vinegar, salt and the beetroot. Put the mixture into jam jars which should be care-fully sealed.

This is delicious with roast meat and even more so with boiled beef.

Carrots.

During the winter one is faced with the difficulty of finding a variety of fresh vegetables at a reasonable price. When I have served my family with cabbage, Brussels sprouts and cauliflower over and over again their patience begins to wear a little thin and I am obliged to turn to carrots—and these, in winter, are not particularly tender. But provided one chooses carrots which are red right through to the centre, and cuts them very thin one can always prevent their remaining hard. A very good tip is to add a pinch of bicarbonate of soda to the cooking water. This is especially useful in the case of woody vegetables such as old carrots. This is why carrots were cooked in Vichy water which is rich in bicarbonate of soda, and hence the name Carottes Vichy. I will explain how to prepare these and I hope you will find the familiar carrot more glamorous in this form.

Carottes Vichy.

> 1 *lb carrots, 2 lumps of sugar, 3½ ozs butter, a good pinch of bicarbonate of soda, slices of bread, butter or lard for frying.*

Scrape the outside of the carrots and wash them in plenty of water. Cut a piece at least ¼-inch thick from the top of each carrot. Cut them in very fine slices or grate them coarsely. Wash once more.

Put the carrots in a saucepan with cold water to cover them, with the sugar and the butter. Put the lid on the pan and simmer for 30 minutes. The carrots are now tender. Remove the lid and turn up the heat so that the water boils furiously. Gradually it evaporates, and the butter begins to sizzle in the bottom of the pan. The carrots are ready.

Serve the carrots with slices of bread which you have fried in butter or lard.

Carrots with Cream.

> Carottes Vichy *prepared as in the previous recipe*, ¼ *pint of fresh cream, chopped parsley.*

Prepare the *carottes Vichy* and just before they are ready to serve, pour the cream into the saucepan and stir. Let it boil for a second, arrange the carrots in a dish and serve them with a dusting of the finest chopped parsley.

Carottes à la Polonaise.

> Carottes Vichy *prepared as before, a small tin of* petits pois, *small* croûtons *of bread fried in butter.*

Prepare the *carottes Vichy* as I have already explained and when they are ready, stir in a small tin of *petits pois* from which you have drained all the liquid.

Heat the carrots once more and serve them with small *croûtons* of bread which you have fried in butter.

Brandade de Carottes.

> 1 *lb carrots, 3 ozs butter, nutmeg, a lump of sugar, 2 table-spoons flour, milk, 2 ozs double cream.*

Scrape the carrots and wash them carefully. Cut them in pieces and put them through a mincer or 'Mouli'. You will have a pulp which oozes a yellowish juice.

Put the carrots in a saucepan with 1½ ozs of the butter and just cover them with water. Add a trace of grated nutmeg and a lump of sugar. Cover the pan and let it cook for 40 minutes. Take off the lid and raise the heat so that the liquid evaporates, stirring from time to time so that the carrots do not stick to the bottom of the pan.

In another saucepan prepare a sauce by mixing the rest of the butter with the flour, over a low fire, and adding just enough milk to make a thick cream. Salt and pepper lightly and add the double cream. Mix this sauce with the carrot purée, warming and stirring so that the whole becomes smooth and creamy with a very agreeable perfume.

Serve this purée with fried sausages or rashers of bacon. I can assure you that it is very, very good. Of course the carrots would be better still round a joint of veal or a roast duck, but one would have to have such luxuries to hand.

Chestnuts.

Looking back to the earliest days of my youth I remember the chestnut sellers at the corners of the Paris streets, close to the wine shops at the onset of winter.

"Hot chestnuts! Hot chestnuts!" cried the Auvergnat with the fur cap as we passed in groups on our way to school, and later to the Lycée. The richest among us bought a sou's worth —in those days, seven chestnuts—and, when it was very cold, he lent a couple to one or two of his comrades, who put a chestnut in each pocket to warm their hands. On arriving at school we gave them back to the 'rich' boy. We had benefited a little from his opulence, and we didn't resent it. In those days humanity was perhaps, in some ways, better than now.

Hot chestnuts! They herald winter with all its rigours, and joys and sorrows too.

But it is not necessary to buy chestnuts ready cooked. One can prepare them very well at home. The chestnut is a perfect food. By itself it is almost enough for a meal. In the Province of Limousin they dine on chestnuts and milk, and they flourish on them too.

Freshly stripped of its prickly shell the chestnut has a beautiful, brilliant colour. To eat it one must strip off the hard outer covering and the thin, inner skin. This is a long and rather troublesome job, so chestnuts do not appear very often on our tables, which is a pity. I suggest the following three methods of peeling chestnuts:

1. Make a circular cut round the outside of each chestnut, making sure that the knife gets right through the shell. Put the chestnuts in boiling water for 5 minutes and peel them whilst they are still hot. The inner and outer covering should come away together.

2. Make a circular cut as before and plunge the chestnuts for 3 minutes into a bath of smoking hot fat. Peel them while they are still hot.

3. Make a circular cut round each chestnut and put them in a hot oven for 10 minutes. Peel whilst they are hot.

Boiled Chestnuts.

Without slitting the skins, put a couple of pounds of chestnuts into 3½ pints of boiling, salted water and cook them for 30 minutes.

Put them on the table with some fresh butter, a jug of hot milk and a bottle of very dry white wine. Everyone helps themselves. You cut the chestnuts in half and, using a teaspoon, scoop out the insides. A dab of butter with each spoonful, a mouthful of milk or wine, and you go happily on until nothing more is left. Not a meal for those who are slimming, but a temptation you will really enjoy falling for.

Finish the meal with a fresh, green salad.

Chestnut Purée with Cream.

> 1½ lbs chestnuts, ¼ pint double cream, 2½ ozs butter, hot milk, nutmeg.

Peel the chestnuts then put them in a saucepan, covered with salted water, and cook for 30 minutes. When they are soft, mash them to a smooth purée. This will be rather dry.

Return the purée to the saucepan and add the butter and cream, stirring over a gentle fire. The butter melts. Little by little, stir in hot milk until the purée begins to swell and form great bubbles of steam which burst and collapse. Taste it and add salt, and pepper and nutmeg to your taste.

Enjoy this with a fried pork chop and a glass of Beaujolais.

Sauté Chestnuts.

Boil, as before, some peeled chestnuts, being careful not to crush them. Drain the chestnuts, and cook them in a frying-pan with goose grease or lard.

Eat them just as they are with a glass of rough red wine.

Chicory.

At least once a week I make a tour of the market. By good fortune I live in a quarter of Paris which has a market every three days. From six in the morning, as the lorries arrive, fruit and vegetables are unloaded and piled in pyramids beneath the awnings of the stalls. Glistening fish contrast with glowing joints of meat; swelling sausages and taut blood puddings flank the pale and melancholy calf's heads. At each step I am hailed by the market people extolling their wares, and jostled by shoppers with their baskets. Each time, I return home with a vivid, colourful impression of bustling life. And that is why I go again and again, although, to be strictly honest I must own that my visits are not solely for pleasure.

I go to market to look for ideas of what to eat and how to reconcile my family's demands with the limitations of the seasons and of my domestic budget.

I can assure you that in the case of vegetables, and especially in winter, this is not easy. My wife doesn't like carrots and my daughter despises turnips and absolutely loathes celeriac. As for me I avoid haricot beans and potatoes for the sake of my waistline, which has already reached respectable proportions. To make a change, I often resort to chicory or, as we in France call them, *endives belges*. This is a very useful vegetable as it can be cooked in so many different ways. Some people say that boiling chicory makes it bitter. This is not true. Certain types of chicory are naturally more bitter than others but gradually, by means of selection, this fault is being overcome. The real disadvantage of boiling chicory is that it turns a sad, grey colour and tends to become too soft. For this reason, many people prefer it braised.

Endives à l'Anglaise.

Since, with considerable truth, the English are suspected of serving every vegetable boiled and soggy, anything called '*à l'anglaise*' will be boiled but need not, in fact, be unappetizing.

Choose firm white chicory with pale yellow tips, tightly closed. Strip off any faded outer leaves, clean them and, with the help of a pointed knife, hollow the base of each. This is the spot where any bitterness will be concentrated.

Plunge the chicory into boiling, salted water for 20 minutes and drain well. Serve it with melted butter.

Endives à la Polonaise.

Boil and drain the chicory as before. Sprinkle it with melted butter and the grated yolks of three hard-boiled eggs.

Braised Chicory.

Chicory, 2 ozs butter, a pinch of caster sugar.

The quantity of chicory you will need depends, naturally, on the number of people you are cooking for. I generally choose a good head for each person. The better the head the more it will weigh so, if you are judging quantities by eye, remember that a smooth, tight head will give a much better helping than the loose, green tipped one of apparently equal size that the greengrocer may try to press on you.

Arrange the chicory in a thick saucepan or deep flameproof dish. Add the butter, cut in pieces, and a pinch of caster sugar. Cover the vegetable with buttered, greaseproof paper and put the lid on the pan.

Leave the pan on a very low fire for 40 minutes. The butter melts and the juice oozes out of the chicory. The sugar turns to a delicate caramel which colours it. Serve on a hot dish or in the flameproof dish in which you have cooked them.

Endives Gratinées.

Cook the chicory as before and put them in a fireproof dish. Sprinkle them with grated Gruyère cheese and let them brown under the grill. .

Endives à la Crème.

Braise the chicory and pour over them ¼-pint of double cream which you have mixed with ½-teaspoon of flour. Spread the cream right through the chicory and then boil for a moment or two.

Serve in a hot dish.

Endives Sauce Mornay.

Whilst your chicory are braising, prepare a sauce using:

2 ozs butter, 1 tablespoon flour, warm milk, 4 ozs grated Gruyère cheese.

Melt the butter and blend it with the flour. Little by little stir in warm milk, keeping the pan over a medium heat, until your sauce is thick and creamy. Salt, and stir in the Gruyère. The sauce tastes very good. Put the chicory into a fireproof dish, cover it with sauce and let it brown in the oven or under the grill.

Chives on Toast.

Chop 3 ozs of chives very finely and mix them with 2 ozs of butter, a little salt, and a dusting of pepper. Spread this fragrant mixture on toast. It is wonderful as an hors d'œuvre or to accompany scrambled eggs.

If you cut the toast in small, convenient pieces this makes a very good cocktail savoury.

Choucroûte.

Choucroûte is very good to eat but it has one disadvantage— its smell. To put up with this—and it will haunt your house for days since the best *choucroûte* dishes are prepared one or even two days before eating—you and your family and even your neighbours will have to be addicts.

Since I rather doubt whether so many devotees of *choucroûte* are conveniently grouped in many parts of this country, and since *choucroûte*, except in tins, is not very easily come by, I shall tell you of just one dish which is quickly prepared and has hardly any smell. On second thoughts, since this is a salad, I shall put it into the next section.

Courgettes à la Poêle.

These delicious baby marrows, which are as delicate as asparagus or new garden peas, are beginning to appear in English shops, though your greengrocer may not have many ideas on how to cook them. Here is a suggestion for a delicious dish.

> 3 *courgettes for each person,* 1 *egg,* 2 *tablespoons flour, milk,*
> 1½ *ozs butter.*

Cut the courgettes, without peeling them, into lengthwise slices about ⅛-inch thick.

Break an egg into a basin and stir in the flour. The mixture is too thick to handle. Gradually, using a wire whisk, beat in milk until you have a thick, but still fluid cream.

Pour the batter into a soup-plate. Melt the butter in a frying-pan and when it is smoking-hot fry the slices of courgettes, which you have dipped in batter, for 3 minutes on one side and 2 minutes on the other. Sprinkle them with salt and a little freshly-milled pepper and serve them on a hot dish. Accompany the courgettes with a lettuce salad which you have dressed with olive oil and lemon juice.

Courgettes à la Grècque.

If you cannot get courgettes this dish can be made equally well with young cucumbers, though, unless you grow your own, these are not easy to come by either.

> 3 *courgettes for each person,* ½ *lb small new onions or*
> *shallots,* 6 *ozs potatoes,* 3 *tablespoons olive oil, lemon juice,*
> *a pinch of caster sugar.*

Cut the courgettes in four lengthwise. Plunge them in boiling water for 10 minutes then lift them out and drain them. Whether you use courgettes or cucumbers you will need a sauce to supplement their flavour.

Chop the onions very fine and simmer them with very little water for 30 minutes. Add the potatoes, peeled and cut in small pieces. When they are tender, put them through a sieve or electric blender. You will have a rather thick purée which must be made a little more liquid by stirring in, bit by bit, the olive oil, salt, pepper, a pinch of caster sugar and enough lemon juice to sharpen the sauce to your taste.

Pour the sauce over the courgettes, chill them for 6 hours or more and serve them as a first course, preferably on a hot evening.

Cucumbers.

Cucumbers are a blessing in summer. They make a refreshing hors d'œuvres and a delightful vegetable and it is a joy to see them escape from their anonymity in a mixed salad, or the hackneyed role of chaperone to a slice of cold salmon. Let us consider a new approach.

Cucumbers with Béchamel Sauce.

A large, rather coarse cucumber, 1½ ozs butter, 2 ozs flour, ¾ pint milk.

Peel the cucumber and slice it in half lengthwise. Remove the seeds with a teaspoon. Cut each half once more lengthwise and then each of the four pieces in three crosswise. Plunge the twelve pieces for 3 minutes into boiling water. Lift them out, drain well and put them on a fireproof dish.

Now you must make a very thick sauce. Melt the butter and work in the flour over a gentle heat. Stir the milk in gradually until your sauce is creamy but still thick, then add salt and plenty of pepper. Heat the cucumber in the sauce for 5 minutes and then taste it.

The flavour of cucumber is fairly strong, but not too pronounced and the dish is excellent. You may like to add a trace more pepper.

Curled Endive with Grilled Sausages.

Curled endive weighing about 2 lbs, 2 ozs butter, milk, ¼ pint double cream, ½ teaspoon flour, 1 lb Chipolata sausages.

One evening I decided that it was time I turned vegetarian, at least for a few hours and, of course, my family must follow my good example. To keep them interested I decided to experiment with some of the rather coarse curled endive which is apt to be so disheartening in an ordinary salad.

First of all, I washed the endive thoroughly while 5 pints of water came to the boil in a large saucepan. Next came the delicate task of fitting all the endive into the saucepan without burning my fingers or swamping the stove. It seemed an impossible task, but finally all the endive was under water and in a moment or two the saucepan was boiling once more.

I let the endive boil for 20 minutes, then tipped it into a colander, refreshed it with cold water from the tap, pressed it with my hands to squeeze out as much water as possible. It was still too wet, so I put the endive in a cloth and wrung it out until it ceased to drip. A little at a time I then put it through a mincing machine (a Mouli would have been even better).

Next, I melted 2 ozs butter in a saucepan and stirred in the purée, thinning it with a few spoonfuls of milk. I salted the purée and tasted it expectantly. After all my trouble it was certainly not exciting. A little more salt might help.

In a little bowl, I mixed $\frac{1}{2}$ teaspoon of flour with $\frac{1}{4}$-pint of double cream, using a wire whisk, and stirred this into the saucepan, warming all the time. Once more I tasted it. This was a great improvement.

At this moment a catastrophe occurred. A friend arrived and invited himself to dinner. I told him of my resolve to turn vegetarian. He threatened to leave, in fact he did leave, shouting over his shoulder, "Wait a minute, I'm coming back!"

And he did come back, with a parcel of sausages. I was lost. Farewell to my good resolutions. I turned on the grill and pricked the sausages with a fork. Soon they were brown and crackling. Meanwhile I warmed up the endive purée and heaped it on my best silver dish. All round it I laid the sausages, crisp and shining. It was a lovely sight and I had no regrets.

Lettuce with Bacon.

This is an unusual dish, not quite a vegetable, not quite a salad, but rather a sort of hot hors d'œuvres.

> *3 green lettuces, 4 ozs fat bacon cut in cubes, 1 tablespoon vinegar.*

Wash the lettuces, separating the leaves. Warm the bacon slowly in a frying-pan, pressing down the cubes with a fork to expel as much fat as possible. Lift the pan from the fire and add the vinegar. Return it to the fire and let it boil for a second.

Meanwhile warm a salad bowl with very hot water. Dry it

and arrange the lettuce leaves in the bowl, pouring over them the contents of the frying-pan. You will need no salt because the bacon is salted, but plenty of freshly-milled pepper.

Eat this at the beginning of the meal with slices of brown toast and a glass of rough red wine.

Mushrooms.

In France, the newspapers have hardly come to the end of the holiday bathing fatalities when they begin the list of victims of poisonous mushrooms. (I wonder how many of you remember the delightful beginning of Sacha Guitry's film, "Le Roman d'un Tricheur"?)

People in England are, on the whole more cautious in experimenting with strange mushrooms and I shall take no risks, and merely give you a couple of ideas for cooking the mushrooms which you buy at your greengrocer's, or have known since childhood if you are lucky enough to live in the country.

It may be of interest, however, to give you some idea of the particular danger of mushroom poisoning. This is caused by two different substances—muscarine and phalline. Muscarine is a poison which causes nausea, vomiting and diarrhœa, but it is not a mortal poison. Phalline provokes none of these symptoms. It is absorbed by the intestine, destroys the red corpuscles of the blood and produces an asphyxia which is always fatal. And this asphyxia does not begin to show until the day after the poisonous mushrooms have been eaten. Medical remedies are practically useless. It is said that the most likely palliative is a plate of minced rabbit flesh, eaten raw. And what with myxomatosis and one thing and another this is not a very helpful suggestion.

Champignons à la Crème.

   1 *lb mushrooms*, 1½ *ozs butter*, ½ *teaspoon flour*, ¼ *pint cream.*

Choose firm, rounded, medium-sized mushrooms and wash them in a large basinful of water. (This applies only to country mushrooms. The cultivated ones are generally so free of earth that they only need wiping.)

Cut the mushrooms, without peeling them, in lengthwise slices. Heat the butter in a medium-sized saucepan and add the mushrooms, which are still dripping. Cover the pan and raise the heat. Take the lid off after 3 minutes. The mushrooms are swimming in juice. Add salt and pepper and leave the pan on the fire so that the juice evaporates.

Mix the cream and flour in a little bowl. When very little liquid is left in the saucepan—only a couple of tablespoons—add the cream. Raise the heat, stirring all the time. The cream thickens and begins to boil.

Serve the mushrooms at once, with, perhaps, an escalope of veal which has been sizzling whilst they were cooking. The mushrooms are exquisite and velvety, a caress for your palate.

If you prefer something a little more robust, try frying them.

Fried Mushrooms.

> ½ *lb small firm mushrooms, lard or vegetable oil for deep-frying, 2 eggs, 5 tablespoons flour, 1 teaspoon baking powder.*

Prepare a batter by whipping together the beaten eggs, flour and baking-powder and adding enough water to make a cream which will coat the back of a spoon. Let it stand for an hour if possible.

Wash the mushrooms and dry them, leaving them whole. Heat the deep-frying-pan until the lard or oil is smoking-hot. Plunge the mushrooms into the batter and drop them, one by one into the hot fat. The batter puffs out, becomes the colour of straw, then golden and then amber. Hardly 3 minutes have passed.

Lift out the mushrooms, drain them on soft paper, sprinkle them with fine salt and garnish them with parsley which you have fried for 10 seconds.

Taste one of the mushrooms—with your fingers, of course. You will burn your tongue, but this is the classic way to sample a *friture*. Inside their crisp, burning jackets the mushrooms are hardly warm and almost raw, full of the delicate, earthy scent of the fields.

Peas.

Returning from Morocco many years ago I learnt, as one should when travelling, something new. Hardly had we left Tangier and before I even had time to feel seasick, I saw the sailors unfurling an immense canvas cylinder about two feet wide and at least thirty feet long. This cylinder was hoisted so that its upper end formed a giant mouth facing the prow of the ship. The lower part of the monster passed through a hatch in the deck to the bottom of the hold. The mouth was flanked by two wings giving the appearance of a huge funnel.

My curiosity was piqued and I enquired its purpose of one of the sailors. "The *petits pois* must have air. Without air they die," he replied. The young sailor explained what I, as a botanist, ought to have known, that peas exhale carbon dioxide and that unless they are supplied with oxygen they rapidly deteriorate. These peas had been grown in Morocco for the Paris market and had to arrive in good condition.

Young peas, freshly picked, have a wonderful flavour and scent, but after a long journey in a confined space they lose nearly all their charm. This applies in greater or less degree to all vegetables. They should be bought fresh and prepared immediately. This advice is sometimes very difficult to carry out, but at least you can avoid throwing away the goodness with the cooking water. Use as little water as possible and a tightly closed pan and never throw away a drop of the liquid that remains. It is full of the virtues of the sun and of the earth.

Green Peas with Lettuce.

> 4 *lbs fresh green peas*, 3 *ozs butter, a lettuce*, ½ *lump sugar.*

To my mind, four pounds of peas is a minimum for four people—as a dish in its own right, of course—and also the maximum.

Shell the peas, discarding any which are wormy. Put them into a heavy saucepan with half the butter and a glass of water. Wash a lettuce and tie it firmly into a bundle. Put it into the saucepan with a few pinches of salt. Cover, and simmer for 20 minutes without lifting the lid, for one must never torment green peas.

Now, taste the juice and a couple of peas. It is not very sweet. The poor little peas have probably had a long journey. It can't be helped. You must commit a sacrilege and sweeten them with half a lump of sugar. No one need know.

The peas are still not soft enough. Let them simmer for another 10 minutes. Before serving, draw the pan off the fire and let the rest of the butter melt in the peas. Taste them. They are excellent.

Green Peas with Cream.

Prepare the peas as before, but instead of adding butter when they are cooked, mix 3½ ozs of double cream with a ½-teaspoon of flour and stir them into the saucepan over the fire. As soon as the cream boils, serve the peas.

Petits Pois à la Polonaise.

>   3 *lbs young green peas,* ½ *lb new carrots,* 3 *ozs butter.*

Shell the peas. Scrape the carrots and cut them in long strips and then crosswise into small cubes not much larger than the peas. Cook the peas and carrots together with half the butter and a glass of water in a covered pan for 40 minutes.

They are a really pretty sight with the apricot colour of the carrots contrasting with the fresh green of the peas. You need not even add sugar, as the carrots which will supply any which the peas have lost during their travels from the earth to your saucepan.

Peppers.

The peppers are a very colourful family. There are small, brilliant red ones which can be a culinary menace. They set your mouth, throat, stomach and intestines on fire. Dried and ground they produce Cayenne pepper.

The 'fire' in the small red peppers is caused by an alkaloid called capsicine. By means of careful selection, horticulturalists have been able to breed a pepper which is much larger and free of this irritant principle. These are the sweet red, green and yellow peppers so much used in the East, and these are the peppers I shall tell you about.

Peppers are a fairly recent importation into France. They were not known to the Romans in spite of their passion for spices. Apicius cites fifty-three spices which were necessary to a self-respecting kitchen. I shall not give you their names in order to show off my learning, but I can assure you that peppers were not among them.

Some people believe that peppers were imported from India in the sixteenth century. Others, basing their theory on the writings of Chanca, the doctor who accompanied the fleet of Christopher Columbus, declare that the pepper came to us from America. In any case, from the sixteenth century onwards the cultivation of peppers spread rapidly in Europe and they were grown in Spain, Moravia, Germany and England. They were used as a condiment to stimulate digestion, and apothecaries employed them in the form of a powder to make hot poultices.

Let us leave the small red peppers to our ancestors and to the apothecaries, and buy the big sweet peppers with their brilliant colours which one can find nowadays at almost any greengrocer's.

Some people say that sweet peppers have no flavour and depend on the sauce with which they are served. It is not true. They have a very subtle taste which you can enjoy most fully if you eat them raw. In the chapter on salads I shall describe how they should be prepared.

Stuffed Peppers.

> 6 *large peppers, a small tin of tunny fish, a cup of brown rice, 1 clove garlic, 1 tablespoon tomato purée, ¼ pint olive oil.*

Heat 2 tablespoons of oil in a saucepan and add the rice, unwashed. Stir for a minute and then pour in exactly 1½ cups of boiling water. Salt, and cover the pan. Cook over a low fire for 18 minutes. Uncover the pan. The rice is heaped on the bottom. That doesn't matter. Stir it with a wooden spoon and you will find that the grains are beautifully separate. Heat it for another 5 minutes with the lid off so that the last of the moisture evaporates. Now the rice is ready. Put it onto a plate and let it cool for 10 minutes.

Open the tin of tunny. Break up the fish with a silver fork and mix it, with all its oil, into the rice. Salt, and add the garlic crushed or chopped very finely and the tomato purée. Add a little more olive oil and mix well, being careful not to crush the rice.

Cut off the stems of the peppers and with a sharp, pointed knife cut out the base of each stem. Scoop out the centre and the seeds with a teaspoon. Fill the peppers with the rice mixture.

Put the rest of the oil into a heavy saucepan and arrange the stuffed peppers carefully in the bottom. Add 2 tablespoons of water and cover the pan. Cook them over a low fire for 30 minutes, then turn the peppers, cover once more and cook for 30 minutes more.

Now take the lid off the pan and raise the heat a little whilst the liquid evaporates. Lift it from the fire and let the peppers cool a little. Arrange the peppers on a dish and pour over them the oil in which they have cooked. They are delicious eaten cold with a finger of white wine, not too dry.

Potatoes.

The potato was introduced to Europe from Peru by the Spaniards in about 1535. They became known in Italy and then in England, and were originally called *taratoufli*, hence the German name for potatoes, *Kartofel* and the word truffles, though they have nothing to do with the truffles which we prize so highly.

In those days potatoes had a bitter, rather disagreeable flavour and they were not very popular. The Burgundians maintained that potatoes caused leprosy, while Turgot on the other hand insisted that the Faculty of Medicine should recommend their use.

Parmentier passed his life campaigning on behalf of the potato. He even asked that the king should wear a potato flower in his buttonhole during a royal reception. It was Parmentier who bred potatoes without bitterness, and from that moment everyone began to eat them.

The Spaniards, in those days masters of the Franche-Comté, introduced the potato to France, and in 1615 they appeared on the table of Louis XIII.

But enough of history. You will already know many ways of cooking potatoes. I shall mention one or two which may be new to you.

Pommes de Terre Soufflées.

It is not easy to make soufflé potatoes and I should advise you not to experiment on the day that you are expecting guests. The potato has to swell, so the slices must be very well cooked inside, whilst the outsides are still elastic enough to stretch before they are allowed to become crisp. The problem appears to be insoluble, but the solution is really quite simple.

If the potatoes are at first cooked in fat which is not very hot they will soften inside without becoming crisp outside. If they are then put into very hot fat, the steam inside the slices of potato will dilate rapidly so that they swell and become fluffy. After this, one only has to wait until the outsides are crisp.

Professional cooks use two deep-frying-pans for their soufflé potatoes, one at medium heat and the other very hot. I shall try to manage with one which contains about 3 pints of vegetable oil.

I take 5 large, waxy Dutch potatoes and wash, peel and dry them. These I cut lengthwise in slices about ⅛-inch thick. The small slices must be discarded. The big ones I range neatly on a cloth, side by side. There are about thirty. I cover them with a second cloth.

The deep-frying-pan is on the fire. As soon as the oil shows the least sign of smoking I lower the heat. When I am sure that there is no smoke I put in half the potatoes, raising the heat as I do so. The oil boils tumultuously and the potato slices float on the surface. The temperature of the fat bath drops considerably. I leave the potatoes for 4 minutes and then lower the heat as much as possible. If it is a gas flame, it should be barely perceptible. After 6 more minutes in this falling temperature the potato slices are soft inside but not coloured on the outside.

Now I raise the heat so that the cooking plate is blazing hot. Watch carefully. Holding the basin by both handles I shake it continuously with rapid, small, jerky movements as if I wished to stop the slices from sticking together. The oil quivers but does not spill. The potato slices turn a pale straw colour. I go on shaking the pan. Now they are browning just at the edges. I lift them out with a wire skimmer, or in the frying basket, and put them onto a dish.

The oil is not smoking, and has not smoked right through the operation, but now I shall heat it until it really does so. Two or three minutes over a blazing fire and I plunge in the potatoes once more, shaking the pan. The potatoes are swelling —or at least most of them. I lift them out and lay them on a cloth, taking care that they do not touch one another. They deflate sadly. Never mind, I carry out the same procedure with the other half of the potatoes.

Now they are all cooked, and lie like limp little invalids in rows of hospital beds. This is the moment to bring them back to life. Just as a beautiful *entrecôte* is sizzling to perfection under the grill, I plunge all my potatoes into smoking oil once more, and they swell up into glorious puffs, crisp on the outside and perfectly soft at the hearts.

This is a wonderful way of cooking potatoes but it is not easy, and in fact I doubt whether it is one to offer any but your closest friends. Either you will spoil the potatoes or you will spend your evening apologizing for neglecting your guests.

La Raclette.

Some people say that there is no such thing as Swiss cooking and that all Switzerland has to offer is the international *cuisine* of the grand hotels. Of course, this is nonsense. But it is true that a lot of the best Swiss dishes come from the mountains and owe a great deal of their charm to fresh milk and butter and cheese, to the sparkling air and the smell of wood-smoke, and for this reason it is impossible to reproduce them in all their simple perfection.

For instance, one evening in a *châlet* high in the mountains, the *patron* speared a lump of Gruyère cheese on a fork and, bending over the wood fire in the huge chimney, he held it close to the flames until the surface began to melt and turn a rich brown. Then, with a neat twist of his knife, he scraped the savoury crust of the cheese over a dish of boiled potatoes.

You may not have a wood fire, nor even a horn-handled knife like my Swiss mountaineer, but you can still put a piece of Gruyére cheese about ¾-inch thick under the grill until it melts, and eat it with boiled potatoes which you have wrapped in a napkin to keep them warm. A couple of turns of the black pepper mill will complete this very simple dish.

Gratin Dauphinois.

There are certain dishes the very name of which always arouses a storm. For instance, I have never spoken of *bouillabaisse* during a lecture without a pure-blooded *Marseillais* jumping up and declaring that my recipe was a heresy.

Happily for me they could never agree on a formula and to add to the confusion a *Toulonnais* would protest that the true *bouillabaisse* came from Toulon.

Not long ago I attended the monthly dinner of the *Académie des Gastronomes*, a grave assemblage composed of forty members each with an especially refined analytical judgment of taste in cooking. They served us a *gratin dauphinois*. I must say that it was abominable and bore no resemblance to the dish which one eats in the Alps of the Dauphiné. We all left, without a pang, the pseudo *gratin* on our plates and the conversation took its course.

First of all, what is a *gratin dauphinois*? It consists of thin slices of potato cooked in the oven in an earthenware dish, swimming in a smooth cream and perfumed with garlic. Now the concoction which was served to us didn't taste of garlic and instead of the cream, it was covered with a sort of over-cooked scrambled egg. Since the *gratin* has to be baked for at least three-quarters of an hour, you can imagine that one must never use eggs when making it. They would, of necessity, be overcooked.

Gravely, three members of the *Académie des Gastronomes* rose to their feet and gave their opinion on the way a *gratin* should be made. All three were *Dauphinois*, or nearly. At the same time one was a senator, another a member of the Council of State and the third, a member of the *Institut Français*.

Not being a *Dauphinois* myself, I could only listen in silence, but I took notes and have adopted the method which I shall give you now. Later I shall explain why I prefer it to the other two.

1½ *lbs white Dutch potatoes*, ¾ *pint milk*, ⅛ *pint double cream*, 4 *cloves of garlic*, ½ *teaspoon flour*.

Ideally this dish should be made in a round earthenware dish—the sort of rough, country dish which one can buy so cheaply in the market places of France. For some reason an oblong dish is not considered quite right.

Chop the garlic very finely. Wash the potatoes, peel them and dry them carefully. Cut them in very fine slices. Unless you have a *mandoline* or cutter this is a tedious business.

Cover the bottom of the dish with sliced potato. Sprinkle with salt, pepper and garlic. Continue with a second layer and so on, until your potatoes are all used up. Meantime, heat the milk and when it is boiling, pour it into the fireproof dish. You will just see it between the slices of potato.

Put the cream into a bowl and mix it with a scant ½-tea-spoonful of flour. Pour it over the potatoes and put the dish into a hot oven (400° F. Gas 5).

After 30 minutes inspect the *gratin*. The milk is boiling gently. Try a slice of potato. It is not yet done. Wait another 20 minutes and try again. The potato is soft. Raise the heat and when the *gratin* is a beautiful golden-brown serve it, being careful to stand the dish on a thick mat, otherwise, being blazing hot, it will damage the surface of the table.

Now let me explain the way the other two methods of making a *gratin dauphinois* vary from that which I have chosen, and why I would not recommend them:

1. The potatoes are par-boiled in their skins for 10 minutes before being sliced.

I see no point in this initial cooking, except perhaps a slight economy in potato. This is balanced, to my mind, by a definite waste of time.

2. No flour is added to the cream.

I tried this, but the cream turned to butter during cooking. The addition of a trace of flour does not affect the flavour of the *gratin* and it prevents the cream from liquifying.

Follow the method I have described, and you can be quite sure of a very pleasant quarter of an hour enjoying the result.

New Potatoes with Tarragon.

I used to fancy myself as a botanist, but my illusions were shattered when I asked a charming young saleswoman for seeds of parsley, chervil and tarragon. "Tarragon does not produce a fertile seed," she replied. "If you want a plant, here you are. In three years it will die. Come back again and see me."

I stared wide-eyed both at the pretty girl and at my towns-man's ignorance, then I carried the plant back to Paris and my little garden. Straight away I looked up tarragon in my medical dictionary and found the following description: "Tarragon (*Artemisia Dranunculus*) a vigorous plant of the compositae family. Native of Tartary and the borders of the Caspian Sea. Propagated by division and by cuttings which root easily. The true tarragon flowers, but produces no fertile seed. The plant frequently found in commerce, *Artemisia Redowskyi*, resembles tarragon in appearance but has no aromatic qualities."

I gazed in wonder at my tarragon plant, offshoot of another plant which in its turn went back in a direct line to the plant which some Roman soldier had plucked in the foothills of the Caucasus and carried home with him. How many tarragon plants for how many hundreds of years had gone to the making of my own small plant!

When you crush the leaves of tarragon it releases a delicate

scent which perfumes everything it touches. It lends an every-
day chicken an aroma of spring, and it turns a dish of potatoes
into a work of art. Try this, you will need:

> 1½ *lbs new potatoes*, 2½ *ozs butter, a heaping tablespoon
> freshly-chopped tarragon.*

Scrape the potatoes and cook them in boiling, salted water.
Drain them and put them into a very hot dish. Add the butter,
which should be soft, not cold and hard from the refrigerator.
Mix the butter with the potatoes and stir in the freshly-chopped
tarragon. Serve immediately and eat very slowly, crushing
the fragrant tarragon leaves between your teeth.

Pumpkins.

It seems that pumpkins have always been known to Western
civilization. The Romans used them a great deal and the
philosopher Taurus is said to have offered his friends a dish of
pumpkin and lentils as an entire meal. His colour sense was
certainly less developed than his philosophy.

Lucullus and Trimalchio served, as a sweet, pumpkin
cooked with honey. This must have tasted as good as it looked.

The giant pumpkin, however, was not used only as a food.
From earliest times it was valued for its therapeutic qualities.
Diosco filled the hollowed out shell of a pumpkin with white
wine. After soaking for two days the liquid possessed, he maintained, laxative qualities. Even today pumpkin seeds are used
with great success as a vermifuge. This virtue was discovered
by an English doctor, Edward Tyson, in 1683.

Pumpkin with Tomato.

> *A piece of pumpkin weighing about* 1 *lb*, ⅛ *pint olive oil,
> a cupful thick tomato purée.*

Cut the pulp of the pumpkin into cubes and fry them in a
little olive oil until they are soft enough to allow the prongs of
a fork to penetrate easily. Arrange the pumpkin on a dish and
cover it with a thick purée of tomatoes.

Sorrel.

In France, any soup to which sorrel has been added is apt
to be called '*potage santé*', but the suitability of the name is
open to discussion, just as is the word 'health' itself. For those

with a lazy intestine sorrel does provoke a healthy reaction, but for sufferers from kidney trouble it only serves to aggravate their disorder.

Horace mentions sorrel as a laxative and Galen cites it as a cure for at least twenty disorders, but ancient records hardly mention it as a food.

Sorrel has a very pleasant acid flavour which gives an agreeable tang to the more tasteless kind of fish or meat. As I said, people with kidney complaints should avoid sorrel, but those with rheumatism will benefit from it. The oxalic acid in the sorrel, during assimilation, liberates potash which helps to reduce the acidity in the blood.

It is quite easy, if you wish, to reduce the oxalic acid in the sorrel by blanching it for 2 minutes in boiling water.

Cultivated sorrel is not widely sold in this country though you can find it in Soho. Wild sorrel has an even sharper taste and makes an interesting addition to a green salad.

Sorrel Purée.

> 1½ *lbs young sorrel, 2 ozs butter.*

Wash the sorrel carefully in several waters. There is no need to throw away the stems. Throw the sorrel into boiling water for 2 minutes, then lift it out and drain it. The beautiful green leaves have turned a dirty yellow. Squeeze the water from the leaves without crushing them too much.

Put the butter in a saucepan and let it melt over a very low fire. Add the sorrel and mix it with the butter and a sprinkling of salt. Slowly it turns into a brownish purée of a not particularly attractive appearance. This combines excellently with scrambled eggs and the milder-flavoured kinds of meat and fish.

Sorrel Fritters.

> ½ *lb sorrel, 2 eggs, 6 ozs flour, beer, oil for deep frying.*

Wash the sorrel carefully and then dry it in a cloth. While the oil in the deep-frying-pan is heating over the fire, put the eggs into a basin and mix in the flour, using a wire whisk. Thin the batter with beer until it is a fluid cream, but still thick enough to coat the back of a spoon.

When the oil is hot, dip the sorrel leaves in batter and drop them, one at a time into the frying-pan. The batter swells.

Put in about ten fritters at a time and when they are golden-brown, lift them out with a wire skimmer and put them on a hot dish with a little soft kitchen paper beneath them to catch the surplus fat. Working fast, make a couple more batches of fritters and serve them, very hot, with escalopes of veal (see *escalopes de veau poêlées*, p. 110). I feel sure you will enjoy them.

Vegetarian Meals.

I am not a vegetarian, but after, for example, the Christmas festivities when I was once invited to three dinners, nibbled at the first, ate the second and made myself ill at the third, I was filled with remorse and decided to do penance. Now penance for a gourmet consists, if not of a fast, at least of a vegetarian meal.

Vegetables are generally considered as an accompaniment to meat or fish. One seldom sees on a menu a dish of carrots, turnips or beetroot standing on its own. Carrots are paired off with boiled beef, and turnips with haggis. As for beetroot, it slips blushing into a bowl of mixed salad.

It is the same with all the vegetables. Chips are paired off with steak or egg, mashed potatoes with sausage, and cabbage with practically anything.

As soon as one advises somebody to diet he is horrified. The household looks askance at this complication of the family catering. The unfortunate victim is sat down to a plate of plain boiled rice or spinach. He has to put up with it while the rest of the family enjoy their normal dinner.

The poor fellow feels that he is an outcast. He becomes neurasthenic. To hell with his doctor and his diet, he feels. And he is quite right, since vegetarian cooking on these lines is devoid of both art and good sense.

A dish, when it arrives at table, must always charm one's eyes as well as one's palate. That is why one garnishes meat dishes with vegetables of various colours. That is how a single dish can afford such a diversity of sensations when we look at it.

When we decide to become vegetarians—even for a time— why don't we prepare garnished dishes of vegetables? A dish of potatoes which looks very dull will appear quite gay when it is surrounded by a garland of lettuce leaves. It is simply a question of visual and gustatory harmony, and it is easy to create a large number of perfect combinations.

Here are some dishes which will refresh you after a surfeit of rich food. Remember them. You may be grateful to me for having made the suggestion.

Spinach en branches *with a turban of tomato sauce.*
Tomatoes à la crème *on potato purée.*
Fried potatoes garnished with watercress.
Savoury rice with sorrel cooked in butter.
Braised chicory surrounded by hot beetroot and cream.
Pilaff of rice with mushrooms.
Noodles with spinach.
Braised lettuce ringed with chopped beetroot.
Carottes Vichy *with lettuce salad.*
Braised turnips with croûtons.
Creamed mushrooms on toast.
Tinned cèpes *with hollandaise sauce.*

In this way one can devise an infinite number of dishes which are both refreshing and a change from one's usual routine.

But, you will say, how can one compose a whole menu with such materials? First of all, you must be content with a limited number of courses, and then you must blend them with an art which is guided by your own appetite.

Here is a vegetarian dinner which I planned for some friends. I think it is rather luxurious, but I wanted it to be specially good so that I could enjoy my penance in good company.

Potage julienne *with rice.*

Fried salsify.
Cèpes sautés, *garnished with watercress.*
Fresh garden peas with cream.
Pineapple and cream cheese.
Fresh fruit.

After having done this agreeable penance, I felt that after a few days I could commit the sin of greed once more. Do like me, and you will merit both salvation and good health.

SALADS

A salad should be the simplest form of food which can be prepared by man—just a raw eatable substance sprinkled with a little salt. Hence the name salad which is derived from the Latin word for salt, *sal*.

The very fact of adding salt to food allows our taste buds to appreciate its flavour. To function properly these must be stimulated by the same percentage of salt which is contained in our blood.

The word salad has changed its meaning, however, and covers a vast range of dishes from delicate leaves of lettuce dressed with a simple vinaigrette, to complex creations containing prawns and truffles and hearts of artichokes, and goodness knows what else.

Salad dressings have progressed from a simple sprinkling of salt, to include oil, vinegar, pepper, herbs, cream, yolks of egg, bacon fat and all sorts of other refinements.

This is a simple book, so I shall describe a few simple salads.

Asparagus and Potato Salad.

> 1½ *lbs cooked asparagus (or a tin of asparagus tips),
> 1 lb new potatoes, ½ cup mayonnaise, an equal quantity
> of double cream.*

Scrape and boil the potatoes and cut them in slices. When they are cold, mix them with the tips of the asparagus. Dress the salad with mayonnaise (p. 189) into which you have stirred an equal quantity of double cream. Add a little salt but no pepper. One must not spoil the subtle flavour of the asparagus.

Raw Carrot Salad.

Fresh raw carrots, especially when young, contain vitamin A. This vitamin, which is also found in butter, cream, cheese, liver and so on, favours growth and is beneficial in various ways. The presence of this vitamin undoubtedly adds greatly to the value of carrots when they are eaten raw, but hardly justifies the craze which almost led people to believe that raw carrots would make women beautiful, men robust, children intelligent and . . . husbands less jealous.

Personally I don't care for raw carrot, but I don't wish to put you off. In fact, I shall make some suggestions which should help you to enjoy them.

Choose young, sound carrots. Wash them and scrape them and dry them in a cloth. Shred them very finely or grate them on a coarse grater, according to your taste, then prepare them each day in a different way. Try dressing them with (one after the other, of course) fresh butter, mayonnaise, gooseberry jelly, thick cream, cottage cheese, rhubarb purée, Brie, tomato sauce. . . . And now it is your turn to think of something.

Cucumber Salad.

A large cucumber, ½ tablespoon vinegar, 2 tablespoons olive oil, chopped tarragon.

Peel the cucumber with a sharp knife, being careful to remove every last shred of green. Slice the cucumber very finely, salt it lightly and put it in a bowl covered with a plate on which you lay a fairly heavy weight.

After 2 hours remove the weight and, pressing down on the plate, tip the bowl so that all the juice runs out. *I* throw the juice away, but if I were a young girl I should keep it to bathe my face. They say that it freshens and lightens the complexion.

The cucumber slices are completely limp. Dress them with the oil, vinegar and tarragon. Before serving taste the salad to make sure the flavour is just as you like it.

Cucumber with Cream.

A large cucumber, 4 ozs thick cream, chopped chervil.

Prepare the cucumber as before and when the slices have been pressed and drained, mix them with the chopped chervil and cream. It is delicious.

Curled Endive with Black Olives.

A head of curled endive, 4 tablespoons olive oil, 1 scant tablespoon wine vinegar, 4 slices of toast, 1 clove garlic, ¼ lb black olives.

Discard the coarse outer leaves of the endive. Wash the rest, shake them vigorously in a salad basket to remove the water and finally dry them delicately in a cloth.

Pour the olive oil into a large salad bowl with the vinegar, salt, and pepper. I do not care for much vinegar in a salad and use it sparingly, but this is a matter of individual taste.

Now cut the crusts from the toast and rub it all over with the clove of garlic, cut in half. There is something so delightful about the natural packaging of garlic, which allows you to rub the pungent juice from the cut surface without soiling your finger tips. Pieces of toast—or bread—rubbed with garlic, are called *chapons*. Sprinkle the olives over the *chapons* and arrange the chicory on top, but do not stir.

Leave the salad to stand for an hour. The oil becomes fragrant with garlic and the olives attract the oil. Stir the salad only at the last moment, when it is already on the table. The pallor of the leaves is flecked with glistening black olives. A slightly mournful colour scheme, you say? Perhaps, but what an incomparable flavour.

Lettuces with Cream.

> *The hearts of* 3 *lettuces,* 5 *tablespoons double cream,* 1 *tablespoon vinegar.*

Wash and dry the lettuce hearts carefully, separate the leaves, and put them into a salad bowl. Mix the cream and vinegar in a small bowl with a little salt. Pour this over the lettuce and scarcely toss it, using a very delicate movement.

Serve this salad with white meat such as roast veal or chicken.

Mushroom Salad.

> 10 *large white mushrooms,* 3 *tablespoons olive oil,* $\frac{3}{4}$ *tablespoon lemon juice.*

Wash and dry the mushrooms, putting the stalks aside for flavouring a soup or stew. Cut the caps in very thin slices and dry them once more. Dress them with oil, lemon juice and salt. I think you will be surprised how good this is.

Sweet Pepper Salad.

> 4 *large sweet peppers,* 2 *green and* 2 *red,* 2 *tablespoons olive oil,* $\frac{1}{2}$ *tablespoon vinegar.*

Cut the stems from the peppers, split them in half length-wise and remove the seeds and the pithy centre. Cut them in small pieces and throw them into boiling water. Five minutes after the water has come to the boil once more, drain the peppers and, when they are cool, dress them with oil, vinegar and salt. This is a much gayer looking salad than that of endive and black olives which I described a little earlier, but the flavour is not nearly so subtle.

Choucroûte Salad.

Many years ago, in Moscow, I was served with a *choucroûte* salad and fried fish. I suggest that you try this salad with sizzling pork chops.

Buy your *choucroûte* in a shop with a brisk turnover and see that it is nice and white. For six people you will need:

> 1 *lb* choucroûte, 4 *tablespoons olive oil*, ½ *teaspoon cumin seeds.*

Put the *choucroûte* in a large bowl of cold water and work it with your fingers. Drain off the water and wash it once more. Now let the *choucroûte* drip in a colander and when you are confident that it can lose no more water, put it into a salad bowl and dress it with the oil, cumin seeds, salt and a little pepper.

Blend the salad, as you eat, with the fat from the hot pork chop. I can assure you that it is excellent.

Spanish Radish with Cream.

The large black Spanish radish has a delicious flavour and makes an excellent addition to a salad either grated, or shaved in very thin slices. In Germany and Austria great spirals of black radish are served as an appetizer with beer. Unfortunately, it is not easy to find in this country though one hopes, as the range of vegetables and salads gradually increases, that it may eventually be found in an ordinary greengrocer's shop.

To make a salad of Spanish radish on its own, peel and grate it and let it stand for a couple of hours, lightly salted so that the juice exudes and can be thrown away. Mix it with thick cream and, if you like delicate contrasts of texture and flavour, accompany it with a plateful of lettuce dressed with oil and vinegar and a glass of orange juice.

Spinach Salad with Hard-Boiled Eggs.

> 2 lbs spinach, 4 hard-boiled eggs, 4 tablespoons olive oil,
> 1 tablespoon vinegar.

If the spinach is tender it can be used whole. If it is coarse, pull the stems off backwards so that they come away with part of the midriff. Spinach must be very carefully washed in a number of waters, especially if it has been picked in rainy weather and is splashed with mud.

When you are quite sure that the spinach is clean and free from grit, plunge it into a large saucepan half full of boiling water. The leaves shrink, go limp and sink to the bottom of the saucepan. The water comes to the boil once more.

After 5 minutes, empty the saucepan into a colander and cool the spinach under the cold tap. Gather up the leaves in the bottom of the colander and work it with your hands so as to expel all the water. This is the secret of preparing spinach.

Leave the spinach to drain for several hours. Meanwhile, chop the hard-boiled eggs.

Put the cold spinach into a bowl and dress it with oil, vinegar, salt and pepper like an ordinary salad. Cover the surface with chopped egg and set the bowl on the dining table, so that everyone can enjoy the fresh white and gold of the eggs on their green background. At the last minute, toss the salad once more. Be sure that you serve it very cold.

Turnip Salad with Capers.

> 2 or 3 young turnips, olive oil, lemon juice, bottled capers.

Wash and peel the turnips and grate them as fine or as coarse as you please. Mix them with 2 or 3 tablespoons of olive oil and a squeeze of lemon juice. Taste as you go. Sprinkle with salt, stir, and add some capers which have been bottled in vinegar.

Watercress with Cheese.

> A bunch of watercress, 4 tablespoons cottage cheese,
> 1 tablespoon double cream.

Put a bunch of watercress through the mincer or 'Mouli', removing beforehand the thick stems. Take four tablespoons of the crushed cress and mix it with the cottage cheese and cream, salting it to your taste. It is marvellous. This makes an excellent spread for cocktail savouries.

SAUCES

The Basic Principles of Sauce Making.

The subject of sauces is so vast and complicated that I propose to limit myself to the basic principles. If you understand these and follow them carefully then you will not only be able to make the sauces which I describe, but to follow intelligently the directions for sauce-making in other cookery books.

Sauces are founded on a *liaison*. Now there are various kinds of *liaisons* in this world, but I propose to stick to those which occur in cookery, that is to say a thickening by which a liquid is given a creamy consistency which not only caresses the tongue, but helps the sauce to cling to the palate, thus prolonging our enjoyment of its flavour.

The two most important substances used for this purpose are starch and yolk of egg. Let us start with starch. This is a white powder which forms almost the entire bulk of any flour. It consists of an infinity of microscopic granules. If you mix the starch with cold water this turns milky, but the granules quickly sink to the bottom and the water becomes clear once more.

If you heat the milky liquid each of the granules swells to a hundred times its original size because it absorbs water. Soon there is no water left. The liquid has turned into a viscous, starchy paste. This paste has served to bind the liquid and you have formed a *liaison*.

To thicken a soup, therefore, one only has to add to it, when boiling, flour mixed with *cold* water, stirring all the time to prevent the formation of lumps. Now the sauce is *lié*.

To make a *sauce liée*, white sauce for example, I make a paste of flour and water and add salt and butter. I taste it. It is detestable. Why? Because flour, even when it has been cooked in water for a long time, has an unpleasant flavour.

What must I do? I shall mask the flavour of the flour by heating it before adding the water. While it is heating the starch turns to dextrine. This substance, like starch, can form a paste, but it can also, like sugar, acquire the very agreeable flavour of caramel.

So I take a saucepan and put it on the fire and melt in it a piece of butter. Then I add the flour, stirring all the time over the heat. If I keep the pan on the fire the flour and butter mixture will turn from cream to gold, to deep yellow, and then deep mahogany brown, and will, of course, finally burn. These changes of colour are due to the degree of caramelization of the dextrine. These stages are called *roux blanc*, *roux blond* and *roux brun* according to whether the colour is pale cream, deep gold or *café au lait*.

If I dilute a *roux blanc* with cold water and heat it, stirring all the time I obtain, after adding salt, a white sauce. Starting with a *roux blond* or a *roux brun* I can produce a *sauce blonde* or a *sauce brune*.

You can imagine therefore how many variations can be produced simply by diluting the *roux* with different liquids and adding various flavours and ingredients to the sauce.

A white sauce diluted with *bouillon* instead of water becomes a *sauce suprême*. Diluted with milk it produces a simple form of *béchamel*. Enrich it with grated Gruyère cheese and you have a *sauce Mornay*; with onion and you obtain *sauce soubise*; with cream it becomes a *sauce Normande*. Add shrimp butter and have made a *sauce Nantua*.

A *roux brun* mixed with bouillon sharpened with a little vinegar and seasoned with chopped gherkins becomes a *sauce piquante*. Dilute it with bouillon and Madeira and you have a *sauce Madère*. In the same way you can make such sauces as *bourguignonne*, *bordelaise*, *Bercy*, etc.

A *liaison* with starch is no longer a mystery to you. Let us go on to a *liaison* with yolk of egg. Yolk of egg, diluted with a liquid which is heated gradually, slowly thickens and attains its maximum viscosity at about 145° F. At 155° F. it hardens and coagulates.

Therefore, to thicken a liquid with yolk of egg mix them together when cold and heat them with care, stirring all the time. Above all don't let the heat rise above 145° F. And how are you to judge this? From time to time, dip your finger into the sauce. When the heat becomes unbearable take care. The egg is just about to coagulate and if this happens, the sauce will curdle, so lift it off the heat at once and serve it immediately.

Sauce Hollandaise.

   2 yolks of egg, 3½ ozs butter.

So many people tell me that they have trouble with *hollandaise* sauce. I never do. They make it in a *bain-marie*, they protest. I make mine *beside* a *bain-marie* and perhaps that is the reason for my success.

What is *hollandaise* sauce? It is a mixture of butter and yolk of egg blended with art—or rather with science. Art demands an impeccable technique; science, a little understanding.

Since art, or a technique founded on instinct, may have caused disappointment, let us try science and attempt to understand what is involved in the making of a *hollandaise* sauce.

If we take melted butter and add yolks of egg blindly we shall obtain a sauce without any creamy consistency. *Hollandaise* sauce is viscous, as a doctor would say, and more viscous than either of its components. How does this occur? It is caused by emulsion. Let us examine this more closely.

Melted butter is liquid. If we examine it under the microscope rapidly, before it has time to cool and harden, we shall see simply a liquid containing no visible particles. On the other hand, if we observe a little warm *hollandaise* sauce under a microscope we see that it consists of millions of tiny spheres which touch one another but remain intact. A liquid which is formed of millions of tiny globules is called an emulsion.

How has the melted butter formed this emulsion? Simply by contact with the yolk of egg which, like soap, bicarbonate of soda, mustard, gum tragacanth and unsweetened condensed milk, has the power of forming an emulsion with fat.

Oil or butter then, when mixed thoroughly with one of these substances will form an emulsion. Butter and yolk of egg will produce a *hollandaise* sauce; oil and yolk of egg, a *mayonnaise*, and oil and mustard a *remoulade* sauce.

The difficulty with a *hollandaise* sauce is the use of hot butter since, as you know, yolk of egg coagulates under the action of heat and then the sauce curdles. So we must be very careful.

And now to work. I put a large saucepan on the fire and bring a couple of pints of water to boil in it. Before me I have a small enamelled saucepan (never aluminium) which will hold about a pint. Besides this there are 2 eggs, and the 3½ ozs butter cut into twelve pieces; a small wire whisk, a glass of cold water and some salt.

I put the egg yolks into the small saucepan with a tablespoon of cold water. Whisking all the time, I add 3 pinches of salt and then, holding the small pan in my left hand and beating briskly with my right, I lower it into the boiling water. In less than 1 minute the yolks begin to thicken. I lift out the small pan and, still holding it, I drop in a piece of butter and whisk this until it melts, *without returning the saucepan to the boiling water*. Now I add a second piece and beat. It melts too. I try a third, but this no longer melts as I beat, so I return the pan to the water. As soon as this melts I remove the pan once more and continue in this way, beating all the time, only holding the small pan in the boiling water just long enough to keep the butter melting.

Now the butter is all used up but the sauce is not very hot. I return the pan to the boiling water, *beating all the time.* The sauce begins to thicken. I test it with the tip of my finger and find that it is still not too hot. I continue warming and beating and try it once more with my finger (after all, I am among friends). The sauce is very hot, though I have not actually burnt my finger. Immediately I empty it into a warm, not hot, sauce-boat and carry it to the table. My finger has acted as a useful thermometer.

Sauce Mousseline.

Make a *hollandaise* sauce as I have described and, just before you finally heat the sauce, fold in ¼-pint of whipped cream. This is delicious with asparagus.

Mayonnaise.

Since we are using a scientific approach to sauce-making let us investigate the preparation of *mayonnaise* in the same way. It may help us to understand why we are not always successful in this simple operation.

Suppose that we examine yolk of egg and olive oil—the two main components of *mayonnaise*—under the microscope. Since the yolk of egg is rather thick we shall dilute it with a trace of water before smearing it on a slide. Now, let us look. It is a fascinating sight. The tiny particles of yolk of egg, under the light, sparkle like stars. They are in constant movement, not because they are alive but because the water gives them all sorts of impulses, a haphazard energy. The sum of this energy which concerns the surface of the particles is called surface tension.

Now let us look at the oil. There is nothing to be seen. It is as if one were looking through perfectly clean, clear glass.

Let us start on the sauce. We break an egg and put only the yolk into a bowl. With the left hand we allow oil to fall into the basin, drop by drop, while with the right we stir as quickly as possible with a fork or a wire whisk. After 10 seconds of beating in the dripping oil we use the microscope once more. The oil has now formed four or five large globules, each surrounded with an infinity of brilliant particles of yolk of egg. The contact of the egg with the oil has forced the latter to divide into globules each of which is perfectly round, since each has a certain surface tension.

Everything which modifies this surface tension forces the oil to divide and re-divide, and yolk of egg possesses this quality.

We continue making the *mayonnaise*, pouring the oil very gently, and stirring very fast. In this way, there is time to surround the oil with yolk of egg. Continually the surface tension is upset. Continually it is forced to break up into smaller and smaller, more and more numerous globules.

When the sauce is ready we look through the microscope once more. As in the case of *hollandaise* sauce we see an infinite number of tiny, separate globules. We have formed an emulsion.

Suppose we pour in the oil too quickly and the sauce curdles. We must start again with another yolk of egg, adding the curdled sauce to it and beating all the time. This time we shall take care to add the oily mixture very slowly indeed.

I have been so absorbed in telling you of the scientific aspect of your *mayonnaise* that I have not mentioned the seasonings. These should be put into the bowl with the yolk of egg and they are very much a matter of individual taste. You will want salt—about a quarter of a teaspoon to start with (it can always be increased later); about half a small teaspoon of French mustard; perhaps a pinch of sugar; a pinch of white pepper; a dusting of Cayenne, and a few drops of lemon juice.

For 1 egg you will want about 1½ tablespoons of white wine vinegar. This can be added during mixing if the sauce becomes too thick before you have finished adding the oil. You will need about a ¼-pint of the best olive oil—that is unless you are making a larger quantity of *mayonnaise*, or are unfortunate enough to have to start at the beginning again with a second egg. Some people like *mayonnaise* very thick, others not, but normally it should be stiff enough to keep its shape, or to coat a piece of fish or hard-boiled egg.

As I say, the seasoning of the *mayonnaise* is a matter of taste and can be the subject of infinite variety. The manner of making it is based on a scientific process which governs its success.

SWEET DISHES

I had always been a little intimidated at the prospect of preparing puddings until one day I realized by a simple mathematical calculation that with three sorts of cream, three kinds of pastry and three different *compotes* one could, by combining them in twos and threes besides eating them on their own, arrive at sixty-three different sweets.

From that day onwards I no longer worried, and thoroughly enjoyed contriving puddings for my family and friends.

First of all, I had to serve my apprenticeship, and I started out to make a *crème anglaise*. This was the moment to consult a volume of classic cookery. I read:

"Take eight yolks of egg, half a pound of caster sugar and three-quarters of a pint of milk. Beat the eggs with the sugar and boil the milk with a vanilla pod. Pour the milk onto the eggs and stir the whole over a low fire until it thickens."

First of all, I found that my cream was very expensive. Eight eggs to ¾-pint of milk, and then the sugar! Anyway, I would have a try. I beat the sugar and eggs, added the milk, stirred them over the fire and the cream began to thicken. It ought to be thicker still, so I continued to heat it. And then, to my horror, I noticed some lumps. My splendid cream was spoilt.

But perhaps it could be saved. I poured the whole thing into a bottle and stoppered it up. Then I shook and shook for five minutes and, blessed relief, the cream was smooth once more. It is an old trick . . . but it doesn't always succeed.

Well, the cream was delicious, but far too expensive. Could I make a cheaper one using at the same time a simpler method? Certainly, by taking advantage of two principles of the chemistry of cooking:

1. The starch which is contained in flour, when it is heated in milk, causes the same creamy thickening as that produced by yolk of egg.

2. The addition of starch to a mixture of milk and yolk of egg allows one to heat up to boiling point without causing

it to curdle. This is because a liquid thickened with starch boils at a temperature below that at which the yolk of egg coagulates.

So I decided to make a *crème anglaise* based on these two observasions, using fewer yolks of egg and a little flour. Not only would this be more economical, but there would be less risk of failure.

In order to avoid the criticism of purists who consider it a crime to add flour to a *crème anglaise*, I shall call my cream a *crème écossaise*. As a matter of fact, I did eat a cream just like this in Scotland and it didn't come out of a packet.

Crème Écossaise.

> *4 yolks of egg, 1 teaspoon flour, 2 ozs caster sugar, 2 or 3 drops of pure vanilla essence, ½ pint milk.*

Put the yolks of egg, flour and sugar into a bowl and mix them with a wire whisk. The egg becomes almost white.

Boil the milk, flavoured with vanilla, for a minute, lift it off the fire and, after a moment or two, pour it, little by little into the bowl, stirring all the time.

Now empty the bowl into the saucepan and stir it over a low fire. The cream thickens rapidly. There is no fear of curdling because of the addition of the flour. When it is thick enough and almost at boiling point pour the contents of the saucepan into a crystal dish and let it cool.

Crème Écossaise au Café.

Make a *crème écossaise* as before, but add to the milk, as well as vanilla, 2 teaspoons of coffee essence, either liquid or in powder form.

Crème Écossaise au Chocolat.

Instead of coffee, this time, stir 3 teaspoons of cocoa or powdered chocolate into the milk, being sure that it is well blended before being poured over the eggs, flour and sugar.

Poires Écossaises.

Peel 2 pears and cook them in well sugared water. When they are tender, lift them out and split them in half lengthwise.

Let them cool and arrange them in a crystal dish. (You can also use tinned pears drained of their juice.)

Pour *crème écossaise* over the pears and sprinkle them with praline, bought at a shop, which you have wrapped in a piece of cloth and crushed with a hammer.

This pudding costs very little but makes quite a luxurious impression.

Mousse de Chocolat.

Chocolate mousse is delicious in itself, so good that it is tempting to eat it over and over again. But even a good thing can be overdone, so when I have explained how to make it, I shall suggest a number of very easy, but subtle variations.

> 6 *ozs good quality block chocolate*, 6 *teaspoons sugar*,
> 6 *eggs*, ¼ *pint double cream.*

Break the eggs, putting the yolks into one bowl and the whites into another. It does not matter if the yolks contain traces of white, but the whites must be absolutely free of yolk, otherwise they cannot be beaten to a snow.

Pour the sugar into the yolks of egg and beat with a wire whisk until you have a whitish mass, then whip in the cream.

Break the chocolate in pieces, put it into a saucepan and add 3 tablespoons of water. Heat over a slow fire, stirring continually with a wooden spoon. The chocolate melts into a thick, syrupy liquid. Lift the saucepan from the fire. Pour a little of the chocolate into the bowl with the eggs, then empty the bowl into the saucepan. Pour the mixture backwards and forwards several times until it is perfectly mixed, then put the saucepan on a low fire. Heat slowly, stirring all the time. The mixture, which had become fairly fluid, thickens once more. Lift it off the fire.

Beat the whites of egg rapidly to a snow and drop this into the saucepan. Take a fork and mix the snow-white mass into the dark brown cream in the pan. Gradually the colours blend.

Pour the mousse into a bowl, scraping out the saucepan. (I can never resist finishing by running my finger round the bowl.) Now I shall suggest how, using the same mousse, one can quickly produce a number of variations.

Mousse with Ground Coffee.

Stir into the mousse a tablespoon of freshly ground, darkly roasted coffee. The flavour of the chocolate and the smooth texture of the mousse make an excellent foil for the tang of the coffee and the pleasant roughness of the granules.

Mousse à l'Orange.

Chop some candied orange peel very finely and mix it with the mousse.

Mousse Montmorency.

Top the mousse with stoned cherries which have been soaked in brandy.

Mousse à la Crème.

Pile whipped cream on top of your mousse. Perhaps it is not fair to give this suggestion a separate title. You might have done this anyhow. But you might not have thought of adding crystallized cherries or pieces of very soft, syrupy marron glacé.

Mousse au Cognac.

Stir some brandy into the mousse—just enough to give it a mysterious but not too decided flavour.

Mousse au Curaçao.

The same procedure again, but this time it is even better.

Mousse aux Noisettes.

Chop some toasted hazel-nuts very finely and mix them with the mousse.

You see what I mean? There is really no end to the things you can do with a mousse.

Pâté à Choux

Pâté à Choux is a soft dough which puffs up when it is subjected to a high temperature and then, when it has trebled or quadrupled its volume, the albumen it contains coagulates under the action of the heat and the pastry becomes stabilized in its new form.

Choux pastry is the basis of a number of excellent dishes and can be fried or baked, mixed with cheese, filled with cream or covered with chocolate, like the famous chocolate éclair. It is not really difficult to make, but it needs care, so I shall explain in detail.

4 *ozs flour*, 3 *ozs butter*, ½ *oz caster sugar*, 4 *eggs*.

Pour ⅜-pint of water into a medium-sized saucepan and add the sugar, butter and a good pinch of salt. Bring to the boil and then lift the saucepan off the fire. Using your left hand, shake the flour into the saucepan little by little, stirring all the time with a wooden spoon.

The flour mixes with the liquid to form a paste. This becomes a very stiff, unappetizing mass. Now put the saucepan on a very low fire stirring the paste with the wooden spoon. Soon it forms a single ball and, as you stir it begins to glisten. When it begins to stick to the bottom of the saucepan, lift it from the fire. All this has taken about 10 minutes.

Put the saucepan on the table and break in an egg. Try to mix it with the paste. This is not easy. The yolk slips away from your spoon. Catch it and break it, and with a little patience you will mix it smoothly into your paste. Repeat this manoeuvre with the second, third and fourth egg. If the paste is too runny the *choux* will not keep their shape, so beat the fourth egg with a fork and add it cautiously, a little at a time, stopping as soon as the paste reaches the consistency of thick Devonshire cream. All this time you have been working air into the paste and it is this air which will make it swell.

Your paste is now ready. It will not run, but it is very soft. You can use this in various ways.

Pets de Nonne.

Heat the oil in a deep-frying-pan and then lower the flame. If you were to put the *choux* pastry into fat which was too hot, the egg in the pastry would coagulate and the surface would become too hard to allow the air in the pastry to expand. For this reason, you should reduce the heat.

Scoop up teaspoonfuls of *choux* pastry and drop them into the deep-frying-pan, detaching them from the spoon with your finger. (You will notice that for me, the finger is one of the most useful implements in the kitchen.)

Drop a dozen little balls of paste into the hot fat and watch them swimming on the surface. They swell gently, become plumper still and roll over and over like small porpoises.

Raise the heat so that they turn golden-brown, then lift them out with a wire strainer and put them on a hot dish. Sprinkle them with icing sugar. Of course you will taste one at once and of course you will burn your tongue. Inside their crisp skin they are soft and very, very good.

It has taken about 10 minutes so far to fry the *pets de nonne* You will finish the rest of the paste in another 10 minutes.

Profiterolles.

Using a teaspoon, arrange small nuts of *choux* paste on a buttered baking sheet. Put this in a hot oven (about 425° F. Gas 6). If the oven were much hotter than this the egg would, as I have explained before, harden too rapidly.

After 20 minutes you will have great big golden puffs with hollow centres. Serve then with a chocolate-flavoured *crème anglaise*.

Choux à la Crème.

Make some *profiterolles* and allow them to cool. Meanwhile, prepare a *crème pâtissière* with:

> 2 *yolks of egg, 2 ozs caster sugar flavoured with vanilla,*
> 1¾ *ozs cornflour, ½ pint milk, the white of an egg.*

Cream the yolks of egg with 1 tablespoon of sugar and then stir in the flour and about 4 tablespoons of milk. Boil the rest of the milk and then lift it off the fire. Stir it into the yolks of egg. When the mixture is well blended, return the pan to the fire and stir until it boils. Now pour it into a basin to cool.

Whip the white of egg until it is stiff, whisk in 1 tablespoon of sugar and then gradually fold in the rest. Whisk up the creamed egg yolks and stir in the white of egg and sugar meringue with gentle movements.

Cut the *profiterolles* in two horizontally and sandwich cream between the two halves. Frost the tops with dry icing sugar.

Merveilles.

Merveilles, like the next two or three recipes, are cooked in a deep-frying-pan. They are small strips of sweet paste which, after frying, are drained and sprinkled with sugar and they can be eaten either hot or cold. Since *merveilles* last for several days it is wise to make a good batch at a time and enjoy them instead of pudding, at tea-time or even, as I do, with your morning coffee.

> 1 *lb flour, 3 eggs, 3 ozs thick cream, 2 small glasses rum,*
> 3 *ozs caster sugar, a little milk, 4 ozs butter, cinnamon.*

Put the flour into a basin, making a hollow in the middle. Into this put the eggs, cream, rum, sugar and half a small teaspoon of salt. Blend them together with a wooden spoon. This is not easy, as the egg yolks slip away from the spoon and the whites are reluctant to mix with the flour. To make things easier, add a couple of tablespoonfuls of milk. Now your paste becomes smooth.

Melt the butter in a small saucepan and pour it, when it is tepid, into the paste. Blend well, and if the paste is rather too liquid sieve in a little more flour. The paste should be fairly firm. Now lift it onto a floured board and knead it with your hands until it is smooth and does not stick to your fingers. Return it to the bowl and let it rest for 30 minutes.

Lift a piece of paste the size of your fist onto a floured board. Roll it out into a round about $\frac{1}{16}$-inch thick and cut it into rectangles about the length and breadth of two fingers. Lay these out side by side on a floured surface and continue rolling and cutting until you have used all the paste.

Heat the deep-frying-pan, which should contain fresh oil, until it is smoking hot, then throw in about 15 *merveilles*. They curl up and colour. When they are pale coffee-coloured lift them out with a wire strainer, and let them drain for 10 seconds on soft kitchen paper or a clean cloth. Arrange them on a dish and sprinkle with sugar mixed with a little cinnamon.

Continue until all the *merveilles* are ready. You should have about three dishes full, crisp and fragrant.

Beignets Soufflés.

> 2 *eggs, milk,* 1 *oz baker's yeast,* $3\frac{1}{2}$ *ozs sugar, 2 ozs*
> *butter, about* 14 *ozs flour.*

Break the eggs into a bowl and beat them with $\frac{1}{8}$-pint of milk and add the yeast which has been dissolved in 2 tablespoons of milk.

Melt the butter and when it is tepid pour it into the bowl

together with the sugar, and a pinch of salt. Add the flour little by little, stirring with a wooden spoon. When the paste has reached the consistency of a thick cream, beat it for 10 minutes. This serves to break down any lumps and to blend the yeast well into the mixture.

Cover the bowl with a clean cloth and leave it in a warm place for 2 hours. The mixture will rise and will probably fill your bowl. Now you must heat the deep-frying-pan until the oil is smoking hot.

Using a dessertspoon, scoop up a small ball of paste and detach it with your finger so that it falls into the hot fat. Make a dozen *beignets* and let them bob and turn in the hot oil for 5 or 6 minutes. They swell, puff out and turn golden-brown. Lift them out with a wire strainer and let them drain. Sprinkle them, while still warm, with sugar flavoured with vanilla.

Continue like this until you have used all the paste. I was able to make about 39 *beignets* with this mixture. Please don't confuse these *beignets* with *Pets de Nonne*, for which I have given you a recipe on page 196. They are quite different.

Bottreaux.

This is a recipe from the Charente and *bottreaux* are rather similar to *merveilles* (p. 197). Since the Charentais cooking is rather heavy, in the middle of a traditional meal they drink a small glass of cognac called '*le coup du milieu*'. This is supposed to help the digestion.

> 12 *ozs flour*, 4½ *ozs sugar*, 2 *eggs*, 5 *ozs butter*, 1 *small glass cognac.*

Mix the flour, sugar, eggs, 2½ ozs of butter and cognac together with 3 tablespoons of water and a pinch of salt, using the tips of your fingers. Use just enough water to make a firm paste which does not stick to your hands. If you should add a little too much, correct this with some more flour. Form the paste into a ball, cover it with a clean napkin and leave it to rest for 1 hour.

Roll out the paste on a floured board and spread over it the rest of the butter which you have softened in a warm place. Fold the paste in three lengthwise, then in three crosswise so that you have a rectangle about 6 inches square. Cover this with the napkin and let it rest for 15 minutes.

Roll out the paste once more and fold it again in three,

crosswise and lengthwise. Let it rest for another 10 minutes. Now roll it out to a thickness of about ⅛-inch and cut it into lozenges about 1½ inches long.

Fry the *bottreaux* in smoking hot fat and serve them while still warm.

Krapfen.

Krapfen are said to have originated in Vienna, though I have eaten them all over Eastern Europe, in Warsaw and Moscow and the St. Petersburg of years ago, and they were always described as local specialities. In fact, they are very similar to English doughnuts, but there is a subtle difference, so I shall tell you how to make them.

> *About 20 ozs flour, 3½ ozs butter (very soft from standing in a warm place), ¼ oz sugar, 1 oz baker's yeast, 3 tablespoons milk, 2 eggs, apricot jam, 5 ozs icing sugar, the white of an egg.*

Warm a medium-sized mixing bowl with hot water. Empty and dry it and when it is lukewarm put the yeast into it and stir in the milk, which you have warmed to blood heat. Mix the yeast and milk with a wooden spoon until there are no lumps and then add 8½ ozs of the flour, stirring first with the spoon and then working with your fingers. The dough clings to your fingers. It is a horrible feeling. Add the sugar and a couple of pinches of salt and go on mixing.

Mix in the butter, still working the paste with your fingers. It begins to firm up and does not cling quite so much. You must persevere, and so that you do not find this too irksome I shall explain why.

The yeast must be spread evenly right through the dough. Each particle of yeast consists of microscopic fungoid growths. These multiply, decompose the sugar in the dough and consume it. They breath the oxygen in the mixture and liberate carbon dioxide. Later, in the warmth, this carbon dioxide expands and the dough rises. If the particles of yeast are evenly distributed the minute bubbles of carbon dioxide will be too. If not, during cooking, the dough will form a great hole in one place whilst in another it will be dense and heavy and unleavened. In order to work the dough properly you must copy the bakers.

Flour a pastry-board, then take up the dough in both hands and throw it on the board with all your strength. Do this again and again for 5 minutes, then put the dough into the mixing bowl, cover it with a hot napkin and stand it in a warm place for 2 hours to prove.

At the end of 2 hours the dough should have tripled in volume. It smells delicious. Once more you must manhandle it. Throw it down on the floured pastry-board again and again for 2 minutes. It will diminish in volume. Never mind. Sprinkle the board with flour once more and put half the dough on it, sprinkling this too with flour. Knead it with your hands, adding flour as you do so, then roll it out to the thickness of a half-crown.

Using a tumbler, cut the dough into rounds and arrange these on a floured cloth. You will be left with a sort of lace-work of paste. Knead this together with the other half of the dough, working in some more flour, and cut this too into rounds. You will now have some scraps. Put these carefully on one side.

Put half the rounds back onto the floured board and on the centre of each a lump of very thick apricot jam the size of a walnut. It is essential that the jam be without any trace of runny juice.

Brush over each of the rounds which are standing on the napkin with the white of an egg which you have mixed with its own volume of water. Lay each of these rounds on top of one of these with apricot jam so that the moist surface is in contact with the jam and the dough which surrounds it. Dip your fingertips in flour and firm the edges very delicately so that the jam is hermetically closed into its little nest. You should have about 21 *krapfen*.

Cover the pastry-board with white paper and set it in a warm place. Wait for two hours and then lift the paper. The *krapfen* are swelling, though the upper half has risen more than the lower. This is quite understandable since the lower half meets the resistance of the pastry-board. To overcome this difficulty, turn them over and wait another hour. Now they have risen all over.

Now heat the deep-frying-pan which should be three-quarters full of oil. The oil must not be too hot and this is where the scraps of dough will prove invaluable. Without waiting for the oil to smoke let a piece of paste fall into the pan. If it remains at the bottom, the oil is not hot enough. If it floats, the temperature is right.

It is important, however, not to make the oil too hot since

this would cause the egg contained in the dough to coagulate and the surface of the *krapfen* to harden so that it would not yield to the pressure of the gas which is formed by the action of the hot oil.

As soon as the oil is hot enough, put 8 *krapfen* into the pan and lower the heat. They swell up and become round as balloons. In 3 minutes the submerged surfaces become golden-brown. Turn them with a wire strainer and fry for another 3 minutes, *always over a low heat*, then lift them out and drain them on soft paper or a cloth. Let them get completely cold while you fry the rest of the *krapfen*.

Whilst the *krapfen* are cooling, sieve the icing sugar into a bowl and mix it with a teaspoon of cold water. Stir it well with a fork until you have a thick cream like toothpaste. Dip each *krapfen* into the sugar so that one half is completely coated and arrange them on a dish sugar-side upwards. The icing sugar quickly dries into a crisp coating. The *krapfen* are ready. To-day they are delicious but tomorrow they will be better still. I wish I could be there to eat them with my breakfast coffee. How many, you say? Oh, I should eat at least ten. Ten, you say, aghast. Yes, ten, but then you will not be surprised to hear that I weigh . . . no, I shall not tell you my weight. I am sure you will not grudge me this innocent coquetry.

Platée de Pommes.

This is a dish which you can very well make with windfall apples. The apples are baked in butter and sugar, covered with a slightly flaky crust. The art is to coat the slices of apple with caramel.

> 2 *lbs apples*, 4 *ozs caster sugar*, 6 *ozs butter, a small glass cognac*, 5½ *ozs flour*, 1 *tablespoon thick cream*.

First of all make the pastry so that it has time to rest while you prepare the apples. Put the flour into a mixing bowl with 3½ ozs of butter, 3 tablespoons of cold water and two pinches of salt. Work the ingredients together with your fingertips. You will not succeed in making a smooth paste but don't worry. Turn it onto a floured board and roll out to a thickness of about ⅜-inch.

Fold the pastry into three lengthwise and then into three crosswise and cover it with a clean napkin. Let it rest for 10 minutes, then roll it out and fold it as before. Cover it with the napkin and turn your attention to the apples. The pastry will wait quite happily.

Peel the apples and cut them in slices about ⅛-inch thick, discarding the cores, of course. Take an oval flameproof dish and spread it with 2 ozs of butter. Arrange half the apple slices evenly in the dish and sprinkle them with half the sugar. Dot this layer with another 2 ozs of butter and cover it with the rest of the apples, sprinkling them with the sugar you have left, and the cognac.

Now roll out the pastry into an oval a tiny bit smaller than the surface of the dish and prick it with a fork in about 20 places. Lay the pastry on the apples taking care that it *does not* touch the sides of the dish. Brush the pastry with double cream and put the dish in a hot oven (425° F.).

The butter melts quickly and the apples exude moisture. Since the pastry does not touch the sides of the dish part of this moisture evaporates. The pastry begins to colour. After a good half-hour everything is cooked—but there is no caramel.

Lift the dish from the oven and put it onto the cooking plate of your stove. The liquid in the dish begins to boil and evaporates rapidly. Suddenly there is a delicious smell of caramel. The pastry crust, however, has softened, so the dish must go back into the oven for 5 minutes.

Now the pastry is crisp once more and ready for the table. Serve each of your guests with apples soaked in butter and caramel, a slice of crust and a little juice. Drink with your *platée* a glass of rather sweet Sauternes.

The Apples of Apicius.

Apicius was a Roman citizen who was born about the year 25 B.C. He was a great gourmet and, as such, his fame has lasted to this day, largely owing to a collection of ten books on Roman cookery said to have been written by him. One day I should like to tell you more about this curious collection, but now I shall only give you one very simple dish made with apples. You must not be startled at its composition. Remember that the Romans did not know sugar and that they left to the barbarians the use of butter. This had been known in Rome since the sixth century B.C., but it was only eaten by the Scythians and the Thracians. The Romans, on the other hand, used and abused olive oil, honey and an enormous number of fragrant spices.

The apples to which Apicius has given his name are hollowed out and filled with honey flavoured with cumin, aniseed or peppermint and wrapped in a sort of pastry made with olive oil. The Romans used then to wrap them in cabbage leaves and cook them in hot ashes. We shall cook them in the oven.

> 2 *large cooking apples, 7 ozs flour, 6 tablespoons olive oil, thick clear honey, powdered cumin or dried mint, a glass dry white wine.*

Peel the apples and core them, taking care not to pierce the skin on the underside. You must make a generous hole. Into the bottom of this hole sprinkle powdered cumin, or failing this, some crushed dried mint. (I think we should leave the peppermint to the Romans.) Now fill the hole with thick, clear honey.

Using your fingertips mix the olive oil and flour with two pinches of salt, adding gradually 3 tablespoons of water. When you have a ball of smooth paste, roll half of it out to a thickness of $\frac{1}{8}$-inch. Place an apple in the centre and, with your two hands, lift the pastry round the apple so that it is completely covered. Snip off the surplus pastry with scissors and firm down the folds with the palm of your hand. Wrap the second apple in the same way and brush the surfaces with olive oil.

Rub a baking-sheet with oil and place the apples on it. Put them into a good, but not too hot, oven (375° F. Gas 4) for 30 minutes. Lift out the apples. They are covered with a magnificent golden crust. Put them on a hot dish and prepare the sauce.

Stir a glass of dry white wine into 4 ozs of honey, heating as you do so, but do not let them boil. Serve the apples on a dish, and the sauce separately. Cut each apple in half and let your guests pour the honeyed wine over the golden crust.

The Romans regarded this dish as a great delicacy, varying its flavour by using honeys from different flowers with the wines which specially suited them.

Country Tarts.

I have learnt a great deal about baking from my neighbour in the country, a charming grandmother who often tells me how her mother, each time she made a batch of bread, used to bake little fruit tarts and give them to her friends. This is not the way to make one's fortune, and the old lady left nothing to her daughter who, resigned but cheerful, ends her little story with a proverb which I have heard from no other lips: "A good heart is sometimes a bad asset."

My kind neighbour gave me her mother's recipe, but I must own that I have modified it a little as, personally, I do not care for lard in pastry. I even broadcast my version over the Paris radio, secure in the knowledge that the old lady would not hear it as, although there is a wireless set in her house, my neighbour is stone deaf. So, apart from this small modification, I shall tell you how fruits tarts were made in the Ile-de-France in 1865.

This recipe is made with fresh bread dough. Ask your baker if he will let you have some freshly-made. You will probably have to arrange this the day before and collect it as soon as possible after it is ready.

½ lb bread dough, 3 ozs butter, 1½ lbs cherries,
5 ozs caster sugar.

Put the dough into a mixing bowl with the butter and work them together with your fingertips. When it is smooth, turn it onto a floured board and roll it out to a thickness of ⅓-inch. This tart should be baked in a flan ring and to line the ring you will need a round of dough 1½ inches bigger than the surface of the finished tart.

Grease the flan ring, and the baking sheet on which it will stand, with a little butter. Lay the pastry over it and, lifting the edges slightly push them delicately against the sides of the ring. Press the palm of your hand against the edge of the ring so that the surplus dough falls away. This can be gathered together, rolled out, and used to make a smaller tart. Prick the dough here and there with a fork.

Remove the stones from the cherries using a new metal hairpin which, if you wish to be meticulous, you can hold for a moment in a flame before starting. Fill the tart with two layers of cherries and sprinkle it thickly with caster sugar. Put it in a very hot oven for 20 minutes. (450° F. Gas 8–9.)

When you open the oven door you will have a shock. It is not a pretty sight. The edges of the tart are slightly burnt and the top layer of cherries blackened in places. The bottom of the tart is filled with very runny juice. Well, it can't be helped. You must not cook it any longer or it will burn. Sprinkle more sugar into the cherries to thicken the juice.

Now slip the tart onto a dish, removing the flan ring. Let it get cold and carry it to table. It will be received without much enthusiasm for, frankly, it is not too prepossessing!

Don't be discouraged. Cut the first slice and the juice will run out. Now try it. What a surprise! The tart is neither crisp nor soggy, and just tinged with cherry juice. The cherries have kept all their flavour and the juice is not sticky—just pure cherry juice. They had some very good ideas in 1865!

Tarte Parisienne.

> *7 ozs flour, 3½ ozs butter, 1 egg, 1 oz caster sugar, 1½ lbs morello cherries, half a small pot of gooseberry jelly.*

Mix everything but the cherries into a smooth paste using the tips of your fingers and roll it out ⅛-inch thick, on a floured board.

Butter a flan case, lay the pastry on it and firm it gently in place with your fingertips. Prick the bottom of the tart with a fork and cut off the surplus pastry by pressing with the palm of your hand on the edge of the ring. Lay a piece of crumpled greaseproof paper in the bottom and cover it with haricot beans.

Heat the oven to 400° F. (Gas 6) and put the tart to bake for 15 minutes. The edges are now golden-brown but when you lift the greaseproof paper you see that the bottom is not cooked. Remove the paper and beans, and return the tart to the oven for a good 10 minutes more.

Meanwhile, stone the cherries, using a new metal hairpin, and put them into a saucepan with a tablespoon of caster sugar and 1 tablespoon of water. Bring them to the boil and let them cook for 5 minutes. Strain off the juice and fill the tart with the half-cooked fruit.

Boil the cherry juice until the water has nearly all evaporated, then mix it with the gooseberry jelly, heating until this melts and mixes with the cherry juice. Pour the melted jelly over the cherries. As it cools it will set. The tart is superb, but my daughter prefers the country tart I have just described . . . and I do myself.

Tarte Alsacienne.

> *7 ozs flour, 3½ ozs butter, 1 egg and 3 yolks of egg, 4 ozs caster sugar, a small glass of Kirsch, 1 lb morello cherries.*

Prepare some pastry as in the previous recipe and line a flan case. Fill the centre with raw, stoned cherries.

Put the egg yolks, the rest of the sugar, the Kirsch and a tablespoon of flour into a bowl and beat them with a wire whisk, adding gradually 1½ glasses of milk. When the mixture is smooth, pour it over the cherries and put the tart into a hot oven (425° F. Gas 7).

After 30 minutes open the oven door gently. The tart is not quite ready yet. Plunge the tip of a knife into the cream. It emerges slightly coated. Let the tart cook for another 10 minutes and test it once more with your knife. The blade remains clean. The tart is puffed up and splendid. Take it out of the oven and don't be disappointed that it falls slightly.

Let the tart cool, then slice it and try it. My favourite is still the simple country tart, though I must admit that this one is very good. You can, if you wish, substitute slices of raw apple for the cherries.

Alsatian Rhubarb Tart.

Rhubarb powder, which was once such a popular laxative, has fallen into neglect, totally outshone by its modern rivals which take up so much of present-day advertizing space.

Before reaching Europe rhubarb—*Rheum palmatum* in Latin —made prodigious journeys from three different sources, China, Persia and, according to ancient writers, Muscovy. The name Muscovy shows that this rhubarb must have reached us well before the time of Peter the Great when Russia, still at loggerheads with the Mongols, called itself the Czarate of Moscow.

From time immemorial the Orientals appreciated the laxative properties of rhubarb. Later, chemists discovered that these were due to the presence of chrisophanic acid which is found in considerable quantities in the root of the plant. The stem and the leaves contain little, but enough to take into account.

One day, during the First World War, when we were very short of vegetables, I prepared for myself and the orderlies attached to my ambulance, a dish of 'spinach', only the spinach was replaced by rhubarb leaves. We all suffered from terrible colic. So beware of rhubarb leaves, they have been the cause of serious poisoning.

There is no need to eat rhubarb in quantities. Just a few

spoonfuls of rhubarb purée or *compote* give a wonderful filip to dishes which are inclined to be a little insipid. It is excellent in tarts and, if you find the traditional English rhubarb tart a little sharp for your taste you will appreciate the Alsatian version, which is sweeter. To make the pastry you will need:

> 7 *ozs flour*, 3½ *ozs butter*, 1 *yolk of egg*, 1 *oz thick cream*,
> 1 *tablespoon sugar*, 2 *pinches salt*.

Mix all the ingredients with your fingers. They are a little dry, so you will need a teaspoonful or so of water. Put the paste onto a floured board and roll it out as before. Line a flan case as I have described in previous recipes.

Wash half a bunch of rhubarb and cut it in pieces.

Make a cream, by mixing in a bowl:

> ¼ *pint double cream*, ½ *glass milk*, 3 *yolks of egg, a tea-
> spoon flour, a scant* 3 *ozs caster sugar*, 2 *or* 3 *drops of
> pure vanilla essence.*

Pour the cream into the tart and cover it with a *single* layer of rhubarb. Put it into a very hot oven (450° F. Gas 8).

Bake the tart for 35 minutes, then lift it out and, while it is still warm, remove it from the flan case. Serve it cold, sprinkled with sugar. I must confess that I prefer this to a '*tarte anglaise*' made with plain stewed rhubarb.

Tarte à la Gelée.

> 1½ *lbs cooking apples*, 6 *ozs caster sugar*, 2 *or* 3 *drops pure
> vanilla essence*, ½ *lb flour*, 3½ *ozs butter*, 4 *pinches of salt*.

Peel and core the apples. You can afford to do this rapidly since, if the peel is rather thick you are not being extravagant. All these trimmings, instead of being thrown away, serve to make excellent jelly for your tart.

Leave 2 apples whole and make the rest into a purée, adding 2 ozs of sugar, vanilla and a ½-glass of water. As soon as the apples break beneath your fork and become fluffy, the purée is ready.

Put the peel, cores and pips of the apples into a saucepan with a glass of cold water. Bring them to the boil and let them cook for 10 minutes.

While the apples are cooking make a *pâte brisée*, mixing the flour and butter with 4 pinches of salt and a scant ¼-pint of water. You may need to add a trace more flour or a few extra drops of water. As soon as the pastry is smooth, roll it out and line a buttered flan case as I have described in the recipe for a country tart on p. 204.

Fill the case with apple purée which you have allowed to cool slightly. Slice the two remaining apples and arrange the slices prettily on the purée. Sprinkle with sugar and put the tart into a good oven (400° F. Gas 5).

Now return to your apple trimmings. Strain the liquid from the saucepan into another small pan, pressing the pulp with a spoon to extract as much juice as possible. Add 4 ozs of sugar and simmer for about 12 minutes. The liquid thickens. You have made the jelly. Draw it off the fire.

A delicious smell is coming from the oven. The edges of the pastry are turning golden-brown but the slices of apple are still white. About 20 minutes have passed. Leave the tart for another 5 minutes. The apples begin to colour. Ten minutes more and the edges of each slice begin to darken. Take the tart out of the oven and let it cool for a quarter of an hour, then remove it from the flan case and set it on a dish.

Wait for an hour until the tart is really cold. The jelly in your small saucepan has set. Warm it slightly so that it melts, and spoon it over the apples. The tart is really superb.

Tarte Pâtissière.

Now supposing that when you were preparing the previous recipe you had inadvertently thrown away the apple trimmings, what would you do? Prepare the tart as before, and put it in the oven filled with apple purée, omitting the slices of apple on top.

While the tart is baking, make a *crème pâtissière*. Heat a cup of milk flavoured with two or three drops of vanilla. Whisk together in a bowl:

> 2 *yolks of egg*, 1 *tablespoon flour*, 3 *tablespoons caster sugar.*

The result will be a stiff cream into which you mix the boiling milk. Pour it all back into the saucepan and stir until the cream is boiling. Let the cream cool a little. When the tart is done and has cooled for a few minutes, remove it from the flan case and spread the tepid cream over the apple purée.

When the tart has cooled completely, sieve some icing sugar over it and, with a red hot poker trace on the sugar a lattice-work of caramel or the initials of some special person. To crown your enjoyment of this delicious tart, I suggest a sip of champagne.

Strawberry Tart.

When the first garden strawberries of the year make their timid appearance they are still small and terribly expensive. How is one to eat them? With cream and a trace of cognac or Maraschino? No, one must savour to the full the flavour of these first fruits of early summer. I like to sprinkle them with pure white sugar and add nothing else to distract from their own fresh fragrance.

It is a strange thing that fresh strawberries, so firm and red and glistening, lose all their charm as soon as they are cooked. They become limp and livid, and their individuality is lost along with their vitamins. So, unless you are making jam, strawberries should never be cooked, not even in a tart, but should appear as if fresh-picked from beneath the leaves which shelter them.

So let us make a strawberry tart, but with fresh strawberries. You will need:

> *A punnet of fresh strawberries, ¼ pint of double cream, half a small pot of gooseberry jelly, 3½ ozs flour, 7ozs butter.*

Put the flour and butter into a bowl with a couple of pinches of salt and work them together rapidly with your fingertips, adding about half a glass of water. You must work lightly and quickly so that the heat of your hands does not melt the butter, and you must stop before the butter and flour are completely blended. Cover the ball of pastry with a clean napkin and let it rest for an hour.

Turn the dough out onto a floured pastry-board and roll it into a strip about ⅛-inch thick. Fold it in three and turn it round so that the open edge is facing you. Repeat once more. Set the pastry aside covered with a napkin for another ten minutes then roll it into a circle about 8 inches in diameter and fill a flan case, tapping it gently into place with your fingertips. Turn the pastry which extends over the edge of the flan inwards, and firm it into place with the back of a fork. Prick the bottom of the tart with a fork and cover it with crumpled greaseproof paper and a layer of haricot beans.

Bake in a hot oven (400° F. Gas 5). After 20 minutes the edges of the tart begin to colour. Take it out of the oven and remove the greaseproof paper and the haricot beans. The pastry is pallid and anaemic-looking. Put it back in the oven for 10 minutes, look at it once more, and when it is a delicate golden-brown take it out and let it cool a little. Whilst still tepid, remove it from the flan case and set it on a dish to cool completely.

Only when your guests have already arrived, spread the bottom of the tart with cream, and cover it with a layer of strawberries which you have cleaned, washed in cold water and dried very carefully with a cloth. Sprinkle them lightly with caster sugar and pour over them the gooseberry jelly which you have melted just sufficiently to allow it to pour. Now your tart appears in all its splendour. Set it to chill.

This tart is bound to rouse the enthusiasm of your friends. First, when it makes its appearance on the table; then when the freshness of the strawberries contrasts with the flavour of the gooseberry jelly and finally when the cream, like a caress, blends in a single sensation the perfume of this most fragrant of all fruits with the delicate, friable texture of the pastry. A strawberry tart is really a work of art.

Clafoutis.

Cherries are full of gaiety, full of Springtime. When the cherry trees are in flower they seem to be covered with snow. In fruit, they seem to be splashed with brilliant blood.

Here are some lines of poetry which, in French, are full of the spirit of spring and the cherry trees. Translated, they would lose their charm, so for those who can enjoy them, I give them just as they are:

> *Quand nous chanterons le temps des cerises,*
> *Et gai rossignol et merle moqueur*
> > *Seront tous en fête!*
> *Les belles auront la folie en tête,*
> *Et les amoureux du soleil au coeur.*
>
> *Quand nous chanterons le temps des cerises,*
> *Sifflera bien mieux le merle moqueur.*

Now I shall tell you how to make *clafoutis*, a dish which comes from the centre of France. It consists of cherries plunged into a sort of thick cream and baked in the oven in an earthenware dish.

> 1½ *lbs cherries, 3 eggs, 2 ozs flour, 4 ozs caster sugar,*
> 4 *ozs thick cream, 2½ glasses milk, a small glass Kirsch.*

Strip the stalks from the cherries, but leave the stones.

Put the fruit into a big fireproof earthenware dish. You will have two or three layers.

Using a wire whisk, beat the eggs and sugar together in a bowl. When they become white and slightly frothy add the flour and a large pinch of salt. Continue to beat briskly, adding the cream and the Kirsch.

Now, little by little, stir in the milk. You will have a thin cream which you pour over the cherries.

Put the dish in a fairly hot oven (about 370° F. Gas 5) and wait for half an hour. The cream thickens. Raise the heat a little. The surface of the *clafoutis* begins to colour. Test it with the tip of a knife. If the knife comes out clean it is ready.

Take the dish from the oven and let it cool. Serve it just as it is for pudding. I should even like to eat it at tea-time. But remember that you left the stones in the cherries, and be careful not to break your teeth.

Piroshki with Cherries.

This is a Polish dish and the *piroshki* are little envelopes of noodle paste each containing some cherries. They should be poached in water and eaten very hot, sprinkled with sugar and thick cream.

> 1¼ *lbs black cherries, 2 eggs, 10 ozs flour, caster sugar and cream.*

Stone the cherries and put them into a shallow bowl.

Beat the eggs with a glass of water using a wire whisk. Add the flour, still using the whisk until the paste becomes too stiff to handle. At this point you must abandon the whisk, scraping it clean. Add a little more flour, mixing with your fingers. You will have a ball of paste, still rather sticky. Put it onto a floured board and knead it with two hands. It no longer sticks to your fingers. The paste is ready. Let it rest for a quarter of an hour.

Scrape the board clean with a knife and sprinkle it with fresh flour. Roll out half the paste to the thickness of a new penny. Working across the top of the circle of paste, make little heaps of 3 or 4 cherries with about an inch between each. Now fold the paste over and press it down between each heap of cherries using the side of your hand. Cut the semi-circles with a wine glass and firm down the edges with your fingertips dipped in flour. You will have five or six *piroshki*.

Trim the edge of the paste and continue folding and cutting until you have used all the paste and all the cherries. You should have about 30 *piroshki*.

Bring 3 or 4 pints of salted water to the boil in a large saucepan and drop in the *piroshki*. Let them boil for 5 minutes then lift them out and drain them. Serve them on a hot plate.

Everyone takes half a dozen or so and eats them, sprinkled with sugar and cream. They should be eaten with a spoon at the end of a light meal.

Cherry Pudding.

The cherry season is very short and one is always touched with sadness when it comes to an end. Sad too is the story of the song which is still passed on from one generation to another, '*Le Temps des Cerises*'. In 1867 a young poet, Jean-Baptiste Clément, sat in a shabby room watching at the death-bed of a friend. To cheer her a little he composed the first verse of the song, which he recited. The dying girl murmured, "It's charming. Go on," and he improvised the whole poem.

The girl died and the poet wept and the song was written. One day the poet suffered from the cold. He went to a publisher and exchanged his poem for an overcoat. Whilst the publisher made two million francs from the song the poet, in a moment of need, pawned the overcoat for fourteen francs, and that is all he got out of his lovely song.

Here is a pudding which can be made with the last transparent red cherries of the season.

2 lbs cherries, ½ lb flour, ¼ lb chopped suet.

Put the flour and suet in a bowl with a pinch of salt. Rub these lightly together with the tips of your fingers. Make a well in the centre of the basin and add cold water, very gradually, with your left hand while you mix with the right. Make a smooth dough and turn it onto a floured board, leaving the basin quite clean. Work the paste lightly with your hands to remove any cracks and then roll it out in one direction only, dusting a little flour beneath the dough when necessary to prevent it sticking to the board. Dust the rolling pin with flour too, but only as much as you need to prevent its sticking otherwise the crust will become hard.

When the paste is about ¼-inch thick fold it over the rolling pin and lift it onto a buttered pudding basin, moulding it gently into a lining. Trim off the surplus paste with scissors, leaving a small margin. Fill the bowl with cherries which you have stripped of their stalks, but not stoned. Add sugar and a pinch of spice.

Make the remaining paste into a ball and roll it out to form a lid. Fold the edges of the lid together with the rim of the suet crust which lines the bowl, so that the cherries are hermetically sealed into the pudding.

Cover the bowl with greaseproof paper and a cloth big enough to reach down to the bottom. Tie firmly with string at the base of the bowl and cut away the surplus cloth and paper with scissors.

Put the bowl into a large saucepan and pour in enough boiling water to reach almost to the rim of the bowl. Cover the saucepan and put it on the fire. Let it simmer for 2 hours, adding water when necessary. Lift the bowl from the saucepan and remove the cloth and the paper. Carry the pudding to table.

Remove the lid of suet crust, cutting it away on a level with the rim of the pudding basin. There is a wonderful smell of cherries. Serve each of your guests with a helping of fruit and a slice of crust fragrant with cherry juice.

Gâteau aux Marrons.

    1 ½ *lbs chestnuts, 4 ozs caster sugar, 4 ozs cooking chocolate, 4 ozs butter.*

With a very sharp knife make an incision round each chestnut starting at the base, passing over the point and down to the base again. Wash the chestnuts carefully and put them into a saucepan of cold water. Bring the water to the boil and let it boil for a minute only, then drain the chestnuts in a colander and refresh them under the cold tap (this, so that you don't burn your fingers).

Take each chestnut in turn and squeeze the shell. The nut pops out white and clean, free of both its inner and outer covering. It really is miraculous.

Put the peeled chestnuts back into the saucepan and cover them with cold water. Bring it to the boil and put the lid on the pan. Simmer the chestnuts for 20 minutes and then test them with the point of a knife. When they are done, drain them and dry them in a cloth.

Put the chestnuts through a sieve or '*Mouli*', add the sugar and let them cool a little. Grate the chocolate and melt it rapidly in very little water, stirring all the time. When it is smooth and creamy add the butter and let it melt. Pour this over the chestnuts and work together with a wooden spoon until you have a soft, tepid mass. This is the same mixture as one uses for the Yule Log (p. 220).

Grease a shallow round bowl with oil, and spoon the chestnut cream into it. You should have a layer about 1½ inches deep. Firm it down with the back of a spoon and stand it in a cool place for 5 hours. Turn the *gâteau* out onto a flat dish. It will have a marvellous flat surface which you can decorate with *crème fouettée*.

> 6 *ozs thick cream, milk, 2 or 3 drops of vanilla, 2 whites of egg, 2 heaping teaspoons icing sugar, grated chocolate.*

Put the cream, which should be very cool, into a bowl and add the vanilla and a couple of tablespoonfuls of milk. Whip with an egg beater. The cream mounts and becomes frothy. If it is too thick, add a teaspoonful of milk. Beat hard for 3 minutes more. It should now form a firm mousse.

Wash the beater in cold water and dry it carefully. This is very important. Put 2 whites of egg in a second small bowl and beat them for 2 minutes. They should be stiff enough to form a point when you lift out the beater. Fold the whites into the whipped cream with a fork and then stir in, very gently, 2 good teaspoonfuls of sieved icing sugar.

Pile the cream onto the chestnut *gâteau* and sprinkle it with grated chocolate.

Pumpkin Gratin.

This dish is Jewish in origin and like many Jewish dishes its history goes back to the earliest culinary records. During the century-long wanderings of the Jewish people this dish has suffered various modifications and it is certainly most doubtful whether the crushed macaroons it contains were used in the time of Moses. Now, *Gratin de Courge* is eaten mainly in Portugal.

> 3 *lbs of pumpkin, 4 ozs shelled almonds, 8 ozs caster sugar, 2 ozs dry macaroons, 2 yolks of egg.*

Cut the pumpkin in two, remove the seeds and the woody fibres and detach the pulp from the skin. Cut the flesh into small cubes and put them into a saucepan. Add 4 tablespoons of water and, when this begins to boil, lower the heat slightly and cook the pumpkin for 10 minutes. The juice runs out and the pumpkin begins to soften. Boil for 10 minutes more. The pulp begins to be soft enough to mash with a fork. Cook for a little while longer and then mash thoroughly. The pumpkin is very fluid, so leave it uncovered on a low fire, stirring constantly with a wooden spoon. Reduce the heat still further as great bubbles of steam will form and burst, splashing the purée over the saucepan edge.

About half an hour has passed and the purée is now very thick. Put it through a sieve.

Blanch the almonds by throwing them into boiling water. Leave them for 5 minutes and empty them into a colander. Hold them for a moment beneath the cold tap. Their skins are all wrinkled and can be easily slipped off with your fingers.

Mince the almonds. In order not to waste any, follow them with a piece of stale bread to drive the last remains of almond out of the mincer. As soon as the bread appears in the holes of the mincer you know that all the almonds have passed through. (You can, of course, use a '*Mouli*' or an electric grater.)

Mix the tepid pumpkin purée, most of the almonds and most of the sugar. Add the yolks of eggs and blend them well together. Rub a fireproof dish with oil and fill it with pumpkin mixture. You should have a layer about 1½ inches deep. Sprinkle this with crushed macaroons and the rest of the almonds and sugar.

Put the dish into a moderate oven (350° F. Gas 5) for a good half hour. Now open the oven door and peep inside. The top of the *gratin* is not yet browned. This is excellent, as the egg should coagulate slowly and the pumpkin thicken still more by evaporation. If you *should* find the surface browned, lower the heat a little.

When an hour has passed, raise the heat to about 425° F. (Gas 5–6). The top of the *gratin* turns golden-brown and then finally a deep, rich brown. Lift it out and let it cool for several hours.

The *gratin* is now a compact mass which can be cut like a soft cake. The slices should be about an inch thick. I think you will enjoy it.

Pumpkin with Sugar.

1 *lb pumpkin, 2 ozs butter, granulated sugar.*

Here is an easy sweet. Cut the pumpkin in cubes about ½-inch square.

Melt the butter in a frying-pan and heat the pumpkin cubes over a gentle fire. After 5 minutes, turn them with a wooden spoon. Cook them for another 10 minutes. When the pulp is soft enough for the tips of a fork to penetrate easily, sprinkle the pumpkin with sugar and toss it over the fire until it is coated with caramel. The pumpkin is now ready to eat.

Madeleines.

Once upon a time, in 1551, shall we say (it is as good a date as any other), there lived a baker who was very jealous—and with good reason, for his wife was extraordinarily pretty. One day he went off on a journey, leaving the shop in the charge of his wife. She, evidently, was desolate at being left to run the business all alone, for she enlisted the help of a handsome young man. He installed himself in the back of the shop and everything proceeded charmingly but for two mishaps: the husband returned unexpectedly, and the young man was not a pastrycook.

To explain the presence of the young man, the wife told her husband that in order to cope with a rush of orders she had been obliged to engage an assistant.

"Very well," replied the husband, "I am prepared to believe your story, but if this young pastrycook cannot prepare eighteen cakes immediately I shall stab him with this cutlass and then slit your throat, Madame." He then withdrew, and the wife trembling, followed him.

The false pastrycook, never having made a cake in his life, stood helplessly staring at the flour and the sugar and prepared himself for death.

In his despair he began to pray, invoking Saint Madeleine, who understands so well those who have sinned. She appeared and made the eighteen cakes in a flash. In exchange, she made the young man swear to behave better in future. Then she disappeared.

The husband came back followed by the wife. He was white with fury and she pale with terror. The young man, smiling and radiant with the grace which he had received, presented them with the cakes which he christened 'Madeleines'. Naturally, neither he nor the wife was slain.

And just to conclude this story on a really moral note I must add that the young man became Saint Honoré, patron saint of pastrycooks. I should not like to swear to the accuracy of my story. I read it in a book called *Le Patissier de Bellone* which was written by Charles Nicolle whose writing was as fine as his scientific work. Some years ago he received the Nobel Prize for medicine.

What is really worth remembering about the story is that Madeleines should be made rapidly. Some cookery books say that the flour, sugar and eggs should be beaten for a long time. I shall break with that tradition and tell you how to make a dozen and a half Madeleines in a few moments.

If you have no madeleine moulds use patty tins or tartlet moulds.

> 2 *eggs*, 4 *ozs flour*, 4 *ozs caster sugar*, 4 *ozs butter*, 1 *teaspoon baking powder*, 1 *teaspoon orange-flower water.*

Brush the inside of the moulds with melted butter. Have on the table before you a mixing-bowl and a small pudding basin. Break the whites into the small basin and the yolks into the mixing bowl. Add to the yolks the flour, sugar, baking powder, orange-flower water and a pinch of salt. Mix with a wire whisk. It is very hard work. The paste is too thick. Add 2 teaspoonfuls of cold water. That is better but it is still too thick to handle easily.

Melt the butter in a small saucepan and pour it into the mixing bowl. Now you can beat the mixture easily. Whip the whites with an egg-beater and fold them into the madeleine mixture using a fork. Now it has become almost a cream.

Pour a tablespoon of this cream into each mould and arrange them on a baking-sheet. Put them into a hot oven (425° F. Gas 6) and wait for 9–10 minutes. The madeleines are browning and rising in gentle curves. Another 3–4 minutes and they are done. Take them out of the oven and prise them from the moulds with the tip of a knife. After 5 minutes the upper sides are dry, and they must be turned. Another 5 minutes and they are ready.

La Galette des Rois.

This is a traditional cake which is eaten on the sixth of January and although it is named after the Three Kings it is evident that the gifts which they brought to the Infant Jesus—gold, frankincense and myrrh—were far more precious than cake.

There are many contradictions in the story of the Three Kings and even their origins are disputed. Tertullian maintains that they came from Arabia whilst others declare that they were Persians. Saint Léon the First gives them definite names—Caspar, Melchior and Balthazar. But no-one mentions the cake.

The origins of the *galette* really lie in the Roman Saturnalia which lasted from the end of December to the sixth of January. This was a time of feasting. The historian Lucian records that not only were the feasting and drinking unrestrained, but everyone had the right to shout and sing in the street the whole night through.

This tradition continued throughout the centuries. At the French Court a king of the revels was chosen from amongst the passers-by in the street: some poor vagabond, perhaps. There are historical records of this revelry. Charles IX, whilst drunk, was seriously wounded. François I celebrated the sixth of January by fasting, and his successors, Henri III, Henri IV, Louis XIII, Louis XIV and Louis XV continued the tradition.

In our day French families celebrate the feast of the Three Kings drinking and laughing and eating the *galette*. The bakers hide a bean inside it and the lucky finder, who risks breaking a tooth, is acclaimed king of the revels, king of the Saturnalia. He laughs and drinks and chooses a queen, and kisses her.

Looking back on my childhood I remember the delicious golden *galette* which I ate from time to time at the Moulin de la Galette on the summit of my dear Butte Montmartre. There was a garden round the windmill with arbours, and a show-case with cardboard pastrycooks rolling out sheets of dough. I wandered amongst the wooden horses while my parents ordered a *galette* and a bowl of hot wine. I knew the Moulin de la Galette when Montmartre still had its vineyards, its streams and its fields of oats.

Do you know that in 1830 there were still twenty windmills on top of the Butte Montmartre? And do you know that on March 30th, 1814 Pierre-Charles Debray, the miller who owned all these mills, fired the last cannon shot which, alas, did not halt the charge of the Russian troops. Montmartre fell, and Pierre-Charles Debray was killed by the Cossacks. His body was hacked in pieces and tied to the sails of the windmill which went on turning until the next day. The following night the wife of this brave gunner was at last able to detach her husband's remains from the sails of the windmill and carry them to the cemetery of the church of Saint Pierre, hidden in sacks of flour. The tomb of Pierre-Charles Debray is still there, and the inscription still says that the miller died on March 30th, 1818, killed by the enemy on the hill below his mill.

Perhaps my digression has wearied you, and I ask your forgiveness. When I think of my dear Butte Montmartre of long ago I could go on and on . . .

But now for the *Galette des Rois*. Put into a basin 10½ ozs flour, 3½ ozs butter.

Mix these with a ½-teaspoonful of salt and ¼-pint of water, using your fingertips. You may need to add a little flour or a little water according to whether the paste is too stiff or too soft. It should feel like fresh putty and should not stick to your fingers.

When the ingredients are *not yet completely blended* stop mixing, and cover the ball of paste with a clean napkin. Let it rest for an hour.

Sprinkle a pastry-board with flour, set the ball of paste in the middle and roll it out to the size of a dinner plate. Fold it in three crosswise and again lengthwise, cover it with the napkin once more and wait for 15 minutes. Repeat this process, waiting another 15 minutes when you have done it.

Roll the pastry out into a round about ⅜-inch thick. Using a flan ring, cut it into a perfect circle and, after making a cut in the surface with the point of a knife, slip a dried bean inside. Put the *galette* onto a buttered baking-sheet and mark it with a trellis pattern, using the back of a knife. Prick the *galette* in ten different places with a fork and brush the surface over with water.

Put it into a very hot oven (450° F.).

After 10 minutes open the oven door gently and look at the *galette*. It is already rising. Shut the door and wait another 10 minutes. What a delicious smell. Your *galette* is marvellous, golden, crinkled and crackling.

Put it on your best dish and carry it to table. Cut it in crisp slices and enjoy your feast.

A Yule Log.

It seems to me that things have changed a great deal since I was a child. In those days the Butte Montmartre was covered with snow in winter. Boys didn't go to winter sports but contented themselves with skating on frozen streams and sliding on their seats down the terrifying slope of the rue Ravignon which was transformed into a sleigh run. That is to say, the poorer ones slid on their trouser seats, whilst the richer ones could boast a few planks fixed, anyhow, onto two bits of wood which served as runners.

What fun it was, and what trouble one got into afterwards when one went home. The snow remained immaculate, as the horse-drawn vehicles could not climb the frozen slopes since in those days they had not yet thought of throwing salt onto the snow to turn it into grimy black mud.

Christmas Eve was celebrated, but it was celebrated at home. There were no cabarets on the Butte in those days. One huddled close together round a steaming cauldron of onion soup beside a roaring, red-hot stove on top of which a fragrant black pudding was waiting.

One Christmas Eve my parents had invited an old friend who was passing through Paris to share our family celebrations. He was an engineer who had lived for many years in Spain and I hardly knew him. He arrived with his wife. Where she came from I don't know, but I remember that she was enormously fat and that she had a horrible southern accent.

The guests arrived. He was wearing a frock coat and she was dressed in black taffeta. He was carrying a superb cake and she, two table-napkins and a loaf of bread. My parents looked surprised. As for me, I was only interested in the cake.

The engineer explained that his wife, native of a small village in the South of France, clung to the customs of her great grandparents. In their day, it seems that they never went out to dine with friends without taking their bread and their table napkins with them. Actually, it is not such a bad idea.

As for the good lady, she told us that on Christmas Eve everyone, before going to midnight mass, sent a log to the house where they were invited. In this way they were sure of enjoying their white and black pudding before a roaring fire.

Perhaps that is the origin of this cake which one sees in the windows of all the pastrycooks in France at Christmas time and at the New Year.

I bought one some years ago and was rather disappointed. It was a great mass of biscuit covered with a layer of *moka* cream flavoured with chocolate. I don't feel the slightest desire to make a similar yule log. But I know of an excellent one which I ate at the house of some charming friends.

This 'log' has the advantage of being made without any special utensils. It almost makes itself with the aid of a saucepan and a sheet of white paper. I must add too that it is delicious and not expensive. You will need:

> 1½ *lbs chestnuts, 4 ozs cooking chocolate, 4 ozs caster sugar,*
> *4 ozs butter, 2 or 3 hazel-nuts, 1½ ozs icing sugar.*

The most difficult part of the operation is peeling the chestnuts. I have explained how to do this in the recipe for *Gâteau aux Marrons* on p. 214 and also how to prepare a chestnut purée. Perhaps you would be kind enough to turn to this page and follow my explanation to the point where you have blended the chestnuts, chocolate, caster sugar and butter together.

Now form this mass into a ball and place it on an oblong piece of white kitchen paper. Grasp one of the long sides with your right hand and the other with your left. Lift each hand in turn so that the ball of paste rolls and gradually turns into a cylinder. Put the cylinder, in its paper, onto a long dish and set it in a cool place for 6 hours.

Slip the log onto a dish. Make streaks with a fork to simulate the bark, and stick the two hazel-nuts into the trunk to look like knots. Sprinkle the log with icing sugar to look like snow.

Slice the log at table. It is sweet and soft and very good. And it has cost so little!

Soft Chocolate Caramels.

I am going to show you how to make forty soft chocolate caramels which, all together, will cost only about 1/6 for you will use:

> 2½ *ozs honey, 2½ ozs butter, 2½ ozs cooking chocolate,*
> 2½ *ozs caster sugar.*

Put the honey, sugar and butter into a small saucepan with the chocolate which you have grated.

Set the saucepan on a very low fire and, if you want to be really cosy, sit down whilst you stir it with a wooden spoon. The butter melts and the chocolate too. The whole thing becomes runny and burning hot. Little bubbles rise from the bottom and burst.

Lower the heat and go on stirring for *exactly* 10 minutes.

Lift the saucepan from the fire. The contents are very liquid. Keep on stirring. The mixture thickens. Stir for 5 minutes and then lift the pan from the fire.

For the next stage you should really have a marble slab. I always carry the saucepan into the dining-room where I have a sideboard with a handsome marble top. Disregarding the proprieties and trusting in my wife's dusting, I wipe the surface over with oil and empty the saucepan onto it, scraping the pan clean with my wooden spoon.

The mass spreads slowly over the marble. I shape the sides by tapping with the spoon so that it forms a rectangle of about 8 by $5\frac{1}{2}$ inches. Then I take a large kitchen knife and cut this into strips about $1\frac{1}{4}$ inches wide, pressing the blade right down to the marble. These I separate from one another by pushing them with the blade of the knife, then I cut each strip into squares of the same measurement as the width, separating one from another.

When they are cold, I put them on a dish. They are pretty and shining and they taste delicious. But goodness, how difficult it is to talk when you have a soft caramel sticking to your teeth. I prefer not to try.

And if you have no marble slab, you say. Well, you might make do with the enamel top of your refrigerator or a plastic pastry-board, but they will not have the wonderful cold solidity of the marble, and I cannot guarantee results. Alas, marble is one of the good things which has almost disappeared from the modern home.

JAM

The English housewife is an expert jam maker and I am not, so I shall only tell you of jam which may be new to you.

Chestnut Jam.

    2 lbs chestnuts, 1 *lb granulated sugar, a vanilla pod.*

With a sharp knife cut from the base of each chestnut, up over the tip and down to the base again, then put them into boiling water for 5 minutes. Slip off the shells and inner skins, and then boil them for 30 minutes. Put the chestnuts through a sieve or '*Mouli*' so that you have a dryish pulp.

Put the sugar into a preserving pan with a very little water. Set the pan on the stove and let the sugar melt. Add a vanilla pod split in two. The syrup should cook for 15 minutes.

Moisten the chestnut purée with just over ¾-pint of water and then stir it into the syrup. Simmer for another 20 minutes, stirring all the time. The jam is ready. Put it into warmed pots and seal it carefully. Like this it is said to keep very well, but I am afraid I can give you no definite assurance on this point as my own chestnut jam is always eaten the week it is made.

A FEW DRINKS

One day, anxious to be in fashion, I caught 'flu. Like a good doctor I put myself to bed, wisely provided with a couple of aspirin tablets and a bottle of brandy.

For six long days I looked at the aspirin, intact in its wrappings, but I must confess that I made a serious attack on the brandy. The result? I was cured.

In fact, I have a blind faith in the medicinal properties of alcohol, and this since the very beginning of my medical studies.

One day, when I was only a student, one of my friends came, post-haste, to seek my very uncertain advice about the condition of his aged mother. She had pneumonia and refused absolutely to trust herself to any doctor but me. She had never been ill in her life and, in this way, had reached the ripe old age of eighty-one.

I arrived to visit her. The diagnosis was easy, but the prognosis was not encouraging. Nevertheless, I agreed to treat her according to the method which I had just learnt at the hospital.

Knowing that the old lady would refuse any kind of medicine, I gave her a little talk on the following lines:

"Now Granma, you must do exactly what I say. I shan't give you any medicine, but you must promise to obey me. I am going to pour some boiling water into a teacup. I shall add a lump of sugar and some lemon rind and a small glass of brandy. Now you must promise me to drink this very hot . . ."

The old lady lifted her eyes to mine. I can see her to this day, with that look of a dying woman. She stared at me and at her son, and then, pointing her finger at me, she said, "He's mad. He's mad. He wants me to put water in my brandy."

In spite of the solemnity of the moment we couldn't help laughing. My friend then explained to me that for the last thirty years his mother had drunk a glass of brandy every day as she played bézique. In order to gain her confidence I had to tell her to put *two* glasses of brandy into her cup of hot water.

She did as she was told, and the next day she was cured. Then, for the next ten years, she drank two glasses of brandy every day, and she died at the age of ninety-one. Who knows? If she had drunk three glasses she might be alive to this day.

So I drank alcohol when I had 'flu and I was cured, and whilst I was under my own treatment I made a comparative study of various alcoholic beverages and in this way gastronomy came to the aid of medicine.

Now I shall tell you how to prepare some of these exquisite medicines. I shall start with the least alcoholic.

An Almost Alcohol-Free Grog.

In spite of the fact that this grog contains very little alcohol it will give you the illusion of being a very strong drink.

Make crosswise cuts on the outside of an orange and strip the peel off in four pieces. Remove any traces of white pith with a sharp knife, and cut the orange peel into tiny pieces.

Warm a teapot, put the peel into it and pour in $\frac{3}{4}$-pint of boiling water. Let it infuse for 6 minutes. Pour out the orange tea, and into each cup measure 15 drops *exactly*, of rum. Do this with a medicine-dropper if you wish.

Taste it. It is exquisite. Your forehead breaks into a gentle perspiration. You are calm and relaxed. It can't be the effect of the alcohol. Could it be the heat? Or imagination perhaps?

Cherry Ratafia.

As long as there are cherries on the trees and in the markets one should enjoy them and then, before they disappear, one should capture the last of the lovely red fruits and preserve them, in sugar or in brandy, like a fetish holding the spirit of the cherry, for the rest of the year.

Here is a liqueur from the *Dauphiné* made with the last black cherries in the orchard.

> $2\frac{1}{4}$ *lbs black cherries,* $3\frac{1}{2}$ *pints brandy,* 2 *cloves, a small piece of cinnamon bark,* 1 *lb* 12 *ozs loaf sugar.*

Strip the stems from the cherries and wash them under the cold tap without removing the stones. Wipe them and dry them with a cloth. Put them into a large glass jar and pour the brandy over them. Add the cloves and the cinnamon, crumbled.

Stopper the mouth of the jar and leave it for two months so

that the cherry juice can mingle with the alcohol. This turns a very dark, almost blackish red. Now you must sweeten the brandy.

Put the sugar into a saucepan with ⅓-pint of boiling water. The sugar melts. Let it boil slowly for 15 minutes over a very low fire. Skim off the traces of scum which form.

Pour the brandy into a large bowl or soup tureen, discarding the cherries which have been exhausted by the alcohol. To this liquid add the syrup which you have allowed to become nearly cold. Mix them together using a ladle. Cover the bowl and wait for 2 hours, stirring every quarter of an hour.

Place a funnel in the neck of a bottle and in the bottom of the funnel a piece of cotton wool.

Ladle the liqueur into the funnel so that it seeps through the cotton wool. In this way, fill three bottles, one after the other. Cork them tightly and put them away in your store cupboard.

Next winter, when summer is only a distant memory, fill your glasses with cherry ratafia and you will all enjoy the illusion that the cherry season has returned once more.

American Grog.

Heat a teapot. Into it put 1 teaspoonful of black Ceylon tea and 2 teacupfuls of boiling water. Let it infuse for 6 minutes exactly, then pour it into two cups.

Add to each cup 2 small teaspoonfuls of cognac, a slice of lemon and a lump of sugar. Stir. Squash the slice of lemon with your spoon so as to extract all the juice. Now drink.

I do not insist upon cognac for this grog. You can replace it with rum, whisky, kirsch or any other natural spirit.

Lait de Poule.

Here is a drink which almost makes me regret the attack of influenza, when I discovered that *lait de poule* is a most efficacious medicine.

> 1 *teacup milk,* 1 *yolk of egg,* 2 *teaspoons caster sugar, nutmeg,* 2 *teaspoons cognac.*

Mix the egg yolk and caster sugar in a small bowl. Boil a cupful of milk with a pinch or two of grated nutmeg. Pour these slowly into the bowl, beating as you do so with a wire whisk. The mixture is ready. Add the cognac, stir and drink immediately while it is still very hot.

FOOD TO REMEMBER

A Lunch in the Country

My house in the country is very small, so tiny that in order to live there I had to move the kitchen into an outhouse which was, once upon a time, the fowl house. Now I cook there, almost in the open air, with the most primitive equipment—an oil stove and a charcoal fire.

On special days, that is to say the days when good friends are coming to lunch, I set up in the garden, against the wall of the house, a charcoal stove with a portable oven. It is primitive enough and simple to handle, but it produces incomparable roasts.

My friends must be given the warmest welcome I can offer, without any pretensions or fuss—no complicated, dressed-up dishes. They will simply share my simple country fare. . . . All the same, they will expect a good meal.

To reconcile these aims I shall give them the very best that is to be found in the village, and cook it in the simplest possible way. So I arrive home with my shopping basket filled with all I need to make:

> *scrambled eggs,*
> *shoulder of lamb roasted on the spit,*
> *mushrooms with thyme,*
> *fresh garden peas with lettuce.*

Besides all this I have bought *fromage à la feuille* and strawberries and cream.

The longest task before me is to shell the fresh garden peas—one pound for each person—which will delight us later. Still, with two of us working and chatting as we go, this won't take too long.

We shall eat at half-past twelve. It is now eleven o'clock.

To avoid being fussed at the last moment I prepare my peas in advance and warm them just before they are served. On

p. 169 I told you how to prepare *petits pois à la laitue.* In my country kitchen I shall cook them in the same way in a splendid old copper pan whose tinned lining is wearing a little thin (not so good for the saucepan, but all the better for the peas, which will remain beautifully green).

I put the peas on the oil stove and leave them undisturbed for 20 minutes. As I have explained to you, if peas are absolutely fresh-picked they need no sugar, but mine were picked the evening before, so when after 20 minutes I lift the lid of the pan, I add a lump of sugar and taste to see if the salt is sufficient. If it is not, I wait until the peas are cooked before adjusting it.

When it is time to serve the peas I re-heat them and add a big lump of butter and 3 tablespoons of double cream. As soon as the butter has melted and the cream is blended with the peas I put them into a hot dish and carry them straight to table. But this will be *after* the roast and as a separate course, naturally.

Mushrooms with Thyme.

At the greengrocer's I found some fresh, white mushrooms. I bought 1 lb, picking out those which were about the size of walnuts. These, too, I prepare in advance, cutting off the sandy ends of the stems and washing them in 10 successive waters until they were quite free from grit.

On the fire I put a copper pan and pour into it 3 tablespoons of olive oil. The oil begins to smoke. I add the mushrooms, cover the pan and let it heat. After 10 minutes I lift the lid. The mushrooms are swimming in the liquid which they have exuded. I go on heating with the lid off. Then I sprinkle the mushrooms with salt and pepper and thyme from my garden, stripping the leaves from the sprigs by rubbing them gently with my fingers.

The water evaporates and the oil begins to splutter. The mushrooms start to brown. I lift the saucepan from the fire. It can wait.

Shoulder of Lamb Roast on a Spit.

My butcher is an artist. He has rolled the shoulder of lamb after boning it. On the surface he has made incisions to look like flowers.

I have threaded this work of art on a spit and, in three

places, inserted a clove of pure white garlic into a small slit made with the point of a sharp knife.

Without the bones, my shoulder weighs 2¾ lbs.

At a quarter to twelve I fill the upright stove with red-hot charcoal and add some coal. I blow with the bellows. The coals are glowing. It is twelve o'clock. I rub the meat over with butter and sprinkle the surface with salt. I put the spit into the *coquille*[1] and stand this in front of the fire. During half an hour the meat turns blond, blushing, golden and ruddy in turn.

Every 10 minutes I turn the spit through a half circle. Finally I pour half a glass of boiling water into the *coquille*. It mixes with the butter. I drench the meat twice with this liquid.

It is half past twelve. My friends arrive. Their nostrils dilate, their faces light up. . . . There is a marvellous smell of roasting meat.

I turn the *coquille* from the fire so that the meat keeps hot. Now I shall make the scrambled eggs.

Scrambled Eggs with Peas.

I beat 12 eggs in a large bowl and salt them. On the fire I put a copper pan. I melt 2 ozs of butter and pour in the eggs. With a wire whisk I beat energetically, scraping the bottom of the saucepan as I beat. Little lumps are formed. I break them. I go on beating. The eggs thicken. . . . They are *almost* ready. I lift the pan off the fire and beat and turn. They are just right. I pour them into a warmed dish and stir in a tablespoon of my peas which are still just warm. I carry my dish to the table.

And now there are a succession of joys:

The eggs with a glass of cider—just like velvet.

The roast with its gravy and the mushrooms which I warmed whilst I was dishing the roast—a rustic cooking with a primitive freshness. With this, a glass of Burgundy.

The peas follow, soothingly bland.

The cheese. . . . The strawberries and cream. . . . The coffee. . . . A thimbleful of plum brandy. . . . Contentment. . . . The joy of living and of loving one's friends.

[1] A curved metal screen combined with a drip-tray which holds the heat of the fire round the hanging meat. The shape is rather like the wicker shelters for single chairs which used to be so popular at the sea-side.

Supper in the High Mountains.

If I were from the *Midi* I should spin you a yarn about how I hunted a chamois. But since I am not, I shall stick to the truth and nothing but the truth. Now, it is true that not so long ago I did go to the high mountains with two chamois hunters who had come to the lonely spot in the Engadine where I often spend my holidays. They were going to stay as long as the chamois season was open, that is to say for three weeks.

So we set out, they with their guns and I with a walking-stick, for the glaciers frequented by the chamois. And we passed through regions where the grass grows as short as if it had been shaved, on rock faces barely covered with top soil.

However, this miserable vegetation nourishes a world of animal life despised by my two hunters: marmots which sit up on their hind legs and whistle to warn their scattered families; roebuck, bounding along followed by their young; foxes nosing about in search of some devilment. At last we reached the glacier and the eternal snows.

The silence of these regions is so awe-inspiring that, for fear of troubling it, one speaks instinctively with a lowered voice.

A whole day passed. My hunters hadn't seen a single chamois, not even through their binoculars. Since we could not spend the night on the glacier we were obliged to sleep in a hut which served as a refuge. And it was there that we dined. This dinner seemed to me quite exquisite. Was it because of the menu? Or was it because of the primitive surroundings in which we found ourselves? I couldn't say. The next day I learnt that the luxury of the meal was something unusual. We had been lucky enough to hit upon the birthday of the *patron's* wife.

I won't bore you by describing the soup, which had no special character. But after this they served us with *boeuf à la bâloise*, a white *risotto* and an apple tart.

I should like you to share my pleasure and so I shall describe just how I make these dishes.

Boeuf à la Bâloise.

To make this braised beef I buy 1½ lbs of rump steak and 1 lb of onions.

The piece of beef should be roughly cube-shaped. With a very sharp knife I cut slices as thin as possible. You can judge of their thickness when I tell you that I make twelve. I peel the onions and cut them in slices crosswise. During the cooking these slices of onions separate into a large number of little bracelets.

In a cast-iron casserole I put a piece of butter the size of a small walnut and 3 ounces of pork fat cut in dice.

I set the casserole on the fire. The pork melts. I add the meat and the onions, pepper, salt and 2 glasses of water. I cover the casserole and bring it to the boil. Now I lower the flame and let the casserole simmer for 2 hours. From time to time I lift the lid and add a little water, and I sniff the steam. The smell is exquisite. As for the taste, you can judge that for yourself.

White Risotto.

This *risotto* is called white in contrast with the Italian *risotto* which is so often coloured yellow with saffron.

I melt a scant 3 ozs of butter in an iron casserole. Into this I put a cupful, exactly, of rice which I have not washed but put into a clean cloth and rubbed between the folds.

I mix the butter and rice and heat them together for 3 minutes. Then, using the same cup, I measure 1½ cupfuls of hot bouillon onto the rice and bring it to the boil. I cover the saucepan, lower the heat and let the rice simmer over a tiny flame for 20 minutes. I lift the lid. The rice is marvellous. It is cooked and all the grains are separate.

I serve the rice in a hot dish. In a deep dish I serve at the same time the *boeuf bâloise* which is covered with onion rings and swimming in a generous amount of sauce. The rice with each helping will be moistened and bound by the sauce.

With this I drink a glass of rough red *vin ordinaire.*

Apple Tart.

This tart is similar to the Alsatian Tart which I described to you on p. 206, but much less thick.

> 7 *ozs flour,* 3½ *ozs butter,* 4 *large cooking apples,* ¼ *pint thick cream,* 3 *yolks of egg,* 1½ *ozs caster sugar.*

I crumble the butter into the flour and mix them with 4 tablespoons of cold water and a couple of pinches of salt. I now have a smooth paste.

I place a flan ring on a buttered baking sheet. On a floured board I roll my pastry out until it is less than ⅛-inch thick, then I lift it onto the flan ring, moulding it with my fingertips. With the palm of my hand I press down on the edge of the ring and cut off the surplus pastry.

My tart is now ready to go into the oven. I shall fill and decorate it.

I core 4 large cooking apples, peel them and cut them into very thin slices.

In a bowl, I beat the cream with the yolks of egg and sugar. I pour this cream into the tart and arrange the apples with art, so that the slices overlap and form a pleasing design. Then I sprinkle the surface with caster sugar and put the tart into the oven.

After 15 minutes I look to see what is happening. Nothing special.

After 25 minutes I take another look. The tart is beginning to turn a faint golden colour at the edges. Ten minutes later a delicious smell comes from the oven. The tart is golden-brown. I lift it from the oven, remove the flan ring and slip the tart onto a dish or better still, a wooden serving board. There it is, this tart from the *Grisons*.

Oh, I nearly forgot to tell you the end of the chamois hunt. The next day my hunters killed a chamois eighteen years old. . . . They could tell its age from the horns, it seems. I attempted to roast a leg of the animal but, alas, it was dry and tough.

Two Good Dishes for Two 'Little' Wines.

Like many Parisians I have no wine cellar. Like many intellectuals I cannot afford the '*grands vins*' which are the glory of France. It is only by the purest chance that a bottle of *Clos Vougeot* or *Château Yquem* strays onto my table. On such an occasion I compose a menu worthy of such a bottle. So I really cannot say that I feel any affection for the '*grands vins*'. I admire and respect them.

On the other hand, I frequently drink those marvellous wines which are called '*petits vins*'. They are not improved by keeping and only ask to be drunk the year that they are made, or the following year. They have the charm of a young face, flushed, smiling and radiant.

The great wines of France have the distinction of an

eighteenth-century *marquise*. The little wines, the gaiety of our beautiful country girls. One can love both of them. And indeed, don't they say that the Pompadour dressed herself as a village maiden to please Louis XV?

I have a bottle or two of pale amber-coloured *Chavignol* and some *Beaujolais*, brilliant red, of last year's vintage.

These light, lively wines require the accompaniment of a simple dish. For the white wine, therefore, I shall devise a fantasy on the theme *Chaudrée de Poissons* about which I told you on p. 72.

Variation on a Chaudrée.

A *chaudrée* is a marvellous fish soup which they make in the Charentes, but a real *chaudrée* requires the wine of the district and special shell-fish.

Since I have neither the one nor the other I shall make my own version of a *chaudrée*. For six people I shall buy a good 3 lbs of fish of various kinds. The less elegant sorts of fish such as conger eel, rock salmon and the heads of gurnards, if you can get them, will all be useful.

These I shall cook in my *Chavignol*. You can use any light white wine which is not too sweet.

I pour 2 bottles of wine into a large saucepan and add the fish-heads, 2 bayleaves, freshly-grated black pepper, a pinch of nutmeg, 2 crushed cloves of garlic and 4 shallots chopped finely. I salt lightly, and let the contents of the pan simmer with the lid on for half an hour. From time to time I skim the pot.

Now I lift out the fish-heads and the bayleaves and put into the saucepan the fish, divided into pieces about as big as an egg. These I boil for 20 minutes, skimming all the time.

In a soup tureen I beat 2 eggs with a fork and add a scant ¼-pint of thick cream. I stand the tureen on the corner of my table and pour the liquid from the fish into a second saucepan, leaving just enough to keep the fish hot over a low flame.

Into the saucepan of *bouillon* I drop, bit by bit, 3½ ozs of butter, beating all the time with a wire whisk. The pan is standing over a tiny flame and I am very careful not to let it boil. When all the butter is blended I pour the very hot broth, little by little, into the soup tureen, beating all the time. The *bouillon* turns white as it mixes with the cream and egg. I put the pieces of fish, very hot, into the broth and carry it to table.

234

Into each plate I put three pieces of fish and a large ladleful of perfumed *bouillon*.

Into the glasses I pour Chavignol, so chilled that there is a delicate mist on the glasses. I watch the faces of my guests. I am happy. They are filled with contentment.

Stuffed Breast of Veal.

Breast of veal is very reasonable in price. I ask my butcher to give me a piece weighing about 3 lbs. Since this democratic cut is composed of several layers of muscle superimposed one on another, the butcher can make a neat pocket by separating with his knife the top layer from the others. Into this pocket I shall put a stuffing composed of:

> *3½ ozs cooked ham, 6 ozs calf's liver, 3 ozs back pork fat, 3½ ozs crumbs from a stale white loaf, 4 ozs mushrooms, a small onion, ½ lb shallots, a bouquet of parsley, chervil and tarragon, a few sprigs of thyme, 1 egg, a little milk, 4½ ozs butter.*

I soak the breadcrumbs in milk and then squeeze them dry. I peel everything which can be peeled and set up my mincing machine. In this, or my '*Mouli*', I mince all the meats, vegetables and the bread. Result—a very smooth pulp.

In a frying-pan I melt 2 ozs butter and add the pulp. I heat, mix, salt, pepper and taste. Exquisite.

When it has cooled a little, I add the egg and mix it in.

I fill the pocket with this stuffing, curving the meat to form a cylinder. With a needle and thread I sew the two edges of the pocket together and tie the cylinder in shape with string.

Into a cast-iron casserole I put a scant 3 ozs of butter and heat it until it melts. Then I fry the meat in the butter until it is golden-brown all over.

In the casserole with the meat I brown 2 or 3 large sliced onions, then add a cupful of boiling water and ¼-lb sliced mushrooms. Now I cover the casserole and let it simmer very gently for 2 hours. From time to time I add a little water.

Before serving I remove the strings and put the roll of meat on a dish. I garnish it with some sauté potatoes, pour the sauce, which is rich with onions, mushrooms and the stuffing which has leaked out, into a small tureen.

I cut the meat in slices and serve everyone with a slice of meat and plenty of sauce. Into very large glasses I pour *Beaujolais* at the fresh temperature of the cellar, as they serve it in Burgundy.

My first dish was a fantasy. This is a symphony.

Lunch by the Sea.

Recently, I succumbed to temptation and allowed myself to be taken for two days to the seaside. The friends who carried me off live on that admirable road which joins Trouville and Honfleur.

Saturday is market day in Honfleur. We set out without any preconceived plans to buy the materials for lunch.

The fishing boats tied up alongside the quays were veiled mysteriously in a very light fog. The reflections of the picturesque houses of the port were hardly visible in the water. The slate-covered bell tower round which the market huddles emerged above the fog into the sunshine. Peasant women, seated grave and silent with their hands folded on their stomachs, offered for sale great blocks of butter and baskets of eggs. Punnets of strawberries perfumed the air.

We pushed our way through the crowds until we reached the fish market. It was a modest enough display. Three fish-sellers offered their wares. But the soles were still quivering and the eels were struggling to escape. The fish had just been brought in from the boats—all except the skate which had been waiting since the day before to lose their first toughness.

The temptation was too great. We decided to eat no meat for lunch and to enjoy the fish and the fruits of the sea. Here is our menu:

> *Hot shrimps,*
> *Mussels with curry,*
> *Skate with hard-boiled eggs,*
> *Lettuce with cream,*
> *Livarot cheese,*
> *Strawberries with lemon,*
> *Cider, coffee and Calvados.*

Hot Shrimps.

Into a large saucepan I poured a bottle of dry cider and $3\frac{1}{2}$ pints of water. I added a handful, but a generous handful, of coarse cooking-salt and plenty of freshly-milled black pepper.

I put the saucepan on the fire and whilst waiting for it to boil I washed the shrimps in plenty of cold water to rid them of any sand. I had bought, I must add, 2 lbs of shrimps.

The water boiled and I threw in the shrimps. Poor things. They died instantly. I let them boil for 5 minutes and drained them in a colander. Then I piled them onto a hot dish and served them with crusty fresh bread and ice-cold butter. And with them the first glass of cider.

Mussels with Curry.

When I was in Honfleur mussels were not yet in season, but all the same some were for sale in the market. They were small, but how delicately flavoured!

I bought 5 pints of mussels, washed them, scraped them and threw away those which were full of mud.

Whilst I was doing this I put on the fire a small saucepan containing a glass of water, 2 small teaspoonfuls of curry powder, 4 onions and 4 shallots chopped finely.

By the time the mussels were washed the onions had been cooking for 10 minutes and I threw them both into a large saucepan and put on the lid. The fire was hot. After 7–8 minutes the mussels opened and released the water in their shells. This water began to boil. In the meantime, I beat together:

> *A teacup thick cream, 1 tablespoon flour, 3 yolks of egg, a handful of parsley chopped very fine, a sprinkling of freshly-milled black pepper.*

I lifted up the saucepan with the mussels and tipped it so that all the water ran into a mixing bowl. The mussels remained in the saucepan. Little by little, I poured some mussel water into the bowl containing the cream, stirring them together carefully. Then, in a medium-sized saucepan I mixed the diluted cream with the rest of the water from the mussels and heated it over a gentle fire, whisking all the time. The liquid thickened slightly. Before it could boil, I moved it off the heat. I served the mussels in a deep dish and the sauce in a small tureen. On the table I laid soup plates and spoons.

At this point a second glass of cider and a small glass of Calvados to make a '*trou*' (a digestive which would encourage our stomachs for the rest of the meal).

Skate with Hard-boiled Eggs.

I put three young skate, caught the day before, into a fish kettle after having cleaned them and washed them carefully. The water was salted, slightly acidulated with vinegar, and perfumed with bayleaves.

Now 10–15 minutes' cooking, during which I put 10 ozs of butter into a frying-pan. It melted. It smoked, and I lifted the pan from the fire. I threw in a handful of parsley, very finely chopped. What a fizzing and foaming! I stirred into the buttery parsley 4 hard-boiled eggs, chopped fine. And then I warmed the mixture once more.

I lifted the skate from the liquid in the saucepan and put them on a dish. Then I sprinkled them all over with the juice of a lemon and carried them to the table. Everyone helped themselves to fish and butter and hard-boiled eggs. A third glass of cider!

Lettuces with Cream.

I trimmed the outside leaves from 2 lettuces and washed them carefully, shaking them dry in the salad basket. Then I dressed them with thick cream, cider vinegar, salt and pepper.

A fourth glass of cider!

With the *Livarot* cheese, however, a glass of good Burgundy.

Strawberries with Lemon.

I removed the stalks from 2 lbs of strawberries, washed them in cold water and left them to drip. I squeezed the juice from a lemon and put it on one side. With a sharp knife I stripped the pith from the skin and discarded it. I was now left with the aromatic yellow skin of the lemon. This I cut into 10 or 12 pieces.

In a large bowl I mixed the rest of the lemon delicately with the strawberries and served them immediately.

I sat back and waited for coffee and Calvados. I did not have to wait for the compliments of my friends, I can assure you. One of them, in a glow of contentment, declared that I should be crowned the King of the Mussels. I was deeply touched.

Food for Camping.

I used to go camping—years ago, when it was not even fashionable, so I can tell you about some simple dishes which you can prepare over the glowing embers of your camp fire or on a paraffin stove.

Brochettes de Viande à la Braise.

To grill a large piece of meat in the open air is rather difficult, so it is better to cut your meat into small pieces and thread them onto a skewer.

For this purpose, there is the widest possible choice of material: beefsteak, fillet from a leg of lamb, shoulder of mutton, escalopes of veal cut very fine, sheep's or calf's liver, and so on.

For two people I cut ½-lb of meat into 8 or 10 pieces. I take as many pieces of thinly-cut fat pork, preferably from the back. I thread these pieces onto skewers or green twigs, alternating meat and fat.

When the fire has died down to glowing embers I lay the two *brochettes* directly onto them, without using a grill. Four minutes on one side and 4 minutes on the other and all that is left to do is to sprinkle the *brochettes* with salt and enjoy them.

Cèpes Grillés.

Cèpes, or *boletus edulis*, are edible mushrooms which are found in deciduous woods in summer and autumn. They are rather large and have bun-shaped caps coloured brown. The underside of the cap is white when the mushroom is young, and later turns yellow-green. The stem is often swollen and the upper part is veined with fine white lines. *Cèpes* are well-known in France and very popular, though in England people are rather timid about picking them, so you have a good chance of finding some in the woods. Be careful, however, to make sure that you avoid any of the poisonous mushrooms. On p. 167 I explained the danger of the poisons they contain.

To return to our *cèpes*. I have often gathered them under oak trees and they are ideal food for the camper. Be sure that they are free from worms, and then just break off the stems and throw the caps straight onto the glowing embers.

After 5 minutes turn them over and leave them for another 5 minutes. Then put the caps on a plate and dust off any ash which may be sticking to them. Sprinkle with salt and eat them with fresh, cold butter which you have set to cool in a nearby stream.

Pea Soup with Onion.

On your paraffin stove melt an ounce or so of butter in your saucepan. When it has melted, add 2 onions cut small. In 6–7 minutes they will be golden-brown.

For two people, add 2 heaping tablespoons of good-quality flour made from dried peas. Then, without waiting, a cup of cold water, stirring all the time. Go on stirring until the soup boils. Cook for another 5 minutes, salt, and pour it into your bowls. Eat the soup with pieces of bread toasted on the embers —floating in your bowl, if you like it this way.

Potatoes Cooked in the Ashes.

Wash 6 medium-sized potatoes and wipe them dry. Put them into the hot ashes. After 20 minutes, lift them out, burning your fingers as you do so, and eat them, skins and all, sprinkled with salt, and dripping with fresh butter.

This is no new idea, you may say. You cooked potatoes like this as children. Granted, but they are so delicious I could not resist the pleasure of describing them once more.

INDEX

SOUPS

Barley with Goose Giblets, 30
Chilled, 30
Fish, 30
Iced Tomato and Cucumber, 33
Mussel, 33
Neapolitan Fish Soup with Rice, 31
Pea with Onion, 240
Pumpkin, 29
Ruby, 31
Tripe, 34

EGGS

Eggs, 35
Bouillabaisse of Eggs, 39
Omelette Basquaise, 38
  with Chipolata Sausages, 38
Poached with Mushrooms, 37
  sur Canapé, 36
  with Tomato, 37
Scrambled with Peas, 230
  with Sorrel, 37
To poach, 36

SOME CHEESE DISHES

Beignets au Fromage, 40
Croûtes au Fromage, 41
Escalopes au Fromage, 41
Fondue, 43
Gougère Comtois, 42
Tranches au Fromage, 42

SAVOURY TARTS, PANCAKES AND OTHER DELICACIES

Canneloni, 49
Flammiche, 46

Friands, 51
Gnocchi, 56
  Choux Pastry, 57
  Semolina, 56
Knèfles à l'Alsacienne, 53
  à l'Italienne, 54
  au Fromage, 54
  gratinées, 54
  Paysanne, 53
Kromeski, 49
Leek Tart, 46
Noodles, à la Tchèque, 59
  with Mushrooms, 59
Onion Tart, 46
Pancakes, 48
  with Ham, 50
Pasta, 58
Piroshki, 54
Quiche Lorraine, 47
  with Mussels, 48
Ramequins, 58
Rice
  Adjem Pilaff, 59
  Salad, 60
Risotto, white, 136, 232
Serniki, 50
Spaghetti à l'Anglaise, 58
  with Tomato Sauce, 59

SEA FISH

Aïoli, 69
Chaudrée, 72
  a variation on, 234
Codling, à la Basquaise, 65
Crawfish, 74
Herrings, stuffed, 66
Langouste à la Crème, 74
Lobster à l'Américaine, 73
  with Mayonnaise, 72
Mackerel, à la Grècque, 66

241

Mussels, 75
à l'Espagnole, 77
fried, 77
Marinières, 76
Niçoises, 76
Salad, 77
with Cream, 76
with Curry, 237
Salt Cod, 66
Aïoli, 69
à la Biscaïenne, 67
Bouillabaisse of, 68
Petits Soldats de Pavie, 68
Salad with Eggs, 68
with Rice, 67
with Spinach, 67
Scallops, 77
Fricasee of, 77
à l'Americaine, 78
St. Jacques, gratine, 79
with Tomato, 79
Shrimps, hot, 236
Skate, 70
Vinaigrette, 71
with Black Butter, 70
with Cream, 71
with Hard-boiled Eggs, 238
Whiting, 62
fried, 64
in White Wine, 64
with Cream, 65

*FROGS, SNAILS AND
FRESHWATER FISH*

Carp, 87
à la Juive, 89
au Lard, 89
stuffed, 87
Eels, 85
grilled, 86
jellied, 87
Maître d'Hôtel, 86
marinated, 86
Frogs, 80
Legs, baked, 82
fried, 82

sauté with Butter, 81
Sauce Poulette, 82
Grey Mullet, with Cucumber, 92
Pike, au Beurre Blanc, 90
Shad, roast, 91
with Sorrel, 92
Snails, 83
en Cassolette, 85
en Coquilles, 84

MEAT

Beef, à la Houssarde, 94
à la Ficelle, 96
Bâloise, 231
Bourguignon, 98
Cheaper Cuts of, 98
Entrecôte, 96
with Red Wine Sauce, 97
Goulash, 101
Hochepot, 100
Mariné à la Crème, 99
Rissoles, French, 103
Sauté with Hard-boiled Eggs, 102
Spanish Stew, 99
Boiled Beef Pâté, 103
Remains of, 101
with Date Sauce, 101
with Horse-radish Sauce, 102
Brains, 117
Croquettes of, 118
en Papillottes, 118
with Black Butter, 117
Brochettes of Meat, 239
Calf's Feet in Jelly, 120
Calf's Head, 119
Madrilène, 120
Tête de Veau Panée, 120
Vinaigrette, 119
Ham Flakes, 125
Pancakes stuffed with, 125
transformation of a Ham Bone, 124
with Flageolets, 126

Kidneys, 121
  Calf's à la Poêle, 122
    with Cream, 122
  Rognon de Boeuf Saignant, 121
Lamb, 103
  Blanquette of, 104
  Boiled Leg of, 105
  Haut de Côtelette aux Haricots, 105
    Pané, 107
  Kebabs with Bacon, 107
  Pigeons Moscovites, 109
  Pilaff, 104
  Shashlik, 107
  Shoulder of, roast on a spit, 229
  Tourte au Mouton, 108
Liver, 123
  Ox, baked, 123
  Sheep's, Brochettes of, 124
Pork, Cabbage stuffed with, 116
  Chops with Rhubarb, 115
    with Green Peppers, 115
Veal, Blanquette of, 114
  Breast of, 235
  Escalopes of, 110
    de Veau Poêlées, 110
    with Olives, 111
    Vénitiennes, 111
  Médaillons, 113
    à la Russe, 114
    with Cream, 114
    with Lemon, 113
  Marengo, 114
  Messicani, 112
  Paupiettes, 111

POULTRY AND GAME

Chicken, Canaille, 130
  Coq au Vin, 132
  Flambé à l'Estragon, 129
  Poule au Pot, 127
  Tamara, 128
  with Cream, 131

Ducks and Ducklings, 133
  Caneton aux Cervelas, 133
    aux Navets, 134
    à l'Orange, 133
Game in General, 138
Goose, 135
  Ragoût with Apples, 136
  roast with Apples and Cervelas Sausages, 135
  with Cabbage, 136
Hare à la Royale, 140
  Civet of, 139
  Roast Saddle of, with Beetroot, 141
  Terrine of, 142
Rabbit, roast with Cream, 137
  with Mustard, 138
  with Turnips, 137
Wild Boar, haunch of, 144

VEGETABLES

Artichokes, 146
  à la Grèque, 147
  à la Juive, 146
  Barigoule, 147
  Sautés à la Crème, 146
Asparagus, 149
  à la Flamande, 150
  à la Polonaise, 150
  au Gratin, 151
  Hollandaise, 150
  with Melted Butter, 150
Aubergines, 151
  à la Grècque, 154
  à l'Orientale, 152
  Caponata Sicilienne, 155
  Caviar, 155
  fried, 153
  grilled, 153
  with Onions, 153
Batavian Endive with Onions, 155
Beetroot, 156
  cold, with Cream, 156
  hot, with Cream, 157
  with Horse-radish, 157

Carrots, 157
  à la Polonaise, 158
  Brandade of, 159
  Vichy, 158
  with Cream, 158
Chestnuts, 159
  boiled, 160
  Purée with Cream, 160
  Sauté, 161
Chicory, 161
  à l'Anglaise, 162
  à la Polonaise, 162
  braised, 162
  gratiné, 162
  with Cream, 163
  with Sauce Mornay, 163
Chives on Toast, 163
Choucroûte, 163
Courgettes à la Poêle, 164
  à la Grècque, 164
Cucumbers, 165
  with Béchamel Sauce, 165
Curled Endive with Grilled
    Sausages, 165
Lettuce with Bacon, 166
  with Cream, 238
Mushrooms, 167
  fried, 168
  with Cream, 167
  with Thyme, 229
Peas, 168
  à la Polonaise, 170
  with Lettuce, 169
  with Cream, 170
Peppers, 170
  stuffed, 171
Potatoes, 172
  cooked in the ashes, 240
  Gratin Dauphinois, 174
  La Raclette, 174
  new, with Tarragon, 176
  soufflé, 172
Pumpkin, 177
  with Tomato, 177
Sorrel, 177
  Fritters, 178
  Purée, 178
Vegetarian Meals, 179

SALADS

Asparagus and Potato, 181
Carrot, raw, 181
Choucroûte, 184
Cucumber, 182
  with Cream, 182
Curled Endive with Black
    Olives, 182
Lettuce with Cream, 183
Mushroom, 183
Spanish Radish with Cream,
    184
Spinach, with Hard-boiled
    Eggs, 185
Sweet Pepper, 183
Turnip with Capers, 185
Watercress with Cheese, 185

SAUCES

Basic Principles of making, 186
Béchamel, 165
Beurre Blanc, 90
Curry, 127
Date, 101
Hollandaise, 188
Mayonnaise, 189
Mornay, 163
Mousseline, 189
Poulette, 82
Red Wine, 97
Vinaigrette, 119

SWEET DISHES

Apples of Apicius, 203
  Platée de Pommes, 202
  Tart, 232
  Tarte à la gelée, 208
  Tarte Pâtissière, 209
Beignets Soufflés, 198
Bottreaux, 199
Cherries, Clafoutis, 211
  Country Tarts, 204
  Piroshki with Cherries, 212
  Pudding, 213
  Tarte Alsacienne, 206
  Tarte Parisienne, 206

Chestnuts, Gâteau aux Marrons, 214
Chocolate Caramels, soft, 222
Choux à la Crème, 197
    Écossaise, 193
Crème Écossaise au Café, 193
    Écossaise au Chocolat, 193
Galette des Rois, 218
Krapfen, 200
Madeleines, 217
Merveilles, 197
Mousse à la Crème, 195
    à l'Orange, 195
    au Cognac, 195
    au Curaçao, 195
    aux Noisettes, 195
    de Chocolat, 194
    Montmorency, 195
    with Ground Coffee, 195
Pâté à Choux, 195
Pears, Écossaise, 193
Pets de Nonne, 196
Profiterolles, 197
Pumpkin Gratin, 215
    with Sugar, 217
Rhubarb, Alsatian Tart, 207

Strawberry Tart, 210
Strawberries with Lemon, 238
Sweet dishes in general, 192
Yule Log, 220

JAM

Chestnut, 224

A FEW DRINKS

Cherry Ratafia, 226
Grog, almost alcohol free, 226
    American, 227
Lait de Poule, 227

FOOD TO REMEMBER

A Lunch in the Country, 228
Supper in the High Mountains, 231
Two Good Dishes for Two 'Little' Wines, 233
Lunch by the Sea, 236
Food for Camping, 238